Not All Those Who Wander Are Lost

Not All Those Who Wander Are Lost

Posts from a
Silicon Valley Entrepreneur

Steve Blank

Published 2010

Printed by Cafepress.com

ISBN 0-9764707-4-8

First printing

Acknowledgments

These stories of my 20+ years as a technology entrepreneur wouldn't have been possible without four extraordinary mentors, each brilliant in his own field: Ben Wegbreit who taught me how to think, Gordon Bell who taught me what to think about, Rob Van Naarden who showed how to get others thinking like me, and Allen Michels who showed me how to turn thinking on my feet into direct and immediate action.

It's possible to read these posts and think that I was the only one at these companies. Nothing could be further from the truth. I've been lucky enough to work with, around and near some extraordinary people: Bill Perry, John Moussouris, John Hennessy, Skip Stritter, Jon Rubenstein, Glenn Miranker, Cleve Moler, Tom McMurray, John Sanguinetti, Alvy Ray Smith, Chris Kryzan, Karen Dillon, Margaret Hughes, Peter Barrett, Bruce Leak, Jim Wickett, Karen Richardson, Greg Walsh, John McCaskey, Roger Siboni, Bob Dorf, Steve Weinstein, Fred Amoroso, Fred Durham, Maheesh Jain, Will Harvey, Eric Ries, Kathryn Gould, Jon Feiber, Mike Maples, Ann Miura-Ko and many, many more.

The last 10 or so years of teaching was made possible by Jerry Engel, formally Director of the Lester Center on Entrepreneurship, at U.C. Berkeley Haas Business School. And at Stanford School of Engineering, Tom Byers, Tina Seelig and Kathy Eisenhardt have made feel at home in the Stanford Technology Ventures Program (STVP). The Columbia Business School allowed me to inflict my theories on their students in their joint MBA program with the Haas Business School. And thanks to my long suffering Teaching Assistants at these schools: Ian Shea, Thomas Haymore, Daisy Chung, David Hutton, Boris Logvinskiy, Eric Carr.

A big thanks to Kris Olson who wrangled the blog into existence and transformed the first set of oral histories into posts - the blog wouldn't have existed without her efforts.

Finally, my wife Alison Elliott not only offered her wise counsel with my weekly obsession with blogging but also added punctuation and complete sentences to my posts.

This is for my daughters who are just figuring out what exactly Dad did for a living.

Preface

This "book" is a collection of blogs I wrote to explain why a "book" I wrote wasn't a book. (Confused? Read on.)

After I retired, I began teaching *Customer Development,* a theory of how to reduce early stage risk in entrepreneurial ventures. The first time I taught the class at the Haas Business School, U.C. Berkeley, I had a few hundred pages of course notes. Students began to ask for copies of the notes so I threw a cover on them and self-published the notes as a "book" at Cafepress.com.

As a pun on my last company as an entrepreneur, E.piphany, I called the book The Four Steps to the Epiphany.

Two years later, Eric Ries mentioned that I could list the book on Amazon. I never imagined more than a few hundred copies would be sold to my students. 15,000 copies later, the horrifically bad proofreading, design and layout is now a badge of honor. You most definitely read the book for the content.

A few years later my teaching assistants at Stanford and Berkeley said, "You tell much better stories than you write." They suggested that sharing those stories on the web was the best way to illustrate some of the more salient points of what even I will admit is a difficult text.

My blog also allowed me to indulge my interest in a few other subjects: The Secret History of Silicon Valley, thoughts on a career as an entrepreneur, observations about family and startups, etc.

These blog posts were written as I thought about them, with little thought about organization by topic. This "book" attempts to remedy that by organizing the 2009 blog posts in a coherent fashion.

Table of Contents

Startup Culture

Am I a Founder? The Adventure of a Lifetime

Posted on June 11, 2009 by steveblank |

When my students ask me about whether they should be a founder or cofounder of a startup I ask them to take a walk around the block and ask themselves:

Are you comfortable with:
- Chaos? Startups are disorganized.
- Uncertainty? Startups never go per plan.

Are you:
- Resilient? At times you will fail – badly. How quickly will you recover?
- Agile? You may find the real opportunities for your company were somewhere else. Can you recognize and capitalize on them?
- Creative / Pattern Recognition – Can you think "out of the box?" Or if not, can you recognize patterns others miss?
- Passionate? Is the company/product the most important thing in your life? 24/7?
- Tenacious? Can you keep going when everyone else gives up? Can you keep giving 200% despite all the naysayers who don't believe in your idea?
- Articulate? Can you create a reality distortion field and have others see and share your vision and passion?

I remind them that they should be bringing some type of domain expertise (technical or business) to the table. This is the minimum feature set for founders.

Other Roles in a Startup

Generic advice given to entrepreneurs assumes that everyone is going to be the founder/co-founder. Yet for every founder there are 10-20 other employees who take the near-equivalent risks in joining an early-stage company. If you're not a founder (by choice, timing or temperament,) you may be an early employee or a later stage startup employee.

And my advice to students who believe they want to do a startup, but are unsure if they want to start one, is to join one that's already raised their first round of funding. Founders *know* they want to start something. If you're unsure, you've just decided.

I believe that founder, early and later stage employees require different risk/personality profile.

The Early Employee

If you're a founder/co-founder, all the attributes I mentioned above are needed in spades. However, if you want to join a startup as an *early employee* (say in the first 25 employees,) you can modify the list above.

You still need to be comfortable with chaos and uncertainty, but by this time the major risk of where the first round of funding is coming from is gone. However, you will be dealing with almost daily change (new customer feedback/insights from a Customer Development process and technical roadblocks) as the company searches for a repeatable and scalable business model. This means you still need to be agile and have a resilient personality.

Early stage employees are "self-starters" and show initiative rather than waiting for other people to tell them what to do or how to do it. (You may be wearing multiple hats in one day.) You have to be passionate about your work, the company and its mission to be working 24/7. But more than likely, you don't need to be as articulate or creative as the founders. They're doing the talking while you're doing the work. And while you do need to be tenacious, you don't need to be the last man standing if the ship goes down.

The Later Employee

If you want to join a startup as a *later employee* (say employee number 25-125, before the company is profitable) you can continue to modify the list above.

You will still need to be comfortable with chaos and uncertainty. And you will be dealing with change, but it won't be the constant daily change the early employees faced with. By now, the company may have found and settled on a repeatable business model. And at this stage of the company rather than everyone doing everything, actual departments may begin to form. However, job responsibilities and organizations will change regularly, and you need to feel comfortable embracing those changes and taking responsibility and ownership.

You'll still need to have a resilient and agile personality as new customer and product opportunities will appear without warning and change your work. But it won't be happening daily. And while you still need to love what you do, your passion doesn't have to extend to tattooing the company's logo on your arm.

The Adventure of a Lifetime

Take the time and think through who you are and what level of challenge you are looking for. You're not joining a big company. Startups are the adventure of a lifetime. But make sure the expectations fit who you are.

Agile Opportunism – Entrepreneurial DNA

Posted on June 29, 2009 by steveblank |

Entrepreneurs tend to view adversity as opportunity.

You're Hired, You're Fired.

My first job in Silicon Valley: I was hired as a lab technician at ESL to support the training department. I packed up my life in Michigan and spent five days driving to California to start work. (Driving across the U.S. is an adventure everyone ought to do. It makes you appreciate that the Silicon Valley technology-centric culture-bubble has little to do with the majority of Americans.) With my offer letter in-hand I reported to ESL's Human Resources (HR) department. I was met by a very apologetic manager who said, "We've been trying to get a hold of you for the last week. The manager of the training department who hired you wasn't authorized to do so – and he's been fired. I am sorry there really isn't a job for you."

I was stunned. I had quit my job, given up my apartment, packed everything I owned in the back of my car, knew no one else in Silicon Valley and had about $200 in cash. *This could be a bad day*. I caught my breath and thought about it for a minute and said, "How about I go talk to the new training manager. Could I work here if he wanted to hire me?" Taking sympathy on me, the HR person made a few calls, and said, "Sure, but he doesn't have the budget for a lab tech. He's looking for a training instructor."

You're Hired Again

Three hours later and a few more meetings I discovered the training department was in shambles. The former manager had been fired because:

ESL had a major military contract to deploy an intelligence gathering system to Korea

- they needed to train the Army Security Agency on maintenance of the system
- the 10 week training course (6-hours a day) hadn't been written
- the class was supposed to start in 6 weeks.

As I talked to the head of training and his boss, I pointed out that the clock was ticking down for them, I knew the type of training military maintenance people need, and I had done some informal teaching in the Air Force. I made them a pretty good offer – hire me as a training instructor at the salary they were going to pay me as a lab technician. Out of desperation and a warm body right in front of them, they realized I was probably better than nothing. So I got hired for the second time at ESL, this time as a training instructor.

The good news is that I had just gotten my first promotion in Silicon Valley, and I hadn't even started work.

The bad news is that I had 6 weeks to write a 10 week course on three 30-foot vans full of direction finding electronics plus a small airplane stuffed full of receivers. "And, oh by the way, can you write the manuals for the operators while you're at it." Since there was very little documentation my time was split between the design engineers who built the system and the test and deployment team getting the system ready to go overseas. As I poured over the system schematics, I figured out how to put together a course to teach system theory, operations and maintenance.

Are You Single?
After I was done teaching each the day, I continued to write the operations manuals and work with the test engineers. (I was living the dream – working 80-hour weeks and all the technology I could drink with a fire hose.) Two weeks before the class was over the head of the deployment team asked, "Steve are you single?" Yes. "Do you like to travel?" Sure. "Why don't you come to Korea with us when we ship the system overseas." Uh, I think I work for the training department. "Oh, don't worry about that, we'll get you temporarily assigned to us and then you can come back as a Test Engineer/Training Instructor and work on a much more interesting system." More interesting than this? Sign me up.

You're Not So Smart, You Just Show Up a Lot
While this was going on, my roommate, who I knew from Ann Arbor where he got his masters degree in computer science, couldn't figure out how I kept getting these increasingly more interesting jobs. His theory, he told me, was this: "You're not so smart. You just show up a lot in a lot of places." I wore it as a badge of honor.

But over the years, I realized his comment was actually an astute observation about the mental mindset of an entrepreneur, and therein lies the purpose of this post.

Congratulations. You're now in Charge of your Life
Growing up at home, our parents tell us what's important and how to prioritize. In college we have a set of classes and grades needed to graduate. (Or in my case the military set the structure of what constituted success and failure.) In most cases until you're in your early 20's, someone else has planned a defined path of what you're going to do next.

When you move out on your own, you don't get a memo that says "Congratulations, you're now in charge of your life." Suddenly you are in charge of making up what you do next. You have to face dealing with uncertainly.

Most normal people (normal as defined as being someone other than an entrepreneur) seek to minimize uncertainty and risk and take a job with a defined career path like lawyer, teacher or fire fighter. A career path is a continuation of the direction you've gotten at home and school – do these things and you'll get these rewards. (Even with a career path you'll discover that you need to champion your own trajectory down that path. No one will tell you that you are in a dead end job. No one will say that it's time to move on. No one will tell you that you are better qualified for something elsewhere. No one will say work less and go home and spend time with your partner and/or family. And many end up near the end of their careers trapped, saying, "I wish I could have, I think I should have.")

Non-Linear Career Path

But entrepreneurs instinctually realize that the best advocate for their careers is themselves and that there is no such thing as a linear career path. They recognize they are going to have to follow their own internal compass and embrace the uncertainty as part of the journey.

In fact using uncertainty as your path is an advantage entrepreneurs share. Their journey will have them try more disconnected paths than someone on a traditional career track. And one day all the seemingly random data and experience they've acquired will end up as an insight in building something greater than the sum of the parts.

Steve Job's 2005 Stanford commencement speech said it best:
Stay Hungry, Stay Foolish.

Lessons Learned

- Trust your instincts.
- Showing up a lot increases your odds.
- Trust that the dots in your career will connect.
- Have a passion for *Doing* something rather than *Being* a title on a business card.

Faith-Based versus Fact-Based Decision Making

Posted on June 5, 2009 by steveblank |

I've screwed up a lot of startups on faith. One of the key tenets of entrepreneurship is that you start your company with insufficient resources and knowledge.

Faith-based Entrepreneurship

At first, entrepreneurship is a Faith-based initiative. There is no certainty about a startup on day-one. You make several first order approximations about your business model, distribution channels, demand creation and customer acceptance. You leave the comfort of your existing job, convince a few partners to join you, and jump off the bridge together.

At each startup I couldn't wait to do this. No building, no money, no customers, no market? Great! Sign me up! We'll build something from scratch.

You start a company on a vision, on a series of Faith-based hypotheses.

Fact-based Execution

However, successfully executing a startup requires the company to become Fact-based as soon as it can.

Think about all the assumptions you've made to get your business off the ground. Who are your customers? What problems do they have? What are their most important problems? How much would they pay to solve them? What's the best way to tell them about our product? Ad infinitum. These customer and market risks need to be translated into facts as soon as possible.

You can blindly continue to execute on *faith* that your hypothesis are correct. You'll ship your product, and you'll find out if you were wrong when you run out of money. Or you can quickly get out of the building and test whether your hypotheses were correct and turn them into facts.

In hindsight, when I was young, this where I went wrong. It's a lot more comfortable to hang on to your own beliefs than to get (or face) the facts because at times facts may create cognitive dissonance with the beliefs that got you started and funded.

This strategy of starting on faith, and quickly turning to facts is the core of the Customer Development process.

Relentless – The Difference Between Motion And Action

Posted on **November 9, 2009** by steveblank |

Never mistake motion for action. - Ernest Hemingway

One of an entrepreneur's greatest strengths is his/her relentless pursuit of a goal. But few realize how this differs from most of the population. Watching others try to solve problems reminded me why entrepreneurs are different.

Progress Report
Last week I happened to be sitting in my wife's office as she was on the phone to my daughter in college. Struggling with one of her classes, my daughter had assured us that she was asking for help – and was reporting on her progress (or lack of it).

She had sent several emails to the resource center asking for help. She was also trying to set up a meeting with her professor. All good, and all part of the "when you're stuck, ask for help" heuristic we taught our kids. But the interesting part for me was learning that in spite of her efforts, no one had gotten back to her.

She believed she had done all things that could be expected from her and was waiting for the result.

I realized that my daughter had confused *motion with action.*

This reminded me of a conversation with one of my direct reports years before my daughter was born.

Status Report
At Ardent, the marketing department was responsible for acquiring applications for our supercomputer. This required convincing software vendors to move their applications to our unique machine architecture. Not a trivial job considering our computer was one of the first parallel architectures, and our compiler required specific knowledge of our vector architecture to get the most out of it. Oh, and we had no installed customer base. I had hired the VP of marketing from a potential software partner who was responsible to get all this third party software on our computer. Once he was on board, I sat down with him on a weekly basis to review his progress with our list of software vendors.

Think Different
I still remember the day I discovered that I thought about progress differently than other people. Our conversation went like this:

Me: Jim, how are we doing with getting Ansys ported?
Jim: Great! I have a bunch of calls into them.

Me: How are we doing on the Nastran port?
Jim: Wonderful. They said they'll get back to me next month.

Me: How about Dyna 3D?
Jim: It's going great, we're on their list.

The rest of the progress report sounded just like this.

After hearing the same report for the nth week, I called a halt to the meeting. I had an executive who thought he was making progress. I thought he hadn't done a damn thing.

Why?

The Difference Between Motion and Action

One of Jim's favorite phrases was: "I got the ball rolling with account x." He thought that the *activities* he was doing – making calls, setting up meetings, etc. – was his job. In reality, these activities had *nothing to do with his job*. His real job – *the action* – was to get the software moved onto our machine. Everything he had done to date was just the *motion* to get the process rolling. And so far the motion hadn't accomplished anything. He was confusing "the accounting" of the effort with achieving the goal. But Jim felt that since he was doing lots of motion, "lots of stuff was happening." In reality, we hadn't gotten any closer to our goal than the day we hired him. We had accomplished nothing – zero, zilch, nada. In fact, we would have been better off if we hadn't hired him, as we wouldn't have confused a warm body with progress.

When I explained this to him, the conversation got heated. "I've been working my tail off for the last two months," he claimed. When he calmed down, I asked him how much had gotten accomplished. He started listing his activities again. I stopped him and reminded him that I could have hired anyone to set up meetings, but I had brought him in to *get the software onto our machine*. "How much progress have we made to that goal?" "Not much," he admitted.

Entrepreneurs are Relentless

Jim's goal was to get other companies to put their software on an unfinished, buggy computer with no customers. While a tough problem, not an insurmountable one for an entrepreneur focused on the objective, not the process.

This was my fault. It had taken me almost two months to realize that other people didn't see the world the same way I did. My brain was wired to focus on the end-point and work backwards, removing each obstacle in my path or going around them all while keeping the goal in sight. Jim was following a different path.

Focused on the process, he defined progress as moving through a step on his to-do list and feeling like progress was being made when he checked them off. The problem was his approach let others define the outcome and set the pace.

The difference between these two ways of thinking is why successful entrepreneurs have the reputation for being relentless. To an outsider, it looks like they're annoyingly persistent. The reality is that their *eyes are on the prize.*

Teaching Moment

If you're not born with this kind of end-goal focus, you can learn this skill.

My wife and I called our daughter back, declared a family "teaching moment," explained the difference between motion and action, and asked her what else she could do to get help for class. She realized that more persistence and creativity was required in getting to the right person. The next day, she was in the resource getting the help she needed.

Lessons Learned

- Most people execute linearly, step by step.
- They measure progress by "steps they did."
- Entrepreneurs focus on the goal.
- They measure progress by "accomplishing their goals."

The Sharp End of the Stick

Posted on May 4, 2009 by steveblank |

The Sharp End of the Stick

At some point in my career as I began to formulate thoughts about *mission and intent*, I started to think about the broader role of marketing in a growing technology company. It became clear to me that the *mission* of marketing in most companies has to be to support sales. While this may seem obvious to anyone not in sales and marketing, trust me, in a technology company, this is a conceptual breakthrough. In my experience, every marketer with an MBA wants to "do strategy." Every marketing communication hire couldn't wait to produce the next great ad or PR program. Every product marketer thought they should help define the product feature set, etc. But without sales, there is no revenue, and without revenue, there is no company. *All the strategic thinking in the world won't make up for a missed revenue plan.*

Sales was the Sharp End of the Stick, and Marketing was the Stick

The epiphany for me was that in any company where I was running the marketing department, marketing's number-one job (its mission) would be to support sales – and to make the (commission-driven) sales VP the highest paid person in the company. We were going to do that by turning marketing into a machine to generate end user demand, drive that demand into our sales channels, and educate our sales channels. And the same time we were also going to do all the other strategic stuff about pricing, positioning, promotion and customer discovery and validation to help engineering understand customer needs. But sales came first.

(By the way, companies that have a single individual as the VP of Sales *and* Marketing have decided that marketing doesn't add any other value then tactical sales support, and the only way to get is to put it under the VP of Sales. That's why you almost never see a marketer as the VP of Sales and Marketing.)

My way of explaining our support and service role to the marketing department was that: Sales is the sharp end of the stick, and marketing at best, is the stick.

But while the sales team works for commission, the rest of the employees have equity (stock) in the company.

If sales revenue and profits are high enough, we could take the company public or sell it, and the stock would be worth more than the paper it was printed on.

In exchange for being the "point" organization, performance of a salesperson is measured continuously, and individuals who fail to deliver quota are removed. If sales as an organization failed to deliver revenue to plan, then all we had were worthless shares. In reality the sales team was working for the rest of the company to make all of our stock valuable.

No one was confused after that.

Who's on the Sharp End?
In an early stage startup, instead of sales being up front, the point departments are likely to be product development and customer development. Later on in this same company's life, sales will become the pointy end, and product development moves to a supporting role. In other companies manufacturing or finance may be the sharp end of the stick. In an IP licensing business, legal and finance are at the sharp end. It varies by company and changes over time. There's no magic formula, but there are always "leading" departments. And all "leading" departments have some type of "consequence-based" feedback loops that make success or failure obvious.

The clearest example is the U.S. military. Combat troops are the "tip of the spear" while everyone else is the logistical tail. No one in the support chain of the troops is confused or resentful as they all understand that the greatest risk is up at the front.

Killing The Company With Equality
I've been on boards where the CEOs took the egalitarian position that "All our departments are equal. No one is more important than any other." The unfortunate corollary is that in these companies, no department believed it was in a supporting or service role.

In these companies, departments that should have been providing support and service instead behaved like they were the "sharp end" organizations. I've encountered finance organizations with budget processes designed to simplify their lives, but not the rest of the company's. Or expense reporting requirements that took hours of a sales teams' time to fill out every week. Sometimes it was the legal department crafting contracts so onerous I wouldn't even sign let alone expect a customer to do so. At times it was human resources with policies that made people leave rather than stay or it was a CIO more interested in standards than deployment.

None of these departments operated with any particular sense of malice – just with the certainty that the company revolved around them. But they were misguided because they lacked a clear *departmental mission statement* that reminded them of the corporate goals. If each department had a mission statement, it would have been clear whether their role was in support or at the sharp end. Having each department develop a mission statement depends on leadership and direction from the CEO.

"Going Out of Business" Strategy

I'm now convinced "all our departments are equal" is a "going out of business" strategy. Not understanding who are the "lead departments" makes companies feel like ponderous, bureaucratic and frustrating places to work. The best people in the "sharp end" organizations simply vote with their feet and leave.

I loved to compete against these companies. Their own internal culture would tie them up in knots, and agile startups could run rings around them.

Don't let this happen to your company. Embrace and then communicate the idea of a lead department(s). Build a company culture where everyone supports the "sharp end of the stick."

Stay agile, stay focused.

Preparing for Chaos – the Life of a Startup

Posted on April 29, 2009 by steveblank |

I just finished reading Donovan Campbell's eye-opening book, "*Joker One*", about his harrowing combat tour in Iraq leading a Marine platoon. This book may be the Iraq war equivalent of "*Dispatches*" which defined Vietnam for my generation. (Both reminded me why National Service would be a very good idea.)

Campbell describes how he tried to instill in his troops the proper combat mentality.

I've paraphrased his speech into the language of a startup. It's eerily similar.

> *Startups are inherently chaos. As a founder you need to prepare yourself to think creatively and independently, because more often than not, conditions on the ground will change so rapidly that the original well-thought-out business plan becomes irrelevant.*
>
> *If you can't manage chaos and uncertainty, if you can't bias yourself for action and if you wait around for someone else to tell you what to do, then your investors and competitors will make your decisions for you and you will run out of money and your company will die.*
>
> *Therefore the best way to keep your company alive is to instill in every employee a decisive mindset that can quickly separate the crucial from the irrelevant, synthesize the output, and use this intelligence to create islands of order in the all-out chaos of a startup.*

Every potential startup founder should think about his/her level of comfort operating in chaos and uncertainty. It may not be for you.

15

Speed and Tempo – Fearless Decision Making for Startups

Posted on April 10, 2009 by steveblank |

"If things seem under control, you are just not going fast enough." - Mario Andretti

I was catching up over breakfast with a friend who's now CEO of his own startup. One of the things he mentioned was that when it came to decision-making he still tended to think and act like an engineer. Each and every decision he made was carefully thought through and weighed. And he recognized it was making his startup feel and act like a big ponderous company.

Speed = Execution Now

General George Patton said, "A good plan violently executed now is better than a perfect plan next week." The same is true in your company. Most decisions in a startup must be made in the face of uncertainty. Since every situation is unique, there is no perfect solution to any engineering, customer or competitor problem, and you shouldn't agonize over trying to find one. This doesn't mean gambling the company's fortunes on a whim. It means adopting plans with an acceptable degree of risk, and doing it quickly. (Make sure these are fact-based, not faith-based decisions.) In general, the company that consistently makes and implements decisions rapidly gains a tremendous, often decisive competitive advantage.

Decision Making Heuristics for the Startup CEO

The heuristic I gave my friend was to *think of decisions of having two states: those that are reversible, and those that are irreversible.* An example of a reversible decision could be adding a product feature, a new algorithm in the code, targeting a specific set of customers, etc. If the decision was a bad call, you can unwind it in a reasonable period of time. An irreversible decision is firing an employee, launching your product, a five-year lease for an expensive new building, etc. These are usually difficult or impossible to reverse.

My advice was to start a policy of *making reversible decisions before anyone left his office* or before a meeting ended. In a startup, it doesn't matter if you're 100% right 100% of the time. What matters is having forward momentum and a tight fact-based feedback loop (i.e. Customer Development) to help you quickly recognize and reverse any incorrect decisions. That's why startups are agile. By the time a big company gets the committee to organize the subcommittee to pick a meeting date, your startup could have made 20 decisions, reversed five of them and implemented the fifteen that worked.

Tempo = Speed Consistently Over Time

Once you learn how to make decisions quickly you're not done. Startups that are agile have mastered one other trick – and that's *Tempo* – the ability to make quick decisions consistently over extended periods of time. Not just for the CEO or the exec staff, but for the entire company. For a startup Speed and Tempo need to be an integral part of your corporate DNA.

Great startups have a tempo of 10x a large company.

Try it.

Killing Innovation with Corner Cases and Consensus

Posted on **April 22, 2009** by steveblank |

I was visiting a friend whose company teaches executives how to communicate effectively. He had just filmed the second of a series of videos called: *Speaking to the Big Dogs: How Mid-level Managers can Communicate Effectively with C-level Executives* (CEO, VP's, General Managers, etc.) As we were plotting marketing strategy, I mentioned that the phrase "Speaking to the Big Dogs" might end up as his corporate brand. And that he might want to think about aligning all his video and Internet products under that name.

We were happily brainstorming when one of his managers spoke up and said, "Well, the phrase 'Big Dogs' might not work because it might not translate well in our Mexican and Spanish markets." Hmm, that's a fair comment, I thought, surprised they even had international locations. "How big are your Mexican and Spanish markets," I asked? "Well, we're not in those markets today but we might be some day." I took a deep breath and asked, "Ok, if you were, what percentage of your sales do you think these markets would be in 5 years?" "I guess less than 5%," was the answer.

Now I mention this conversation not because the objection was dumb, but because objections like these happen all the time when you're brainstorming. And when you are brainstorming, you really do want to hear all ideas and all possible pitfalls. But entrepreneurial leaders sometimes forget that in startups, you can't allow a "corner case" to derail fearless decision making.

Corner Cases

  A corner case is an objection that may be:

- technically reasonable
- may have a probability of occurring
- *its probability of occurring is lower than your probability of running out of money.*

I've noticed that *corner case comments are directly proportional to the intelligence of the people in the room.* The smarter the team, the more objections you'll have – and they'll all be technically and theoretically possible.

Corner Cases and Consensus are For Large Companies

Carefully considering each and every possible outcome before you proceed with a decision is something large companies with large revenues, shareholders and employees need to do.

18

Unlike large corporations, startup meetings are not about achieving consensus for every objection raised. They are about forward motion, momentum and feedback loops (i.e. Customer Development.)

Calculate the Odds

The heuristic I suggest is: hear the corner case objections, make the objector calculate the odds. If the potential damage estimate is low (probability of the event occurring multiplied by its ability to put you out of business,) keep the meeting focused and move on. If you do this consistently, your team will catch on.

You'll be spending your time on what matters, rather what's theoretically possible. For a startup, "No Corner Cases" needs to be an integral part of your corporate DNA.

Focus on Speed and Tempo. Any startup that's striving for consensus on corner cases instead of speed and tempo will be out of business.

The "Good" Student

Posted on April 7, 2009 by steveblank |

I saw an article in the New York Times about Google's hiring practices that reminded me of the differences between great big successful technology companies and small scrappy startups.

The New York Times

February 28, 2009

One candidate got a C in macroeconomics. "That's troubling to me," Ms. Mayer says. "Good students are good at all things."

Marissa Mayer
Google

I love Google. I think its one of the smartest companies out there. And it hires very smart people from the best schools. If you meet their criteria of a "good student", you ought to go to work there. Or Microsoft or IBM.

Nothing makes me happier then to see my students getting great grades (and as they can tell you, I make them very work hard for them.)

But what I remind them is that great grades and successful founders/technology entrepreneurs have at best a zero correlation (and anecdotal evidence suggests that the correlation may actually be negative.)

BTW, by the standards mentioned in the *Times* article, the following people would never have been interviewed or hired at Google.

College Dropouts - Bill Gates, Steve Jobs, Larry Ellison

These guys realized that *customers don't ask to see your transcript.*

There's a big difference between being an *employee* at a great technology company and having the guts to start one. You don't get grades for having resiliency, curiosity, agility, resourcefulness, pattern recognition and tenacity.

You just get successful.

Touching the Hot Stove – Experiential versus Theoretical Learning

Posted on August 13, 2009 by steveblank |

I'm a slow learner. It took me eight startups and 21 years to get it right, (and one can argue success was due to the Internet bubble rather then any brilliance.)

In 1978 when I joined my first company, information about how to start companies simply didn't exist - no Internet, no blogs, no books on startups, no entrepreneurship departments in universities, etc. It took lots of trial and error, learning by experience and resilience through multiple failures.

The first few months of my startups were centered around building the founding team, prototyping the product and raising money. Since I wasn't an engineer, my contribution was around the team-building and fund raising.

I was an idiot.

Customer Development/Lean Startups

In hindsight startups and the venture capital community left out the most important first step any startup ought to be doing – hypothesis testing in front of customers- from day one.

I'm convinced that starting a company without talking to customers is like throwing your time and money in the street (unless you're already a domain expert).

This mantra of talking to customers and iterating the product is the basis of the *Lean Startup Methodology* that Eric Ries has been evangelizing and I've been teaching at U.C. Berkeley and at Stanford. It's what my textbook *Four Steps to the Epiphany* on Customer Development describes.

Experiential versus Theoretical Learning

After teaching this for a few years, I've discovered that subjects like Lean Startups and Customer Development are best learned experientially rather than solely theoretically.

Remember your parents saying, "Don't touch the hot stove!" What did you do? I bet you weren't confused about what hot meant after that. That's why I make my students spend a lot of time "touching the hot stove" by talking to customers "outside the building" to test their hypotheses.

However, as hard as I emphasize this point to aspiring entrepreneurs every year, I usually get a call or email from a past student asking me to introduce them to my favorite VC's. The first questions I ask is: "So what did you learn from testing your hypothesis?" and "What did customers think of your prototype?" I know these questions will be on top of the list that VC's will ask.

At least 1/3 of the time the response I get is, "Oh that class stuff was real interesting, but we're too busy building the prototype. I'm going to go do that Customer Development stuff after we raise money."

Interestingly, this response almost always comes from first time entrepreneurs. Entrepreneurs who have a startup or two under their belt tend to rattle off preliminary customer findings and data that blow me away (not because I think their data is going to be right, but because it means they have built a process for learning and discovery from day one.)

Sigh. Fundraising isn't the product. It's not a substitute for customer input and understanding.

Sometimes you need a few more lessons touching the hot stove.

Burnout

Posted on July 20, 2009 by steveblank |

If you hang around technology companies long enough, you or someone you know may experience "burnout" – a state of emotional exhaustion, doubt and cynicism. Burnout can turn productive employees into emotional zombies and destroy careers. But it can also force you to hit the pause button and perhaps take a moment to reevaluate your life and your choices.

Hitting "burnout" changed the trajectory of both ends of my career in Silicon Valley. This post, which is divided in two parts, is the story of the first time it happened to me.

Zilog

Zilog was my first Silicon Valley company where you could utter the customer's name in public. Zilog produced one of the first 8-bit microprocessors, the Z-80 which competed at the time with Intel's 8080, Motorola 6800, and MOS Technology 6502.

I was hired as a training instructor to teach microprocessor system design for the existing Z-80 family and to write a new course for Zilog's soon to be launched 16-bit processor, the Z-8000. Given the hardware I had worked on at ESL, learning microprocessors wasn't that hard but figuring out how to teach hardware design and assembly language programming was a bit more challenging. Luckily while I was teaching classes at headquarters, Zilog's field application engineers, the technical engineers working alongside our salesmen, would work side-by-side with our large customers as they designed their systems with our chips. So our people in the field could correct any egregious design advice I gave to customers who mattered.

Customers

The irony is that Zilog had no idea who would eventually become its largest customers. Our salesmen focused on accounts that ordered the largest number of chips and ignored tiny little startups that wanted to build personal computers around these chips, companies like Osborne, Kaypro, Coleco, Radio Shack, Amstrad, Sinclair, Morrow, Commodore, Intertec. Keep in mind this is still several years before the IBM PC and DOS. And truth be told, these early systems were laughable; at first having no disk drives (you used tape cassettes,) no monitors (you used your TV set as a display,) and no high level programming languages. If you wanted your own applications, you had to write them yourself. No mainframe or minicomputer company saw any market for these small machines.

Two Jobs at Once

When I was hired at Zilog part of the deal was that I could consult for the first six months for my last employer, ESL.

Just as I was getting settled into Zilog, the manager of the training department got fired. (I was beginning to think that my hiring managers were related to red-shirted guys on Star Trek.) Since the training department was part of sales, no one really paid attention to the four of us. So every day I'd come to work at Zilog at 9, leave at 5 go to ESL and work until 10 or 11 or later. Repeat every day, six or seven days a week.

Meanwhile, back at ESL the project I was working on wanted to extend my consulting contract, the company was trying to get me to return, and in spite of what I had done on the site, "the customer" had casually asked me if I was interested in talking to them about a job. Life was good.

But it was all about to catch up to me.

Where Am I?

It was a Friday (about three quarters through my work week) and I was in a sales department meeting. Someone mentioned to me that there were a pile of upcoming classes heading my way and warned me "remember that the devil is in the details." The words "heading my way" and "devil" combined in my head. I immediately responded, "well that's OK, I got it under control – as long as the devil coming at me isn't an SS-18." Given that everyone in the room knew the NATO codename for the SS-18 was SATAN, I was thinking that this was a witty retort and expected at least a chuckle from someone.

I couldn't understand why people were staring at me like I was speaking in tongues. The look on their faces were uncomfortable. The VP of Sales gave me a funny look and just moved on with the agenda.

VP of Sales? Wait a minute.. where am I?

I looked around the room thinking I'd see the faces of the engineers in the ESL M-4 vault, but these were different people. Who were these people? I had a moment of confusion and then a much longer minute of panic trying to figure out where I was. I wasn't at ESL, I was at Zilog. As I realized what I had said, a much longer panic set in. I tried to clear my head and remember what else I had said, like anything that would be really, really, really bad to say outside of a secure facility.

As I left this meeting I realized I didn't even remember when I had left ESL or how I had gotten to Zilog. Something weird was happening to me. As I was sitting in my office looking lost, the VP of Sales came in and said, "You look a bit burned out. Take it easy this weekend."

"Burned out?" What the heck was that? I had been working at this pace since I was 18.

Burnout
I was tired. No I was more than tired, I was exhausted. I had started to doubt my ability to accomplish everything. Besides seeing my housemates in Palo Alto, I had no social life. I was feeling more and more detached at work and emotionally drained. Counting the Air Force I had been pounding out 70 and 80-hour weeks nonstop for almost eight years. I went home and fell asleep at 7pm and didn't wake up until the next afternoon.

The bill had come due.

Recovery
That weekend I left the Valley and drove along the coast from San Francisco to Monterey. Crammed into Silicon Valley along with millions of people around the San Francisco Bay, it's hard to fathom that 15 air miles away was a stretch of California coast that was still rural. With the Pacific Ocean on my right and the Santa Cruz Mountains on my left, Highway 1 cut through mile after mile of farms in rural splendor. There wasn't a single stoplight along 2-lane highway for the 45 miles from Half Moon Bay to Santa Cruz. Looking at the green and yellows of the farms, I realized that my life lacked the same colors. *I had no other life than work.* While I was getting satisfaction from what I was learning, the sheer joy of it had diminished.

As the road rolled on, it dawned on me that there was no one looking out for me. There was no one who was going to tell me, "You've hit your limit, now work less hours and go enjoy yourself." The idea that only I could be responsible for taking care of my happiness and health was a real shock. How did I miss that?

At the end of two days I realized:

This was the first full weekend I had taken off since I had moved to California 3 years ago.

I had achieved a lot by working hard, but the positive feedback I was getting just encouraged me to work even harder.

I needed to learn how to relax without feeling guilty.

I needed a life outside work.

And most importantly I needed to pick one job not two. I had to make a choice about where I wanted to go with my career–back to ESL, try to work for the Customer or stay at Zilog?

More about that choice in the next post.

Lessons Learned

> - No one will tell you to work fewer hours.
> - You need to be *responsible* for your own health and happiness.
> - Burnout sneaks up on you.
> - Burnout is self-induced. You created it and own it.
> - Recovery takes an awareness of what happened and
> - A plan to change the situation that got you there.

The Road Not Taken

Posted on July 23, 2009 by steveblank |

At Zilog I was figuring out how to cope with job burnout. And one of my conclusions was that I needed to pick one job not two. I had to decide what I wanted to do with my career – go back to ESL, try to work for the Customer, or stay at Zilog?

While it may seem like an easy choice, few people who love technology and who work on black projects leave. These projects are incredibly seductive. Let me explain why.

National Efforts

In World War II, the U.S. put its resources behind a technical project that dwarfed anything every built – the atomic bomb. From a standing start in 1942, the U.S. scaled up the production of U-235 and plutonium from micrograms to tens of kilograms by 1945. We built new cities in Hanford, Oak Ridge and Los Alamos and put 130,000 people to work on the project.

During the cold war, the U.S. government kept up the pace. Hundreds of thousands of people worked on developing strategic weapons, bombers, our ICBM and SLBM missile programs, and the Apollo moon program. These programs dwarfed the size that any single commercial company could do by itself. They were *national* efforts of hundreds of companies employing 10's or 100's of thousands of engineers.

ESL – National Technical Means of Verification

The project I was working on at ESL fit this category. The 1970's and '80's were the endgame of the cold war, and the U.S. military realized that our advantage over the Soviet Union was in silicon, software and systems. These technologies that allowed the U.S. to build sensors, stealth and smart weapons previously thought impossible or impractical would give us a major military advantage. Building these systems required resources way beyond the scope of a single company. Imagine coming up with an idea that could work only if you had your own semiconductor fab and could dedicate its output to make specialized chips just for you. Then imagine you'd have to get some rockets and put this reconnaissance system in space – no, make that several rockets. No one laughed when ESL proposed this class of project to "the customer."

If you love technology, these projects are hard to walk away from.

The Road Not Taken

At first, I thought my choice was this: working on great technology at ESL or continuing to work on these toy-like microprocessors at Zilog.

But the more I thought about it, the choice wasn't about the hardware or systems. There was something about the energy and passion Zilog's customers had as they kept doing the most unexpected things with our products.

While I couldn't articulate at it at the time (it would take another 25 years,) at ESL the company and the customer had a *known problem* and were executing to building a *known solution*, with a set of desired specifications and PERT charts telling them what they needed to do and in what order to achieve the goal. There was a ton of engineering innovation and coordination along the way, and the project could have failed at any point. But the insight and creativity occurred at the project's beginning when the problem and solution was first being defined. Given where I was in the hierarchy, I calculated that the odds of me being in on those decisions didn't look high – ever.

In contrast, my customers at Zilog had nothing more than a set of visions, guesses and hallucinations about their customers: who they were, what they wanted to achieve and what was the right path to get there. At these startups both the *problem and solution were unknown.*

Startups were not just smaller versions of a large company, they were about invention, innovation and iteration - of business model, product, customers and on and on. Startups were doing discovery of the problem and solution in real-time. I could see myself doing that – soon.

Unbeknownst to me, I was facing a choice between becoming an entrepreneur or working for a large company.

I chose a path and never looked back.

———

> Two roads diverged in a yellow wood,
> And sorry I could not travel both
> And be one traveler, long I stood
> And looked down one as far as I could
> To where it bent in the undergrowth;
>
> Then took the other, as just as fair,
> And having perhaps the better claim,
> Because it was grassy and wanted wear;
> Though as for that the passing there
> Had worn them really about the same,

And both that morning equally lay
In leaves no step had trodden black.
Oh, I kept the first for another day!
Yet knowing how way leads on to way,
I doubted if I should ever come back.

I shall be telling this with a sigh
Somewhere ages and ages hence:
Two roads diverged in a wood, and I—
I took the one less traveled by,
And that has made all the difference.

Robert Frost – The Road Not Taken – 1916

Lessons Learned

- There is no "right" choice for a career.
- There's only the choice you make.
- Don't let a "career" just happen to you.
- A startup is not a smaller version of a large company.

Ask and It Shall be Given

Posted on July 27, 2009 by steveblank |

Once I recovered from burnout at Zilog, I was working less and accomplishing more. I even had time to find a girlfriend who was a contractor to the company. One of her first comments was, "I didn't know you even worked here. Where were you hiding?" If she only knew.

What's the Worst that Can Happen?

Our small training department had been without a manager for months and finding a replacement didn't seem to be high on the VP of Sales list. We four instructors would grumble and complain to one another about our lack of leadership. Then it hit me – no one else wanted to be manager. What was the worst that could happen? I walked into the VP of Sales' office and with my knees trembling, I politely asked for the job. I still remember him chuckling as I nervously babbled on what I good job I would do, what I would change for the better in the department, why I was qualified, etc. He said, "You know I figured it would be you to come in here and ask for the job. I was wondering how long it would take you." I was now manager of Training and Education at Zilog.

All I had to do was ask.

From that day forward, in my business and personal relationships, I would calculate the consequences of a "No" for an answer against the benefits of getting a "Yes." The math said that it was almost always worth asking for what you want. And the odds in your favor are even higher, as most of your peers wouldn't even get into the game due to some unspoken belief that in a meritocracy, good things will come to those who wait. Perhaps if you have a union job based on seniority, but not in any startup I've ever seen.

For entrepreneurs good things come to those who ask.

What's Marketing?

As part of the sales organization, I thought I kind of figured out what the function of the sales department was. (In reality it would be another 20 years.) And I understood engineering since I interacted with them almost daily. And since Zilog still had a semiconductor fab next door, I learned what manufacturing did in a chip company, as every training class wanted to see their chips being made. But the one group that had me stumped was something called "marketing." "Explain it to me again," I'd ask.

31

After a year and a half of running training and teaching the new Z-8000 and its peripheral chips, I began to figure out that one of the jobs of marketing was to translate what engineering built into a description that our salesmen could use to talk to potential customers. I distinctly remember this is the first time I head the phrases "features and benefits." And since I saw our ads (but didn't quite understand them,) I knew marketing was the group that designed them, in an effort to get customers to think our products were better than Intel and Motorola's.

But Intel was kicking our rear.

One day I heard there was an opening in the marketing department for a product marketing manager for the Z-8000 peripheral chips. The department had hired a recruiter and was interviewing candidates from other chip companies. I looked at the job spec and under "candidate requirements," it listed everything I didn't have: MBA, 5-10 years product marketing experience, blah, blah.

I asked for the job.

The response was at first less than enthusiastic. I certainly didn't fit their profile. However, I pointed out that while I didn't have any of the traditional qualifications, I knew the product as well as anyone. I had been teaching Z8000 design to customers for the last year and a half. I also knew our customers. I understood how our products were being used and why we won design-in's over Intel or Motorola. And finally, I had a great working relationship with our engineers who designed the chips. I pointed out it that it would take someone else 6 months to a year to learn what I already knew – and I was already in the building.

A week later Zilog had a new product marketing manager, and I had my first job in marketing.

Now all I needed to do was to learn what a marketer was supposed to do.

MBA or Domain Expert
Years later when I was running marketing departments, I came up with a heuristic that replicated my own hire: *In a technology company it's usually better to train a domain expert to become a marketer than to train an MBA to become a domain expert.* While MBA's have a ton of useful skills, what they don't have is what most marketing departments lack – customer insight. I found that having a senior marketer responsible for business strategy surrounded by ex-engineers and domain experts makes one heck of a powerful marketing department.

Entrepreneurs Know How to Ask

Successful entrepreneurs have the ability to ask for things relentlessly. In the face of rules that stand in their way they find a way to change the rules. (To an entrepreneur comments like: "You need an MBA, we don't fund companies like yours, we don't buy from start-ups, you have to go through our vendor selection committee" are just the beginning of a negotiation rather than the end.) Entrepreneurs are fearless, persistent and uninhibited about *asking* – whether it's asking to assemble a team, get financing, sell customers, etc. or whatever is necessary to build a company. If you are on the path to be a successful entrepreneur, hopefully you are already asking for things you want/need/aspire to. If not, don't wait. Get started asking. It is a skill you need to either have or develop.

Lessons Learned

> Ask, and it shall be given you; seek, and you shall find;
> knock, and it will be opened to you.
>
> King James Bible, New Testament – Matthew 7:7

Selling with Sports Scores

Posted on June 25, 2009 by steveblank |

When I was a young marketer, I learned how to listen to customers by making a fool of myself.

Twenty-eight years ago I was the bright, young, eager product marketing manager called out to the field to support sales by explaining the technical details of Convergent Technologies products to potential customers.

The OEM Business

Convergent's business was selling desktop computers with our own operating system and office applications to other computer manufacturers – most of them long gone: Burroughs, Prime, Monroe Data Systems, ADP, Mohawk, Gould, NCR, 4-Phase, AT&T. These companies would take our computers and put their name on them and resell them to their customers.

Business customers were starting to ask for "office automation solutions" – word processing, spreadsheets, charting software on a desktop. This was just before the IBM PC hit the desktop so there were no "standard" operating systems or applications for desktop platforms. Computer hardware companies were faced with their customers asking for low-cost (relatively) desktop computers they had no experience in building. Their engineering teams didn't have the expertise using off-the-shelf microprocessors (back then "real" computer companies designed their own instruction sets and operating systems.) They couldn't keep up with the fast product development times that were enabled by using standard microprocessors. So their management teams were insisting that they OEM (buy from someone else) these products. Convergent Technologies was one of those OEM suppliers.

Their engineers hated us.

I was traveling with Convergent's regional sales manager who had called on these companies, gotten them interested and now needed someone from the factory to provide technical details and answer questions about how the product could be configured and customized.

See How Smart I Am

As the eager young marketer on my first sales call, as soon as we shook hands, I was in front of the room pitching our product and technical features. I knew everything about our operating system, hardware and applications – and I was going to prove it. I talked all about how great the new products were and went into excruciating detail on our hardware and operating system and explained why no one other than our company could build something so brilliantly designed. (This being presented to another company's proud engineering team who was being forced to buy product from us because they couldn't build their own in time.) After I sat down, I was convinced the only logical conclusion was for the customer to tell us how many they wanted to buy.

The result wasn't what I expected. The customers didn't act particularly excited about the product and how brilliantly I presented it. I do believe some actually rolled their eyes. They looked at their watches, gave our sales guy a quizzical look and left.

After the meeting our sale rep took me aside and asked if "perhaps I wouldn't mind watching him on the next call."

Sports Scores

The next day, as I drove to our next meeting, our sales guy was intently reading the sports section of the newspaper and as I glanced over, he seemed to be writing down the scores. I wondered if he had a bookie. When we got to the meeting he reminded me to be quiet and follow his lead.

We shook hands with the customers, but instead of launching into a product pitch (or better, letting me launch into the pitch,) he started asking about their families. He even remembered the names of their wives and kids and some details about schools or events. (I couldn't believe it. Here we were wasting precious time, and the dumb sales guy is talking about other stuff.)

Just as I thought we were going to talk about the product, he mentioned the previous nights football game. (Damn, another five minutes down the tube as the whole room chimed in with an opinion as we talked about something else unimportant.)

The Customer is a Genius

Then instead of talking about *our* products, he segued the conversation into *their* products. He complemented their elegantly designed minicomputers and made some astute comment about their architecture (now I'm rolling my eyes, their computers were dinosaurs) and asked who were the brilliant designers. I was surprised to see that they were in the room. And soon the conversation were about architectural tradeoffs and then how customers didn't appreciate the elegant designs and how the world was going to hell in a handbasket because of these commodity microprocessors. And our sales guy was agreeing and commiserating. (And I'm thinking why is he doing all this? Just tell these idiots that the world has passed them by, and they need to buy our stuff and let's get an order.)

The engineers spoke about all the pressure they were getting from management to build desktop personal computers rather than their traditional minicomputers. Their management wanted these new systems on a schedule that was impossible to meet. Then our sales guy said something that made me stop breathing for a while. "I bet if your management team would give you guys the resources, you guys could build desktop computers better than anyone, even better than us." There's a unanimous agreement around the table about how great they were, and how bad management was.

The Consultative Sale

Our sales guy then quietly asked if there was any way we could help them. (Help them?!! We're here to sell them our stuff. Why can't we just present what we got and they'll buy it?) The VP of Engineering said, "Well we don't have the resources or time, and as long as you know we could build better computers then you guys, why don't you tell us the details about your computers."

I had just watched a master of the consultative sale.

Engineers as Salesmen

I thought (and still do) that this sales guy walked on water. He had spent 12 years at DEC, first as a hardware engineer designing part of the PDP-16, then as the marketing manager for the LSI-11 and then in sales.

Making sales calls with him taught me what a world-class salesperson was like. It also made me understand what kind of support sales people needed from marketing and what marketing programs were wasted motion.

It also made me realize that there are times you don't want any sales people in your company.

Startups and Sales

If you read this post you can come away with the impression that every startup with a direct salesforce needs a consultative sales team. Not true.

The answer depends on your answer to two questions:

- Which step in the Customer Development process are you in?
- What Market Type is your startup?

Customer Development and Selling Strategy

If you've just started your company, you are in customer discovery. If you've tried to slog your way through my book on Customer Development, you know that I'm insistent that the founders need to be the ones getting outside the building (physically or virtually) to validate all the initial hypotheses of the business model and product. If you hire a VP of Sales with the idea that they can do customer discovery, you violated the first principle of Customer Development. This isn't a step the can be outsourced to a non-founder.

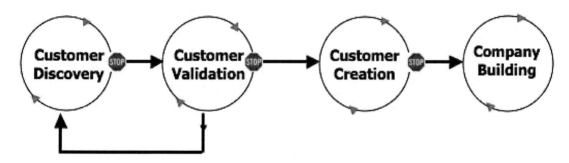

Hiring a VP of Sales in customer discovery typically sets a startup back. It's only after you're done with customer discovery and are in the final steps of customer validation (when you are building a repeatable and scalable sales process) that you start hiring a sales executive.

The next thing you need to do is match your sales team with your market type.

Market Type and Sales Teams

If you remember from a previous post, startups fall into four Types of Markets. You need to hire the right type of sales people for the type of market.

If you are in a New Market delivering what Clayton Christensen calls disruptive innovation, the market doesn't even have a name and customers have no clue on how your product works or how it could help them. This market cries out for a sales force that can help educate and guide customers to making the right choices. Your sales team is an extension of your marketing department. The same is true if you are in an existing market and trying to sell to a niche or a segment of the market based on your knowledge of their particular needs. Both New Markets and Resegmented Niche Markets required a skilled consultative sales force.

This is very different from the sales team you would hire to sell in an existing market or a cheaper product.

```
┌─────────────────────────────────────────────────────────┐
│                   Types of Markets                       │
│                                                          │
│   •  Existing Market                                     │
│        o           Faster/Better – High End              │
│   •  Resegmenting an Existing Market                     │
│        o   Niche = Marketing/Branding driven             │
│        o   Cheaper = Low Cost/Low End                    │
│   •  New Market                                          │
│        o           Never been done before                │
└─────────────────────────────────────────────────────────┘
```

If you're in an existing market and you have a superior product, by all means tout your features and specifications. However, your product itself will be doing a lot of the selling. If it is demonstrably better as you claim, your marketing department needs to communicate this competitive advantage, and your sales curve should look linear as you take share from the existing incumbents.

If you are resegmenting an existing market a product with a cheaper alternative, by all means tout your price. Your marketing department should be all over this. In both cases you really don't need a skilled/consultative sales force. A sales team with a great Rolodex will do.

Lessons Learned

```
┌─────────────────────────────────────────────────────────┐
│   •  Get out of the building (physically or virtually.)  │
│   •  Sales calls aren't your IQ test or PhD defense.     │
│   •  Stop talking and listen to the customer's problem.  │
│   •  Hire a sales team at the Customer Validation step.  │
│   •  Match the sales team to market type.                │
└─────────────────────────────────────────────────────────┘
```

Love/Hate Business Plan Competitions

Posted on **May 7, 2009** by steveblank |

I love business plan competitions.

I hate business plan competitions.

I Love Business Plan Competitions

I had a breakfast with a friend who has founded a few companies in Thailand and started the New Ventures Program at a Thai university. He was visiting Stanford and mentioned how proud he was that several of his Thai students were here in the States for a business plan competition.

For those of you who don't know, business plan competitions are held by universities who get their students to enter and compete. The goal is to see who has the best business idea. Local venture investors and/or companies offer cash prizes for the winners. In exchange, these VCs/companies get early looks at new deal flow and offer aspiring entrepreneurs feedback and advice on their business plan.

These competitions started in the early 1980's at the University of Texas and have sprouted like mushrooms in the last ten years. Just Google the term and you'll be amazed. Almost every university, region and car wash now has a business plan competition; the rules, who can participate, how large the prizes and who are the judges vary by school.

Over scrambled eggs and diet coke, I listened to this seasoned startup veteran describe the excitement of his students who came to the U.S. to compete. I finally understood how valuable these contests can be for students in cities or countries without a venture capital or entrepreneurial infrastructure. At a university business plan competition, for the first time they can swim in the sea of expertise that we/I take for granted in the middle of Silicon Valley. Win, lose or draw, these students have a life changing experience where they can network and get smarter as they see what good startup thinking looks like.

I love business plan competitions (and with my valley-centric bias, I think Berkeley and Stanford have two of the best.) If you are outside of Silicon Valley, you ought to jump into them with both feet. You'll learn a lot.

I Hate Business Plan Competitions

Yet this same conversation reminded me why every time students at Berkeley or Stanford tell me they've entered a technology business plan competition, I question whether they are wasting their time.

For all the reasons why business plan competitions are wonderful for students from outside the U.S., or even outside of Silicon Valley, I am left speechless when a student in a 50-mile radius of Sand Hill Road (who tells me they're serious about starting a company) thinks their time is better spent entering one.

I have seen students spend well over a year refining a business plan competition pitch when they have could have gotten the same advice within a month by literally stepping out the door and aggressively pursuing it. And with the other 11 months, they could have been well into actually building a company.

In the real world, most business plans don't survive the first few months of customer contact.

And even if they did – *customers don't ask to see your business plan.*

Here's a simple heuristic: if you are one of the lucky few who are within one- or two-degrees of separation of venture capital and startup resources (law firms, patent attorneys, etc.) and you are chasing a technical business plan competition, *you are signaling that you really don't want to start a company.* (And that may be fine with you. Just don't confuse the time you're spending with actual progress in building a company.)

I hate business plan competitions when they encourage students to write a "winning plan" rather than teaching them how to get out of the building and use locally available resources to start a company.

The Elves Leave Middle Earth – Sodas Are No Longer Free

Posted on December 21, 2009 by steveblank |

Sometimes financial decisions that are seemingly rational on their face can precipitate mass exodus of your best engineers.

We Hired the CFO

Last week as a favor to a friend, I sat in on a board meeting of a fairly successful 3½ year-old startup. Given all that could go wrong in this economy, they were doing well. Their business had just crossed cash flow breakeven, had grown past 50 employees, just raised a substantive follow-on round of financing and had recently hired a Chief Financial Officer. It was an impressive performance.

Then the new CFO got up to give her presentation – all kind of expected: Sarbanes Oxley compliance, a new accounting system, beef up IT and security, Section 409A (valuation) compliance, etc. Then she dropped the other shoe.

"Do you know how much our company is spending on free sodas and snacks?" And to answer her own question she presented the spreadsheet totaling it all up.

There were some experienced VC's in the room, and I was waiting for them to "educate" her about startup culture. But my jaw dropped when the board agreed that the "free stuff" had to go.

"We're too big for that now" was the shared opinion. But we'll sell them soda "cheap."

Unintended Consequences

I had lived through this same conversation four times in my career, and each time it ended as an example of unintended consequences. No one on the board or the executive staff was trying to be stupid. But to save $10,000 or so, they unintentionally launched an exodus of their best engineers.

This company had grown from the founders who hired an early team of superstars, many now managing their own teams. All these engineers were still heads-down, working their tails off, just as they had been doing since the first few months of the company. Too busy working, most were oblivious to the changes that success and growth had brought to the company.

The Elves Leave Middle Earth – Sodas Are No Longer Free

One day the engineering team was clustered in the snack room looking at the soda machine. The sign said, "Soda now 50 cents."

The uproar began. Engineers started complaining about the price of the soda. Someone noticed that instead of the informal reimbursement system for dinners when they were working late, there was now a formal expense report system. Some had already been irritated when "professional" managers had been hired over their teams with reportedly more stock than the early engineers had. Lots of email was exchanged about "how things were changing for the worse." A few engineers went to the see the CEO.

But the damage had been done. The most talented and senior engineers looked up from their desks and noticed the company was no longer the one they loved. It had changed. And not in a way they were happy with.

The best engineers quietly put the word out that they were available, and in less than month, the best and the brightest began to drift away.

What Happened?
Startups go through a metamorphosis as they become larger companies. They change from organizations built to learn, discover and iterate to ones that can execute adroitly once they have found product/market fit.

Humans seem to be hard-wired for numbers of social relationships. These same numbers also define boundaries in growing an organization – get bigger than a certain size, and you need a different management system. The military has recognized this for thousands of years as they built command and control hierarchies that matched these numbers.

Wake Up Call
The engineers focused on building product never noticed when the company had grown into something different than what they first joined.

The sodas were just the wake-up call.

As startups scale into a company, founders and the board need to realize that the most important transitions are not about systems, buildings or hardware. They are about the company's most valuable asset – its employees.

Great companies do this well.

Lessons Learned

- Be careful of unintended consequences when you grow.
- Recognize the transition boundaries in company size.
- Preserve and manage an Innovation Culture.

Stories from the Trenches

Raising Money Using Customer Development

Posted on November 5, 2009 by steveblank |

Getting "funded" is the Holy Grail for most entrepreneurs. Unfortunately in early stage startups the drive for financing hijacks the corporate DNA and becomes the *raison d'être* of the company. Chasing funding instead of chasing customers and a repeatable and scalable business model is one reason startups fail.

This post describes how companies using the Customer Development model can increase their credibility, valuation and probability of getting a first round of funding by presenting their results in a "Lesson Learned" venture pitch.

It should go without saying that this post is not advice, nor is it recommendation of what you should do, it's simply my observation of how companies using Customer Development positioned themselves to successfully raise money from venture investors.

Product Development – Getting Funded as The Goal

In a traditional product development model, entrepreneurs come up with an idea or concept, write a business plan and try to get funding to bring that idea to fruition. The goal of their startup in this stage becomes "getting funded." Entrepreneurs put together their funding presentation by extracting the key ideas from their business plan, putting them on PowerPoint/Keynote and pitching the company – until they get funded or exhausted.

Concept ➭ **Business Plan** ➭ **Seed or Series A** ➭ **Execute**

What are Early Stage VC's Really Asking?

When you present to a VC, there are two conversations going on: the one you are presenting and the one that investors are thinking as they are listening to your presentation. (If they're not busy looking at their Blackberry/iPhone.)

A VC listening to your presentation is thinking, "Are you going to blow my initial investment or are you going to make me a ton of money? Are there customers for what you are building? How many? Now? Later? Is there a profitable business model? Can it scale?" And finally, "Is this a team that can build this company?"

The Traditional VC Pitch

Entrepreneurs who pursue the traditional product development model don't have customer data to answer these questions. Knowing this, venture firms have come up with a canonical checklist of what they would like to see. A typical pitch to a venture firm might cover:

- Technology/Product
- Team
- Opportunity/Market
- Customer Problem
- Business Model
- Go to Market Strategy
- Financials

Given that the traditional pitch has no hard customer metrics (and VC's don't demand them,) you get funded on the basis of intangibles that vary from firm to firm: Do you fit the theme or thesis of the venture firm? Did the VC's like your team? Do they believe you have a big enough vision and market. Did the partner have a good or bad day, etc.? Tons of advice is available on how to pitch, present and market your company.

I believe all this advice is wrong. It's akin to putting lipstick on a pig. The problem isn't your pitch, it's your fundamental assumption that you can/should get funded without having real customer and product feedback. No amount of learning how to get a VC meeting or improving your VC demo skills will fix the lack of concrete customer data. You might as well bring your lucky rabbit's foot to the VC meeting.

Customer Development –Getting Funded After Finding a Repeatable Model

In contrast, if you are following a Customer Development process, you have a greater chance of getting listened to, believed and funded.

Just as a refresher. The first step in Customer Development is Customer Discovery; extracting hypotheses from the business plan and getting *the founders* out of the building to test the hypotheses in front of customers. Your goal is to preserve your cash while you turn these guesses into facts and search for a repeatable and scalable sales model. Your proof that you have a business rather than a hobby comes from customer orders or users for your product even thought it is buggy, unfinished and has a minimum feature set.

If you're following Customer Development, you are now raising money because even with this first rev of the product, you think you've found product/market fit, and you want to scale.

What VC's Really Want But Don't Know How to Ask For

Mike Maples at Maples Investments observes that the quality of pitches from entrepreneurs get better as you climb the "Hierarchy of Proof."

1. On the bottom, and least convincing are statements about your "idea."

2. Next are hypothesis – "I think customers will care about x or y, "

3. Better are facts from customers – "We interviewed 30 customers with 20 questions,"

4. Even better is "Customer Validation"– "We just got $50K from a customer" or "We got 100,000 users spending x minutes on our site,"

5. Finally if you're ever so lucky – "Everyone's buying in droves, and we're here because we need money to scale and execute"

If you've actually been doing Customer Development, at a minimum you're at step 3 or 4. If not, you don't have enough data for a VC presentation. Get out of the building, get some more customer feedback, spin your product and go back and read the book.

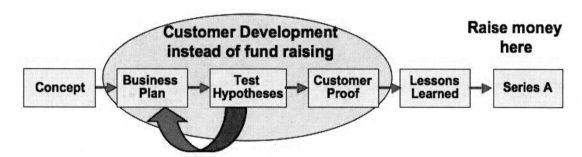

Lessons Learned – A New Type of VC Pitch

A Customer Development fundraising presentation tells the story of your journey in Customer Discovery and Validation. While your presentation will cover some of the same ground as the traditional VC pitch, the heart of the presentation is the *Lessons Learned from our Customers* section. The overall presentation looks something like this:

- Market/Opportunity
- Team
- Lessons Learned Slide 1
- Lessons Learned Slide 2
- Lessons Learned Slide 3
- Why We're Here

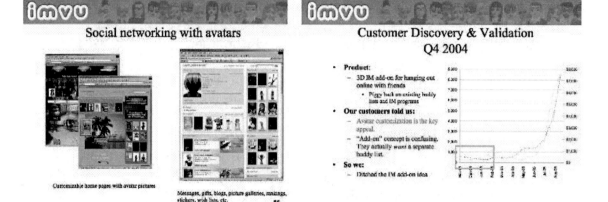

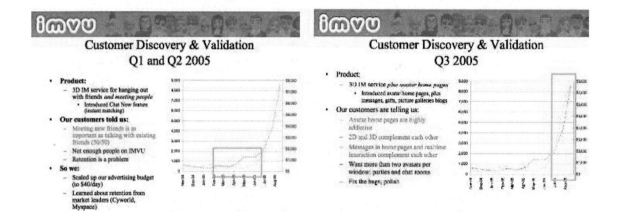

IMVU's Original VC Presentation - Will Harvey & Eric Ries

Here's What We Thought, What We Did, What We Learned

Notice that each of the *Lessons Learned* slides has three major subheads and a graph:

- *"Here's What We Thought"*
- *"Here's What We Did"*
- *"Here's What Happened"*
- *A Progress Graph*

Here's What We Thought is you describing your initial set of hypotheses. *Here's What We Did* allows you to talk about building the first-pass of the product's minimum feature set. *Here's What Happened* is the not so surprising story of why customers didn't react the way you thought they would. *A Progress Graph* on the right visually shows how far you've come (in whatever units of goodness you're tracking – revenue, units, users, etc.)

48

Telling the Customer Discovery and Customer Validation story this way allows you to take VC's on your journey through all the learning and discovery you've done. After three of these slides, smart VC's will recognize that by iterating on your assumptions you have dramatically reduced risk– on your nickel, not theirs. They will realize that you have built a startup that's agile, resilient and customer-centric.

Your presentation doesn't have a single word about Lean Startups or Customer Development. There is no proselytizing about any particular methodology, yet the results are compelling.

This is a radical departure from a traditional VC pitch. It will blow the minds of 70-80% of investors. The others will throw you out of their office.

Guaranteed Funding – Not

Will this type of presentation guarantee you funding? Of course not. Even if you have the worlds best *Lessons Learned* slides you might find out that your particular market (i.e. consumer Internet) might have a really, really high bar of achievement for funding.

In fact, just trying to put three *Lessons Learned* slides together showing tangible *progress will make most startups realize how hard really doing Customer Development is.*

Try it.

Lessons Learned – A New Type of Venture Capital Pitch

Posted on November 12, 2009 by steveblank |

I joined the board of Cafepress.com when it was a startup. It was amazing to see the two founders, Fred Durham and Maheesh Jain, build a $100 million company from coffee cups and T-shirts.

But Cafepress's most memorable moment was when the founders used a *Lessons Learned* VC pitch to raise their second round of funding and got an 8-digit term sheet that same afternoon.

Here's how they did it.

Fail Fast and Cheap

Fred and Maheesh had started 9 previous companies in 6 years. Their motto was: "Fail fast and cheap. And learn from it." Cafepress literally started in their garage and was another set of experiments - only this time it caught fire. They couldn't keep up with the orders.

Tell the Story of the Journey

The company got to a point where additional capital was needed to expand just to keep up with the business (a warehouse/shipping center collocated with UPS, etc.) Rather than a traditional VC pitch, I suggested that they do something unconventional and tell the story of their journey in Customer Discovery and Validation. The heart of the Cafepress presentation is the *Lessons Learned from our Customers* section. Their presentation looked like this:

- Market/Opportunity
- Lessons Learned Slide 1
- Lessons Learned Slide 2
- Lessons Learned Slide 3
- Why We're Here

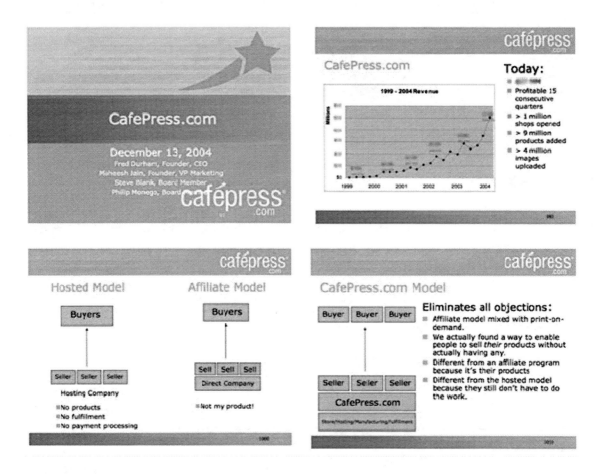

Telling the Cafepress Customer Discovery and Customer Validation story allowed Fred and Maheesh to take the VC's on their journey year by year.

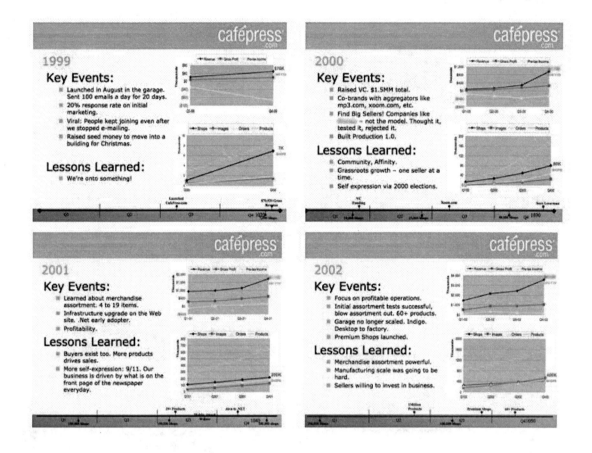

After these slides, the VC's recognized that this company had dramatically reduced risk and built a startup that was agile, resilient and customer-centric.

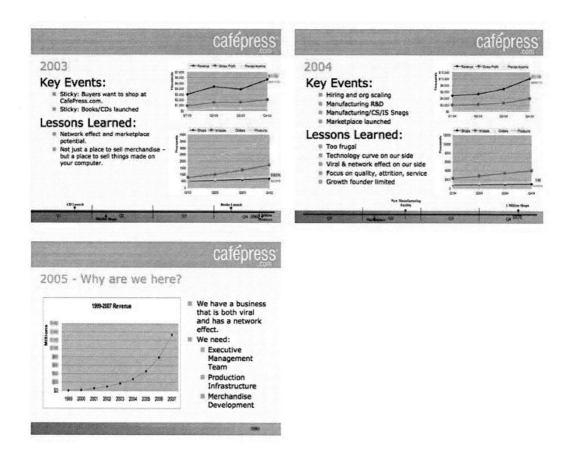

The presentation didn't have a single word about Lean Startups or Customer Development. There was no proselytizing about any particular methodology, yet the results are compelling.

The VC firm delivered a term sheet for an 8-digit second round that afternoon.

Your results may vary.

Can You Trust Any VC's Under 40?

Posted on September 14, 2009 by steveblank |

Over the last 30 years Wall Street's appetite for technology stocks has changed radically, swinging between unbridled enthusiasm to believing they're all toxic. Over the same 30 years, Venture Capital firms have honed their skills and strategies to match Wall Street's needs to achieve liquidity for their portfolio companies.

You have to wonder: does the VC you have on your board today have the right skill set to help you succeed in today's economic environment?

What Do VC's Do?

One of the biggest mistakes entrepreneurs make is misunderstanding the role of venture capital investors. There's lots of lore, emotion, and misconceptions of what VC's do or don't do for entrepreneurs. The reality is that VC's have one goal – *to maximize the amount of money they return to their investors.* To do this, they have to accomplish five things;

1) get deal flow – via networking and legwork, they identify likely industries, companies and teams with the potential for rapid growth (less than 10 years.)

2) evaluate those companies and teams on the basis of technology, market opportunity, and team. (Each VC firm/partner has a different spin on what to weigh more.)

3) invest in and take equity stakes in exchange for capital.

4) help nurture and grow the companies they invest in.

5) liquidate their investment in each company at the highest possible price.

Going Public

VC's make money by selling their share of your company to some other buyer – hopefully at a large multiple over what they originally paid for it. From 1979 when pensions funds began fueling the expansion of venture capital, the way VC's sold their portion of your company was to help you take your company "public." Your firm worked with an investment banking firm that underwrote and offered stock (typically on the NASDAQ exchange) to the public. At this Initial Public Offering, your company raised money for its use in expanding the business.

In theory when you went public, everyone's shares were now tradable on the stock exchange, but usually the underwriters required a six-month "lockup" during which company insiders (employees and investors) couldn't sell. After the end of the lockup, venture firms sold off their stock in an orderly fashion and entrepreneurs sold theirs and bought new cars and houses.

Five Quarters of Profitability
During the 1980's and through the mid 1990's, startups going public had to do something that most companies today never heard of – they had to show a track record of increasing revenue and consistent profitability. Underwriters who would offer the stock to the public typically asked for a young company to show five *consecutive* quarters of profits. There was no law that said that a company had to, but most underwriters wouldn't take a company public without it. (On top of all this it was considered very bad form not to have at least four additional consecutive quarters of profits *after* an IPO.) While there was an occasional bad apple, the public markets rewarded companies with *revenue growth and sustainable profits*.

What this meant for entrepreneurs and VC's was simple, profound and unappreciated today: VC's worked with entrepreneurs to *build* profitable and scalable businesses. In this time, building a successful business meant building a company that had paying customers quarter after quarter. It did not mean building a startup into a company to flip or hype on the market with no earnings or revenue, but building a company that had paying customers.

Venture Capitalists on your board brought your firm their expertise to build long-term sustainable companies. They taught you about customers, markets and profits.

The world of building profitable startups as the primary goal of Venture Capital would end in 1995.

The IPO Bubble – August 1995 – March 2000
In August 1995 Netscape went public, and the world of start ups turned upside down. On its first day of trading, Netscape stock closed at $58/share, valuing the company at $2.7 billion for a company with less than $50 million in sales. (Yahoo would hit $104/share in March 2000 with a market cap of $104 billion.) There was now a public market for companies with no revenue, no profit and big claims. Underwriters realized that as long as the public was happy snapping up shares, they could make huge profits on the inflated valuations regardless of whether or not the company should have ever been public.

And some companies didn't even have to go public to get liquid. Tech acquisitions went crazy at the same time the IPO market did. Large companies were acquiring technology startups just to get in the game at the same absurd prices.

What this meant for entrepreneurs and VC's was simple– the gold rush to liquidity was on. The old rules of building companies with sustainable revenue and consistent profitability went out the window. VCs worked with entrepreneurs to *brand, hype and take public un*profitable companies with grand promises of the future. The goals were "first mover advantage," "grab market share" and "get big fast." VCs or entrepreneurs who talked about building profitable businesses were told, "You just don't get the new rules." And to be honest, for four years, these were the new rules. Entrepreneurs and VCs made returns 10x, or even 100x larger than anything ever seen. (No value judgments here, VCs were doing what the market rewarded them for, and their investors expected – maximum returns.)

(And since Venture Capital looked like anyone could do it, the number of venture firms soared as fast as stock prices.)

Venture Capitalists on your board developed the expertise to get your firm public as soon as possible using whatever it took including hype, spin, expand, and grab market share because the sooner you got your billion dollar market cap, the sooner the VC firm could sell their shares and distribute their profits.

The boom in Internet startups would last 4½ years until it came crashing down to earth in March 2000.

The Rise of Mergers and Acquisitions — March 2003 -2008
After the dot.com bubble collapsed, the IPO market (and most tech M&A deals) shutdown for technology companies. Venture investors spent the next three years doing triage, sorting through the rubble to find companies that weren't bleeding cash and could actually be turned into businesses. With Wall Street leery of technology companies, tech IPOs were a receding memory, and mergers and acquisitions became the only path to liquidity for startups and their investors. For the next four or five years, technology M&A boomed, growing from 50 in 2003 to 450 in 2006.

What this meant for entrepreneurs and VCs was a bit more complex– the IPO market was all but closed (with the Google IPO in 2004 as a brilliant exception), but it was possible find a *buyer* for your company. The valuations for acquisitions were nothing like the Internet bubble, but there was a path to liquidity, difficult as it was. (Every startup wanted to believe they could get acquired like YouTube for $1.4 billion.) VCs worked with entrepreneurs to build their company with an eye out for a chance to flip it to an acquirer. The formula for exits was a variation of the formula they used in the Internet bubble, morphing into: brand, hype and sell the company.

In the fall of 2008, the credit crisis wiped out mergers and acquisitions as a path to liquidity as M&A collapsed with the rest of the market.

So what's left?

2009 – Back to The Future

The bad news is that since the bubble, most VC firms haven't made a profit. It may just be that the message of building companies that have predictable revenue and profit models hasn't percolated through the VC business model, perhaps in direct proportion to the number of "freemium" and "eyeballs" web deals funded.

It may be that the venture business will have to return to the old days of helping entrepreneurs build companies – not hype them, not spin them, but actually make them worth something to customers and investors.

The question is: do VC's still have what it takes to do so?

Next time you sit in a board meeting with your VCs, step back a bit from the moment and listen to their advice like you are hearing them for the first time. Are these VC's who know how to build a company? Is the advice they are giving you going to help you build a repeatable and scalable revenue model that's profitable quarter after quarter?

Or were they trained and raised in the bubble and M&A hype and still looking for some shortcut to liquidity?

Are Those My Initials?

Posted on December 3, 2009 by steveblank |

In my 21 years of startups I've had my ideas "stolen" twice. Once it almost mattered. This is about the time it didn't.

Worries from the garage

One of the worries I hear from entrepreneurs (not just my students) is that Customer Development means getting out of the building and sharing what you are working on. What if, gasp, someone steals my idea? Then all my hard work will be for nothing.

This actually happened to me twice in my career.

The first time was at Rocket Science Games. I was positioning the company as the second coming of the video games businesses at the intersection of "Hollywood Meets Silicon Valley." This was a great positioning. It helped us raise lots of money and get tons of press. I had a wonderful set of slides that illustrated (to me) this inevitable trend. At the end of the presentation was one "uber" chart I had labored over for months that laid out all the converging trends in the industry. I used it in all presentations and gave it at industry conferences.

Are those my initials on the slide?

Fast forward nine months. My co-founder, head of business development and I were in Japan raising money. We were sitting in the conference room of a large well-respected media firm when the CEO breezed in to give us an overview of who they were and how forward thinking their firm was. I thought highly of this firm and was in awe of their content and films so I was a bit blown away when the CEO got to the finale of their presentation. It was, as he explained, the sum of *their* strategy and strategic thinking for online media. And the slide was

My slide.

Not a summary of my slide or a Japanese copy of my slide, but my actual slide. I stood up from my seat, and walked around the boardroom table to get closer to the screen just to be sure. The CEO was beaming at my interest in the details of the slide. Examining the slide, I pointed to the bottom right and said to our translator, "Tell him my initials are still on the bottom." The interpreter's face went white, and after a lot of "I can't tell him that," he did.

We weren't sure if we should feel insulted or complimented, but after a few deep breaths and a lot of kicking under the table, my smart VP of business development used it as an opportunity to point out how honored we were that there was an obvious strategic alignment between the two companies. (I sat there smiling tightly.) Given the potential for a cross-cultural meltdown, all parties behaved politely. The CEO turned out to be a very nice guy and rented a big bus to take his staff and all of us sightseeing, dinner and drinking around Tokyo. (I'm sure when he got back to the office he was handing out a personalized knife to the executive on his staff who had borrowed my slide.)

In the end, the CEO couldn't get his board to give us the cash in exchange for the Japanese distribution rights and some equity. We ended up raising money from Sega.

I heard later that the slide disappeared from his presentation.

—

The next time one of my ideas was "borrowed," it was a little less benign and more like the nightmare founders fear. More in the next post.

Lessons Learned

- If you present slides publicly, assume everyone including your competitors will have them.
- If you present slides privately, assume a high probability that your competitors will acquire them
- Do *not* put your trade secrets, proprietary algorithms, patentable technology, secret sauce, etc. on presentation slides – ever.
- That still leaves you tons to talk about in a first and even second meeting.
- For slides that contain diagrams or drawings that you created, make sure your initials and date are on them.

They Raised Money With My Slides?!

Posted on December 7, 2009 by steveblank |

In my 21 years of startups, I had my ideas "stolen" twice. See the last story for the first time it happened. This time it was serious.

As a reminder, this post is not legal advice. It's not even advice. It's just a story about what happened to me.

Customer Development

We were starting Epiphany, my last company. I was out and about in Silicon Valley doing what I would now call Customer Discovery, trying to understand how marketing departments in large corporations worked. The initial hypothesis for Epiphany (from my much smarter partner Ben) was that as departments in the enterprise (manufacturing, finance, customer support sales) became automated, the marketing department would eventually get its turn.

I remember presenting our ideas for Marketing Automation to one VP of Marketing in a large Silicon Valley company. His enthusiastic response was, "This will revolutionize marketing departments!" He continued: "I'd like to convince my boss so our company can be your first customer." I should have been suspicious when he said, "I'd like to take a copy of your presentation to show him." Caught up in the enthusiasm of hearing what a great idea we had, I violated one of my cardinal rules, and left him a hard copy.

Fast Forward

Fast-forward nine months. After talking to tons of customers and almost as many VC's, we got Epiphany funded as a company that was going to automate Marketing Departments. After a ton of unreturned phone calls, I had written off the enthusiastic VP of Marketing who wanted to show my slides to his boss and moved on with building our company.

By now we had found a few customers and learned a lot more about the market from them and other prospects. Our business model changed as we realized that to become a large company, we needed to automate more than just a few marketers. As we were out looking for our Series B round, our company had gotten the attention of "name of big VC firm here" that wanted a play in enterprise software.

Are These Your Slides?

During the due-diligence process, I sat down with one of the partners who pulled out a set of slides and asked me: "Have you seen these?" I quickly leafed through them and replied, "Sure they're our original slides. Why?" He said, "Look again." They had all my words from a year ago, but hey wait a minute, there's someone else's logo on my slides?! What's going on? He said, "That's what we're trying to figure out. These guys just got funded, and they sound a lot like you guys." Luckily I had the original slides and could prove who came first. Still the fact was a competitor had raised money using our idea and our slide deck.

And who was this competitor? The VP of Marketing who a year earlier had wanted a hard copy of our slides. He was now CEO of a new company in our market.

I felt like I had just been kicked in the stomach.

Disbelief, Anger, Resignation and Acceptance

My cofounders and I went through the stages of disbelief, anger, resignation and acceptance. Here was a competitor who had appropriated our idea and gotten funded. (Welcome to the Internet bubble.) There was lots of venting as we talked about bringing lawsuits and issuing nasty press releases.

We consciously didn't ask potential customers to sign a Non-Disclosure Agreement (NDA). In Customer Discovery we were learning as much from them as they did from us. And we figured that unless litigation was going to be our business strategy, NDA's would have inhibited the back-and-forth that made us smarter. We concluded that, at least for us in this market, an NDA would be a bigger impediment than asset. Now we started asking ourselves, "Did we make a mistake? Would have getting a signed confidentially agreement deterred this person?" On further reflection, (and his track record since) not in the least. But that still left us with a problem. What should we do about this competitor copying our strategy?

Finally, we concluded, "You can't drive forward by looking in the rear-view mirror."

Our competitor was executing on hypotheses we had developed 9 months ago, and their strategy remained static. We, on the other hand, had moved on. We had discovered detailed information about what customers really needed and wanted and turned our original hypotheses into facts. We had validated our new assumptions by a set of orders, and we had pivoted on our business model (i.e. we had radically changed our model based on customer feedback.) Our original idea had been nothing more than an untested set of hypotheses. Truth be told, *we were no longer the company in those stolen slides.*

While the common wisdom said that our success was going to be determined by which company executed better, the common wisdom was wrong. In a startup, success isn't about just execution, it's how well we could take our original hypothesis and *learn, discover, iterate* <u>and</u> execute.

Never Get Even, Get Ahead

With a set of orders from brand name customers, we had growing confidence that we had achieved product/market fit. We were within three months of formally announcing our company and products at a major industry trade show. We made sure our competitor knew this. In fact, we made sure they knew what day at the show we were going to announce. Just as we predicted, they picked the day before us for their announcement in an effort to preempt our company launch with theirs. We made sure they heard how shocked and upset we were that they were going to beat us to an announcement in our market.

Our competitor announced on a Monday solidifying their position in the small market we had abandoned because we realized it was unprofitable and would not scale.

We announced the next day, positioned as a player in a much larger and broader market with new positioning, strategy and customers.

Our copycat competitor was now publicly locked into a company and product strategy that was obsolete and untenable.

Over the next two years we left them in the dust.

_____

While how you iterate and execute your idea is more important than the idea itself, there are parts of your intellectual property a startup does need to protect.

Lessons Learned

- Your business concept is not a company. Lots of people have ideas. Typically they are just a set of untested hypotheses.
- Successful companies are about *the learning, discovery, iteration* on your initial ideas. If someone can do a better job iterating hypotheses and executing than you can, you deserve to fail.
- No business plan survives first contact with customers.
- The real value is finding the product/market fit. That's not found in a set of slides.

The Best Defense is a Good IP Strategy

Posted on December 10, 2009 by steveblank |

Early on in my career I took a "we're moving too fast to deal with lawyers" attitude to patents and Intellectual Property (IP.) That changed when I joined the board of a startup, and we sued Microsoft and Sony on the same day for patent infringement – and won $120 million.

A few caveats, this post is not legal advice, it's not even advice, and it deals with law in the United States. Outside the U.S. your results will vary depending on your distance to a consistent and predictable legal system.

At one of my entrepreneurship classes at Stanford, Dan Dorosin, of Fenwick & West LLP guest lectures about startups and Intellectual Property. Most of this post is from Dan's lecture. (But there are no guarantees that I got it right.) It may seem full of legal definitions and terms but my two takeaways are: 1) Entrepreneurs need to know about these legal options, 2) Consulting an intellectual property attorney is a good move even before you get funded.

Intellectual Property

Intellectual property gives you rights to stop others from using your creativity.

The assets you can protect may include your "core technology" like source code, hardware designs, architectures, processes, and formulas. Or it can be your brand, logo or domain name. You can protect business processes, know how, customer information, product road map. Protection is also available for content such as music, books, or film.

Type of IP	What is Protectable	Examples
Trademark	Branding (i.e. Nike swoosh)	marks, logos, slogans
Copyright	Creative, authored works; expressions (not ideas)	software, songs, movies, web site content
Trade Secrets	Secrets with economic value(i.e. the Coke recipe)	non-public technology customer lists, formula
Contract, NDA	As defined in the contract	technology, business information
Patent	Inventions	new technology

For some of these assets, you get protection automatically. For other classes, to get full protection, you should/must go through a registration, application or examination process.

Trademark

A trademark protects branding and marks, it gives you the right to prevent others from using "confusingly similar" marks and logos. Trademark protection lasts as long as you are using the mark. The more you use the mark, the stronger your protection. Trademark registration is optional, but has significant advantages if approved.

Copyright

A copyright protects creative works of authorship; typically songs, books, movies, photos, etc. Copyright gives you the right to prevent others from copying, distributing or making derivatives of your work. It protects "expressions" of ideas but does not protect the underlying ideas. (If your product is software, copyright is also used to prevent someone from stealing your software and reselling it as machine and/or source code.) Copyright protection lasts practically forever. Registration is optional, but is required to sue for infringement.

Contract

A contract is a binding legal agreement that is enforceable in a court of law. There's no official registration process. You have whatever protection is defined in the contract (e.g., a Non Disclosure Agreement gives you certain rights to protection of your confidential information.) The protection lasts for the time period defined in the contract.

Patents

A patent is a government granted monopoly to prevent others from making, using or selling your invention – even if the other parties infringement was innocent or accidental.

Just about anything can be patented: circuits, hardware, software, applied algorithms, formulas, designs, user interfaces, applications, systems. Scientific principles or pure mathematical algorithms cannot be patented.

Your invention must be "non-obvious." The test for non-obvious is: given the prior art at the time of the invention, would a typical engineer 1) identify the problem, and 2) solve it with the invention? You must be "first" to patent. In the U.S. that means, "first to invent" while outside U.S. it means "first to file." You must file in U.S. within one year of sale, offer for sale, public disclosure or public use.

Your patent application has to include a written description with details of the claims of the invention. The details have to allow others to duplicate your invention from your description and has to the "best mode" in describing critical techniques/technologies. And it has to identify all prior art.

Patent protection lasts typically for 15-20 years. It requires a formal application and examination process. Each patent filing will cost your company $10-30k and take 1-4 years. Filing of patents is frequently of major interest to people funding your company.

(There's something called a "provisional patent." It's an alternative to a full patent. It allows you to claim "first to file" and use the term "patent pending." Provisional patents get into the patent office quickly and cheaply. However they automatically expire after one year and no patent rights are granted. Provisional patents are a good placeholder because they are cheap to file and doesn't get in the way of your other patent efforts.)

Key Idea #1 – Intellectual Property Creates Value

Intellectual Property is an asset for you company. You need to acquire, protect and exploit it. An intellectual property strategy will map out:

- Who are the key players and technologies in its market(s)?
- What are the most important ideas and inventions that need patents (or provisional patents?) Start filing these early!
- What are the important patent applications that come next?

Key Idea #2 – Your Intellectual Property Needs Are Unique

What type of intellectual property matters to your company, and what you should do to protect it is highly company/industry dependent, requiring unique analysis and/or protection. For example if you are a:

- Medical device company – patents are key
- Web 2.0/social network start up – trademark and copyright are more likely
- Enterprise software company – copyright and trade secrets are probable
- Biotech/phama – don't leave your bedroom until you have a patent counsel

Make sure you understand Intellectual Property for your *specific industry*.

Four Common Intellectual Property Mistakes by Start-Ups

1. Founders Didn't Make Clean Break with Prior Employer

Under California law, employers may own inventions that are "related to employer's reasonably anticipated R&D." It's a very subjective standard, and since startups don't often have resources or time to spend in lawsuits large companies use threats of litigation to ensure you don't take anything. Therefore the best advice is "take only memories." If you're at a university, they may have patent policies that apply, too.

2. Your Company Cannot Clearly Show That it Owns its Intellectual Property

Take the time to create a well documented, clear chain of title to your intellectual property. If you are using independent contractors make sure you have written agreements assigning work created. Make sure you have Employee Invention Assignment Agreements. (If you hire subcontractors or friends to do some work, get assignment agreements as well.)

3. Your Company Lost Patent Rights due to Filing Delays/Invention Disclosures

In the U.S. patent rights are forfeited if you wait greater than 1 year after:

- Disclosure in a printed publication: Red flags: White paper, journal/conference article, Web site
- Offer for sale in the U.S.: Red flags: Start of sales effort, Price list, price quotation, Trade show demonstration, Any demonstration not under NDA
- Public use in the U.S.

In most foreign countries there is no one-year grace period.

4. Your Company Grants "Challenging" Licenses to Intellectual Property

Startups acquiring their first customers may give special licensing terms in key markets, territories, etc. For example, a grant of "most favored nations" license terms or other licensee-favorable economic terms can make your intellectual property less valuable to future buyers of your company. Or you may cut a deal that you can't assign or transfer (or can't get out of) if you get acquired.

Lessons Learned

> - Protecting your startups intellectual property should be a strategy not an after the fact tactic.
> - You need a plan for trademarks, copyright, trade secrets, contracts/NDA's and patents before you get funded.
> - Your intellectual property may be an additional revenue stream or may add substantial value to your company.

Elephants Can Dance – Reinventing HP

Posted on June 22, 2009 by steveblank |

I was at the Stanford library going through the papers of Fred Terman and came across a memo from 1956 that probably hasn't been seen or read in over 50 years. It had nothing to do with the subject I was looking for so I read it, chuckled, put it back in the file and kept leafing through the other papers. About a minute later, I did a double-take as it hit me what I had just read. (I'll show you the memo in a second. But first some background.)

Things Change

In 1956 Hewlett Packard (HP) was a 17-year old company with $20 million in test equipment sales with 900 employees. It was still a year away from its IPO.

Its latest product was an oscilloscope, the HP 150a.

In March of 1956, Fred Terman, the Stanford professor who encouraged Bill Hewlett and David Packard to start HP, wrote Bill Hewlett asking for help.

Terman, who now was the Provost of Stanford, had joined the U.S. Army Signal Corps advisory board, and the Army was going to acquire their first computer for research. No one in the Army Signal Corps knew much about computers. (To be fair in 1956 not too many people in the world knew much either.) So the Army asked Terman for help.

Fred Terman wrote to Bill Hewlett asking if he or anyone at Hewlett Packard could help them figure out these "computers."

Hewlett's answer, in the memo I discovered in the Stanford library, is below.

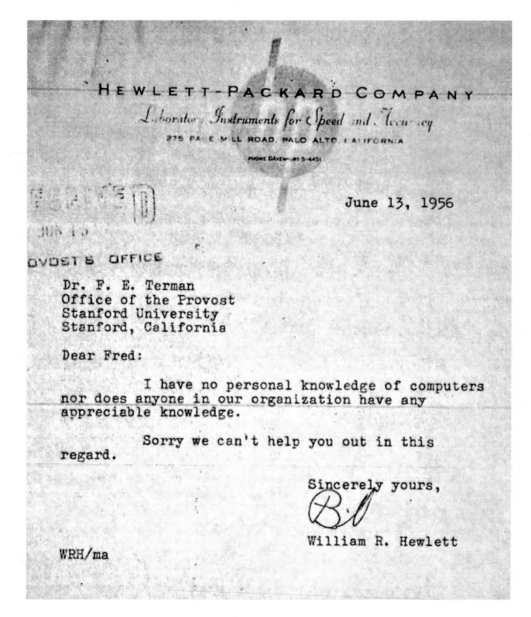

HEWLETT-PACKARD COMPANY

Laboratory Instruments for Speed and Accuracy

275 PAGE MILL ROAD, PALO ALTO, CALIFORNIA

PHONE DAVENPORT 5-4451

June 13, 1956

PROVOST'S OFFICE

Dr. F. E. Terman
Office of the Provost
Stanford University
Stanford, California

Dear Fred:

I have no personal knowledge of computers
nor does anyone in our organization have any
appreciable knowledge.

Sorry we can't help you out in this
regard.

Sincerely yours,

William R. Hewlett

WRH/ma

*I have no personal knowledge of computers
nor does anyone in our organization have any*

We Changed Our Mind

In 1966, 10 years after Hewlett's memo, Hewlett Packard's revenue and headcount had grown ten fold; $200 million and 11,000 employees – all from test and measurement equipment. That year HP introduced its first computer, the HP 2116A, as an instrument controller for HP's test and measurement products. (Hewlett's partner Dave Packard wanted to get into the computer business.) It was priced at $22,000 – equivalent to about $140,000 in 2009 dollars.

Thirty-three years after introducing its first computer, Hewlett Packard split into two separate companies. The original Hewlett Packard which made test and measurement products was spun-out and renamed Agilent. The remaining company kept the Hewlett Packard name and focused on computers.

Agilent is a $5.8 billion dollar test and measurement company.

Hewlett Packard (HP) at a $118 billion is the largest PC and notebook manufacturer in the world. That's a pretty long way from a company that said it knew nothing about computers.

Elephants Can Dance

HP's complete makeover made me wonder about other large companies that reinvented themselves.

Intel was founded in 1968 to make memory chips (bipolar RAM) but 17 years later they got out of the memory business and become the leading microprocessor company.

IBM had a near death experience in 1993, and moved from a product-centric hardware company to selling a complete set of solutions and services.

After failing dismally at making disposable digital cameras in 2003 Pure Digital Technologies reinvented their company in 2007 to make the Flip line of camcorders.

Apple was a personal computer company but 25 years after it started, it began the transformation to the iPod and iPhone.

A few carriage makers in the early part of the 20th century made the transition to become car companies. A great example is William Durant's Durant-Dort Carriage Company. In 1904 Durant took over Buick, and in 1908 he created General Motors by acquiring Oldsmobile, Pontiac, and Cadillac.

Elephant Graveyard

Reinvention of large companies, while making for great case studies, are rare. For the first 25 years, HP's business model was static. It got bigger by inventing new test and measurement equipment, and it hired people who knew how to execute that strategy. Of course HP did ship new products and innovate, but their center of innovation was sustaining innovation around the core of their existing business. (Clayton Christensen describes this brilliantly in the *Innovators Dilemma*.)

However, no markets last forever. Technology changes, culture changes, customer needs change, more agile competitors emerge, etc. So what causes some big companies to reinvent themselves, and others to remain static?

Creative Destruction

Most established companies fall into the seductive trap of following short-term profits all the way into the ground – leaving behind only their t-shirts and coffee cups. It's not the executives are stupid, it's just that there are no incentives (or corporate DNA) for doing otherwise. General managers of divisions are compensated on division P&L not long-term innovation. CEO's and the executive staff are watching the corporate bottom line and earnings per share. Wall Street wants quarterly earnings.

It's a pretty safe bet that left to their own devices, most large corporations wouldn't last more than a generation without major reinvention. And venture capital and entrepreneurship has made life even tougher for the modern corporation. Over the last 35 years, venture capital has funded nimble new entrants (on a scale never imagined by Schumpeter) who exist to exploit discontinuities in technology or customer behavior. Startups have forced an accelerated cycle of creative destruction for large companies that didn't exist in the first half of the 20th century.

Cultural Revolution at Large Corporations – the Founders Return

Of the companies that do reinvent themselves, it's interesting that often *its the founder or an outsider that has the insight to make the radical changes*. At HP the founders were still at the company and still running the business. It was David Packard who wanted to get into the commercial computer business – over the objections of his co-founder Bill Hewlett and most of the company. Packard had the stature and authority to encourage the shift and the internal political acumen to acquire a minicomputer company and label the first HP computer as a "instrument controller."

At Apple the company reinvented itself on Steve Job's return. Howard Shultz came back at Starbucks, Michael Dell reengaged at Dell. Outsiders like Lou Gerstner at IBM and Jon Rubenstein at Palm were brought in to reinvent their companies.

Lessons Learned

- It's the founders that can reinvent a company by seeing market shifts that professional managers focused on execution can not.
- If the founders aren't around, bring in outsiders with fresh insights.

Customer Development Manifesto

The Leading Cause of Startup Death:
The Product Development Diagram

Posted on August 27, 2009 by steveblank |

When I started working in Silicon Valley, every company bringing a new product to market used some form of the Product Development Model. Thirty years later we now realize that it's one of the causes of early startup failure. This series of posts is a brief explanation of how we've evolved from Product Development to Customer Development to the Lean Startup.

The Product Development Diagram

Emerging early in the twentieth century, this product-centric model described a process that evolved in manufacturing industries. It was adopted by the consumer packaged goods industry in the 1950s and spread to the technology business in the last quarter of the twentieth century. It has become an integral part of startup culture.

At first glance, the diagram, which illustrates the process of getting a new product into the hands of waiting customers, appears helpful and benign. Ironically, the model is a good fit when launching a new product into an *existing*, well-defined *market* where the basis of competition is understood, and your customers are known.

The irony is that few startups fit these criteria. (None of mine did.) We had no clue what our market was when we first started. Yet we used the product development model not only to manage product development, but also as a road map for finding customers and a planning tool to time our marketing launch and sales revenue plan. The model became a catchall tool for all schedules, plans, and budgets. Our investors used the product development diagram in our board meeting to see if we were "on plan" and "on schedule." Everyone was using a road map that was designed for a very different location yet they were surprised when they end up lost.

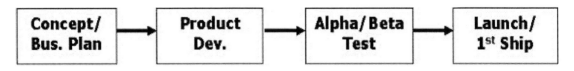

Product Development Diagram

To see what's wrong with using the product development model as a guide to building a startup, let's first examine how the model is currently used to launch a new product. We'll look at the model stage-by-stage.

Concept and Seed Stage

In the Concept and Seed Stage, founders capture their passion and vision for the new company and turn them into a set of key ideas, which quickly becomes a business plan, sometimes on the back of the proverbial napkin. The first thing captured and wrestled to paper is the company's vision.

Then the product needs to be defined: What is the product or service concept? What are the features and benefits? Is it possible to build? Is further technical research needed to ensure that the product can be built?

Next, who will the customers be and where will they be found? Statistical and market research data plus potential customer interviews determine whether the ideas have merit.

After that there's a discussion of how the product will reach the customer and the potential distribution channel. The distribution discussion leads to some conclusions about competition: who are they and how they differ. The startup develops its first positioning statement and uses this to explain the company and its benefits to potential investors.

The distribution discussion also leads to some assumptions about pricing. Combined with product costs, an engineering budget, and schedules, this results in a spreadsheet that faintly resembles the first financial plan in the company's business plan. If the startup is to be backed by venture capitalists, the financial model has to be alluring as well as believable. If it's a new division inside a larger company, forecasts talk about return on investment. In this concept and seed stage, creative writing, passion, and shoe leather combine in hopes of convincing an investor to fund the company or the new division.

Product Development

In stage two, product development, everyone stops talking and starts working. The respective departments go to their virtual corners as the company begins to specialize by functions.

Engineering focuses on building the product; it designs the product, specifies the first release and hires a staff to build the product. It takes the simple box labeled "product development" and makes detailed critical path method charts, with key milestones. With that information in hand, Engineering estimates delivery dates and development costs.

Meanwhile, Marketing refines the size of the market defined in the business plan (a market is a set of companies with common attributes), and begins to target the first customers. In a well-organized startup (one with a fondness for process), the marketing folk might even run a focus group or two on the market they think they are in and prepare a Marketing Requirements Document (MRD) for Engineering. Marketing starts to build a sales demo, writes sales materials (presentations, data sheets), and hires a PR agency. In this stage, or by alpha test, the company traditionally hires a VP of Sales who begins to assemble a sales force.

Alpha/Beta Test

In stage three, alpha/beta test, Engineering works with a small group of outside users to make sure that the product works as specified and tests it for bugs. Marketing develops a complete marketing communications plan, provides Sales with a full complement of support material, and starts the public relations bandwagon rolling. The PR agency polishes the positioning and starts contacting the long lead-time press while Marketing starts the branding activities.

Sales signs up the first beta customers (who volunteer to pay for the privilege of testing a new product), begins to build the selected distribution channel, and staffs and scales the sales organization outside the headquarters. The venture investors start measuring progress by number of orders in place by first customer ship.

Hopefully, somewhere around this point, the investors are happy with the company's product and its progress with customers, and are thinking of bringing in more money. The CEO refines his or her fund-raising pitch and hits the street and the phone searching for additional capital.

Product Launch and First Customer Ship

Product launch and first customer ship is the final step in this model, and the goal the company has been driving towards. With the product working (sort of), the company goes into "big bang" spending mode. Sales is heavily committed to building and staffing a national sales organization; the sales channel has quotas and sales goals. Marketing is at its peak. The company has a large press event, and Marketing launches a series of programs to create end-user demand (trade shows, seminars, advertising, email, and so on). The board begins measuring the company's performance on sales execution against its business plan (which typically was written a year or more earlier, when the entrepreneur was looking for initial investments).

Building the sales channel and supporting the marketing can burn a lot of cash. Assuming no early liquidity (via an IPO or merger) for the company, more fund raising is required. The CEO looks at the product launch activities and the scale-up of the sales and marketing team, and yet again goes out, palm up, to the investor community. (In the dot-com bubble economy, the investors used an IPO at product launch to take the money and run, before there was a track record of success or failure.)

The Leading Cause of Startup Death

If you've ever been involved in a startup, the operational model no doubt sounds familiar. It is a product-centric and process-centric model used by countless startups to take their first product to market. It used to be if you developed a plan that looked like this, your investors would have thought you were geniuses.

In hindsight, both you and your investors were idiots. Following this diagram religiously will more often than not put you out of business. The diagram was developed to be used by existing companies doing product line extensions - *not startups creating new markets or resegmenting existing ones*. Most experienced entrepreneurs will tell you that the model collapses at first contact with customers.

VC's who still believe in the product development model in the 21st century offer no value in building a company other than their Rolodex and/or checkbook.

Reasons for the Revolution (Part 1)

Posted on August 31, 2009 & September 3, 2009 by steveblank |

This post makes more sense if you read the previous post – *The Leading Cause of Startup Death: The Product Development Diagram.*

After 20 years of working in startups, I decided to take a step back and look at the product development model I had been following and see why it usually failed to provide useful guidance in *activities outside the building* – sales, marketing and business development.

Every startup has some methodology for product development, launch and life-cycle management. At their best, these processes provide detailed plans, checkpoints and milestones for every step in getting a product out the door: sizing markets, estimating sales, developing marketing requirements documents, prioritizing product features. Yet at the end of the day even with all these processes, 9 out of 10 of new products are failures.

So what's wrong the product development model? The first hint lies in its name. This is a *product* development model, not a marketing model, not a sales hiring model, not a customer acquisition model, not even a financing model (and we'll also find that in most cases it's even a poor model to use to develop a product.) Yet startup companies have traditionally used this model to manage and pace not only engineering but also non-engineering activities.

In this post I'm going to describe the flaws of the product development model. In the next few posts that follow, I'll describe more specifically how this model distorts startup sales, marketing and business development - and how thinking of a solution to this commonly used model's failures led to a new model – the Customer Development Model – that offers a new way to approach startup activities outside the building. Finally, I'll write about how Eric Ries and the Lean Startup concept provide the equivalent model for product development activities inside the building and neatly integrates customer and agile development.

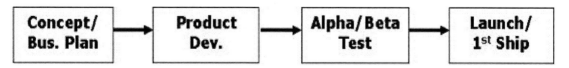

Canonical Product Development Diagram

1. Where Are the Customers?

To begin with, the product development model completely ignores a fundamental truth about startups and new products. The greatest risk in startups —and hence the greatest cause of failure—is *not* the technology risk of developing a product but the risk of developing *customers* and *markets*. Startups don't fail because they lack a product; *they fail because they lack customers and a profitable business model.* This alone should be a pretty good clue about what's wrong with using the product development diagram as the sole guide to what a startup needs to be doing. Look at the Product Development model and you might wonder: Where are the customers?

The reality for most startups today is that the product development model focuses all attention on activities that go on inside a company's own building. While customer input may be a checkpoint or "gate" in the process, it doesn't drive it.

2. The Focus on a First Customer Ship Date

Using the Product Development model also forces sales and marketing to focus on the end point of the process – the first customer <u>ship</u> date. Most sales and marketing executives hired into a startup look at the "first customer ship date," look at the calendar on the wall, and then work backwards to figure out how to do their job in time so that the fireworks start the day the product is launched.

The flaw in this thinking is that "first customer ship" is simply the date when engineering thinks they "finished" the 1.0 release of the product. The *first customer ship date does not mean that the company understands its customers, how to market or sell to them or how to build a profitable business.* (Read the preceding sentence again. It's a big idea.)

Even worse, a startup's investors are managing their financial milestones by the first customer ship date as well.

The product development model is so focused on building and shipping the product that it ignores the entire process of testing your basic hypothesis about your business model (customers, channel, pricing, etc.) *before you ship*. Not testing these hypotheses *upfront* is a fundamental and, in many cases, fatal error most startups make.

Why? Because it isn't until after first customer ship that a startup discovers that their initial hypotheses were simply wrong (i.e. customers aren't buying it, the cost of distribution is too high, etc.) As a result the young company is now saddled with an expensive, scaled-up sales organization trying to execute a losing sales strategy and a marketing organization desperately trying to create demand without a true understanding of customers' needs.

As Marketing and Sales flail around in search of a sustainable market, the company is burning through its most precious asset - cash.

3. The Focus on Execution Versus Learning and Discovery

The product development model assumes that customer's needs are known, the product features are known, and your business model is known. Given this certainty, it's logical that a startup will hire a sales and marketing team to simply *execute* your business plan. You interview sales and marketing execs for prior relevant experience and their rolodexes, and hope they execute the playbook that worked for them in prior companies.

All of this is usually a bad idea. No one asks; Why are we executing like we know what we are doing? Where exactly did the assumptions in our startup business plan come from? Was the sales revenue model based on actually testing the hypotheses outside the building? Or were they a set of spreadsheets put together over late night beers to convince an investor that this is going to be a great deal?

No newly hired sales and marketing exec is going to tell a founder, "Hey my prior experience and assumptions may not actually be relevant to this new startup." Great sales and marketing people are great at execution – that's what you hired for. But past experience may not be relevant for your new company. A new company needs to test a series of hypothesis before it can successfully find a repeatable and scalable sales model. For startups in a new or resgemented market, these are not merely *execution* activities, they are *learning and discovery* activities that are critical to the company's success or failure.

4. The Focus on Execution Versus Agility

The product development diagram has a linear flow from left to right. Each step happens in a logical progression that can be PERT charted with milestones and resources assigned to completing each step.

Anyone who has ever taken a new product out to a set of potential customers can tell you that the real world works nothing like that. A good day in front of customers is two steps forward and one step back. In fact, the best way to represent what happens outside the building is more like a series of recursive circles—recursive to represent the iterative nature of what actually happens in a learning and discovery environment. Information and data are gathered about customers and markets incrementally, one step at a time. Yet sometimes those steps take you in the wrong direction or down a blind alley. You find yourself calling on the wrong customers, not understanding why people will buy, not understanding what product features are important. Other times potential customers will suggest a new use for the product, new positioning or even a much better idea.

The ability to learn from those missteps, *to recognize new opportunities, and to rapidly change direction* is what distinguishes a successful startup from those whose names are forgotten among the vanished.

5. The Outsourcing of Founders' Responsibility

The Product Development model separates founders from deeply understanding their customers and market. The responsibility for validating *the founders'* original hypotheses is delegated to employees – the sales and marketing team.

This means the founders are isolated from *directly* hearing customer input – good, bad and ugly. Worse, founders really won't understand whether customers will buy and what features are saleable until after first customer ship.

When an adroit and agile founder gets outside the building and hears for the nth time that the product is unsellable, he will *recognize, regroup and change direction*. A process to give the founders *continuous customer interaction* – from day one – is essential.

6. The Focus on a Finished Product Rather than a Minimum Feature Set

The passion of an entrepreneur coupled with the product development diagram drives you to believe that all you need to do is build the product (in all its full-featured glory) and customers will come. A Waterfall development process reinforces that inanity. The reality is quite different. Unless you are in an Existing Market (making a better version of what customers are already buying,) you'll find that your hypothesis about what features customers want had no relationship to what they really wanted.

Most startup code ends up on the floor.

7. Investor Focus on a Broken Model

Ask VC's why they use the Product Development model to manage a startup and you get answers like, "It's the way my firm has always done it. Why change something that has worked so well over the last three decades?" Or, "Look at our returns, its always worked for us." Or at times an even more honest answer, "My senior partners say this is the only way to do it."

Some firms correctly point out that, "It's fine if 8 out of 10 of our companies fail if the remaining two return 20x our money. That's a better return than having 10 out of 10 companies succeed and each return 2x our money. Therefore we don't want startups doing anything but swinging for the fences."

The fallacy is that the product development model is the most efficient model for new ventures swinging for the fences – this year, last year, last decade or since the first startup met their first investor.

80

Venture portfolio companies don't succeed because they used the Product Development model, *they succeeded in spite of using it. The fact is most successful startups abandon the product development model as soon as they encounter customers.*

Today, startups using the product development model iterate and learn and discover by burning investor cash. When cash is tight, they go out of business – or they adopt a more efficient model.

Reasons for the Revolution (part 2)

Posted on September 3, 2009 by steveblank

8. The Lack of Milestones for Sales, Marketing and Business Development
The one great thing about the product development methodology is that it provides an unambiguous structure with clearly defined milestones. The meanings of alpha test, beta test, and first customer ship are pretty obvious to most engineers. In contrast, sales and marketing activities before first customer ship are adhoc, fuzzy, and don't have measurable, concrete objectives. They lack any way to stop and fix what's broken (or even to know if it is broken.)

What kind of objectives would a startup want or need for sales and marketing? Most sales executives and marketers tend to focus on execution activities because at least these are measurable. For example, some startup sales execs believe hiring the core sales team is a key objective. Others focus on acquiring early "lighthouse" customers (prominent customers who will attract others.) Once the product begins to ship, startup sales execs use orders and revenue as its marker of progress in understanding customers. (Freemium models have their own scorekeeping.) Marketers believe creating a killer web presence, corporate presentation, are objectives. Some think that hiring a PR agency, starting the buzz and getting coverage in hot blogs or on the cover of magazines at launch are objectives.

While these objectives provide an illusion of progress, in reality they do little to validate the business plan hypotheses about customers and what they will buy. They don't help a startup move toward a deep understanding of customers and their problems, discovering a repeatable road map of how they buy, and building a financial model that results in profitability.

9. The Use of a Product Development Model to Measure Sales
Using the product development diagram for startup sales activities is like using a clock to tell the temperature. They both measure something, but not the thing you wanted.

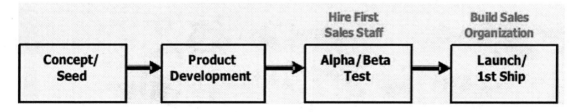

The product development diagram from a sales perspective.

A VP of Sales looks at the diagram and says, "Hmm, if beta test is on this date, I'd better get a small sales team in place before that date to acquire my first 'early

82

customers.' And if first customer ship is on this date over here, then I need to hire and staff a sales organization by then." Why? "Well, because the revenue plan we promised the investors shows us generating customer revenue from the day of first customer ship."

I hope this thinking already sounds inane to you. The plan calls for selling in volume the day Engineering is finished building the product. What plan says that? Why, the business plan, crafted with a set of hypotheses now using the product development model as a timeline for execution. This approach is not predicated on *discovering* the right market or *learning* whether any customers will actually shell out cash for your product. Instead you use product development to time your readiness to sell. This "ready or not, here we come" attitude means that you won't know if the sales strategy and plan actually work until after first customer ship. What's the consequence if your stab at a sales strategy is wrong? You've built a sales organization and company that's burning cash before you know if you have demand for your product or a repeatable and scalable sales model. No wonder the half-life of a startup VP of Sales is about nine months post first customer ship.

"Build and they will come" is not a strategy, it's a prayer.

10. The Use of a Product Development Model to Measure Marketing
The head of Marketing looks at the same product development diagram and sees something quite different.

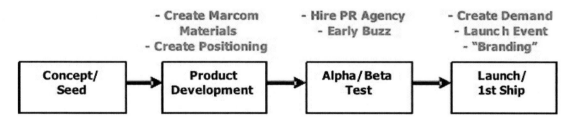

The product development diagram from marketing's perspective.

For Marketing, first customer ship means feeding the sales pipeline with a constant stream of customer prospects. To create this demand at first customer ship, marketing activities start early in the product development process. While the product is being engineered, Marketing begins to create web sites, corporate presentations and sales materials. Implicit in these materials is the corporate and product "positioning." Looking ahead to the product launch, the marketing group hires a public relations agency to refine the positioning and to begin generating early "buzz" about the company. The PR agency helps the company understand and influence key bloggers, social networks, industry analysts, luminaries, and references. All this leads up to a flurry of press events and interviews, all geared to the product/web site launch date. (During the Internet bubble, one more function of the marketing department was to "buy" customer loyalty with enormous advertising and promotion spending to create a brand.)

At first glance this process may look quite reasonable, until you realize all this marketing activity occurs before customers start buying—that is, before the company has had a chance to actually test the positioning, marketing strategy, or demand-creation activities in front of real customers. In fact, all the marketing plans are made in a virtual vacuum of real customer feedback and information. Of course, smart marketers have some early interaction with customers before the product ships, but if they do, it's on their own initiative, not as part of a well-defined process. Most marketers spend more of their time behind their desks inside the building then outside talking to potential customers.

This is somewhat amazing since *in a startup no facts exist inside the building – only opinions.*

Yet even if we get the marketing people out from behind their desks into the field, the deck is still stacked against their success. Look at the product development diagram. When does Marketing find out whether the positioning, buzz, and demand creation activities actually work? After first customer ship. The inexorable march to this date has no iterative loop that says, "If our assumptions are wrong, maybe we need to try something different."

11. Premature Scaling
The Product Development model leads Sales and Marketing to believe that by first customer ship, come hell or high water, they need fully staffed organizations leads to another disaster: premature scaling.

Startup executives have three documents to guide their hiring and staffing; a business plan, a product development model and a revenue forecast. All of these are execution documents – they direct the timing and hiring of spending as if all assumptions in the business plan are 100% correct. As mentioned earlier there are no milestones that alert a startup to stop or slow down hiring until you have proven until you understand you customers. Even the most experienced executives succumb to the inexorable pressure to hire and staff to "plan" regardless of the limited customer feedback they've collected to this point in Alpha and Beta test.

Premature scaling is the immediate cause of the startup Death Spiral.

The Startup Death Spiral

Posted on September 7, 2009 by steveblank |

This post describes how following the traditional product development can lead to a "startup death spiral." In the next posts that follow, I'll describe how this model's failures led to the Customer Development Model – offering a new way to approach startup sales and marketing activities.

12. The Startup Death Spiral: The Cost of Getting Product Launch Wrong

By the time of first customer ship, if a startup does not understand its market and customers, failure unfolds in a stylized ritual, almost like a Japanese Noh play.

Three to six months after first customer ship, if Sales starts missing its numbers, the board gets concerned. The VP of Sales comes to a board meeting, still optimistic, and provides a set of reasonable explanations – "Our pipeline looks great, but orders will close next quarter" or "We've got lots of traffic to our site. We just need to work on conversion." The board raises a collective eyebrow. The VP of Sales goes back and exhorts the troops to work harder.

To support sales, Marketing tries to "make up a better story," and the web site and/or product presentation slides start changing (sometimes weekly or even daily). Morale in Sales and Marketing starts to plummet.

Meanwhile, if you have a direct sales force, smart salespeople realize that the sales strategy and marketing materials the company headquarters provided don't work. Each starts inventing and testing their own alternatives about how to sell and position the product. They try different customers, different customer contacts, different versions of the presentations, etc. Instead of a Sales team organized to sell with a consistent and successful sales roadmap generating revenue, it is a disorganized and unhappy organization burning lots of cash.

You're Just Not Selling it Right

By the next board meeting, the VP of Sales looks down at his shoes and shuffles his feet as he reports that the revenue numbers still aren't meeting plan. Now the board collectively raises both eyebrows and looks quizzically at the CEO. The VP of Sales, forehead bathed in sweat, leaves the board meeting and has a few heated motivational sessions with the sales team.

Fire the First VP of Sales

By the next board meeting if the sales numbers are still poor, the stench of death is in the air. No one wants to sit next to the VP of Sales. Other company execs are moving their chairs to the other side of the room. Having failed to deliver the numbers, he's history. Whether it takes three board meetings or a year is irrelevant; the VP of Sales in a startup who does not make the numbers is called an ex-VP of Sales.

Now the company is in crisis mode. Not only hasn't the sales team delivered the sales numbers, but now the CEO is sweating because the company is continuing to burn cash at what now seems like an alarming rate. Why is it only alarming now? Because the company based its headcount and expenses on the expectation that the Sales organization will bring in revenue according to plan. The rest of the organization (product development, marketing, support) has been burning cash, all according to plan, expecting Sales to make its numbers. Without the revenue to match its expenses, the company is in now danger of running out of money.

Blame it On Marketing

In the next 3-6 months, a new VP of Sales is hired. She quickly comes to the conclusion that the company's positioning and marketing strategy were incorrect. There isn't a sales problem; the problem is that marketing just did not understand its customers and how to create demand or position the product.

Now the VP of Marketing starts sweating. Since the new VP of Sales was brought on board to "fix" sales, the marketing department has to react and interact with someone who believes that whatever was created earlier in the company was wrong. The new VP of Sales reviews the sales strategy and tactics that did not work and comes up with a new sales plan. She gets a brief honeymoon of a few months from the CEO and the board.

In the meantime, the original VP of Marketing tries to come up with a new positioning strategy to support the new Sales VP. Typically this results in conflict, if not outright internecine warfare. If the sales aren't fixed in a short time, the next executive to be looking for a job will not be the new VP of Sales (she hasn't been around long enough to get fired), it's the VP of Marketing—the rationale being "We changed the VP of Sales, so that can't be the problem. It must be Marketing's fault."

Time for an Experienced CEO

Sometimes all it takes is one or two iterations to find the right sales roadmap and marketing positioning that connects a startup with exuberant customers ready to buy. Unfortunately, more often than not, this is just the beginning of an executive death spiral. If changing the sales and marketing execs doesn't put the company on the right sales trajectory, the investors start talking the "we need the right CEO for this phase" talk. This means the CEO is walking around with an unspoken corporate death sentence. Moreover, since the first CEO was likely to have been one of the founders, the trauma of CEO removal begins. Typically, founding CEOs hold on to the doorframe of their offices as the investors try to pry their fingers off the company. It's painful to watch and occurs in a majority of startups with first-time CEOs after First Customer Ship.

In flush economic times, the company may get two or three iterations to fix a failed launch and bad sales numbers. In tougher times, investors are tighter with their wallets and make the "tossing good money after bad" calculations with a more frugal eye. A startup might simply not get a next round of funding and have to shut down.

Any of this sound familiar?

Market Type

Posted on September 10, 2009 by steveblank |

Not All Startups Are Alike

There's an urban legend that Eskimos-Aleuts have more words to describe snow than other cultures. While that's not true, it is a fact that entrepreneurs only have one word for "startup." This post points out that the lack of adequate words to describe very different "types" of startups can lead not only to confusion in execution but also at times to disaster.

The product development model treats all startups like they are in an *Existing Market* – an established market with known customers. With that implicit assumption, startups hire a VP of Sales with a great rolodex and call on established mainstream companies while marketing creates a brand and buzz to create demand and drive it into the sales channel (web, direct salesforce, etc.)

Most startups following the Product Development Model never achieve their revenue plan and burn through a ton of cash not knowing what hit them.

They never understood Market Type.

Why does Market Type matter?

Depending on the *type of market* it enters, a startup can have very different rates of customer adoption and acceptance, and their sales and marketing strategies will need to be dramatically different. Even more serious, startups can have radically different cash needs. A startup in a *New Market* (enabling customers to do something they never could before,) might be unprofitable for 5 or more years, (hopefully with the traditional hockey stick revenue curve,) while one in an Existing Market might be generating cash in 12-18 months.

Handspring in a Existing Market

As an example, imagine it's October 1999 and you are Donna Dubinsky, the CEO of a feisty new startup, Handspring, entering the billion dollar Personal Digital Assistant (PDA) market. Other companies in the 1999 PDA market were Palm, the original innovator, as well Microsoft and Hewlett Packard.

In October 1999 Donna told her VP of Sales, "In the next 12 months I want Handspring to win 10% of the Personal Digital Assistant market." The VP of Sales swallowed hard and turned to the VP of Marketing and said, "I need you to take end user demand away from our competitors and drive it into our sales channel." The VP of Marketing looked at all the other PDAs on the market and differentiated Handspring's product by emphasizing its superior expandability and performance. End result? After twelve months Handspring's revenue was $170 million. This was possible because in 2000, Donna and Handspring were in an *Existing Market*. Handspring's customers understood what a Personal Digital Assistant was. Handspring did not have to educate them about the market. They just need to persuade customers why their new product was better than the competition – and they did it brilliantly.

Palm in a New Market

What makes this example really interesting is this: rewind the story 4 years earlier to 1996. Before Handspring, Donna and her team had founded Palm Computing, the pioneer in Personal Digital Assistants. Before Palm arrived on the scene, the Personal Digital Assistant market did not exist. (A few failed science experiments like Apple's Newton had come and gone.) But imagine if Donna had turned to her VP of Sales at Palm in 1996 and said, "I want to get 10% of the Personal Digital Assistant market by the end of our first year." Her VP of Sales might had turned to the VP of Marketing and said, "I want you to drive end user demand from our competitors into our sales channel." The VP of Marketing might have said, "Let's tell everyone about how fast the Palm Personal Digital Assistant is and how much memory it has." If they had done this, there would have been zero dollars in sales.

In 1996 no potential customer had even heard of a Personal Digital Assistant. Since no one knew what a PDA could do, there was no latent demand from end users, and emphasizing its technical features would have been irrelevant. What Palm needed to do first was to educate potential customers about what a PDA could do for them. In 1996 Palm was selling a product that allowed users to do something they couldn't do before.

In essence, Palm created a *New Market*. In contrast, in 2000 Handspring entered an Existing Market. ("Disruptive" and "sustaining" innovations, eloquently described by Clayton Christensen, are another way to describe new and existing Market Types.)

The lesson is that even with essentially identical products and team, Handspring would have failed if it had used the same sales and marketing strategy that Palm had used so successfully. And the converse is true; Palm would have failed, burning through all their cash, using Handspring's strategy. *Market Type changes everything.*

Market Type Changes Everything

Here's the point. Market Type changes how you evaluate customer needs, customer adoption rate, how the customer understands his needs and how you should position the product to the customer. Market Type also affects the market size as well as how you launch the product into the market. As a result, *different market types require dramatically different sales and marketing strategies.*

The standard product development model is not only useless, it is dangerous. It tells the finance, marketing and sales teams nothing about how to uniquely market and sell in each type of startup nor how to predict the resources needed for success.

The Path of Warriors and Winners

Posted on **September 17, 2009** by steveblank |

Most startups lack a process for discovering their markets, locating their first customers, validating their assumptions, and growing their business. A few successful ones do all these things. The difference is that the ones that succeed invent a Customer Development model. This post describes such a model.

The Customer Development Model

Customer Development is designed to solve the problems of the Product Development model I described in the four previous posts. Its strength is its rigor and flexibility. The Customer Development model divides all the customer-related activities in the early stage of a company into their own processes and groups them into four easy-to-understand steps: Customer Discovery, Customer Validation, Customer Creation, and Company Building. These steps mesh seamlessly and support a startup's ongoing product development activities. Each step results in specific deliverables.

The Customer Development model is *not* a replacement for the Product Development model but rather a *companion* to it. As its name should communicate, the *Customer Development model focuses on developing customers* for the product or service your startup is building.

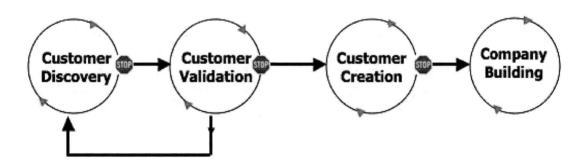

The Customer Development Model

Four Steps

While startups are inherently chaotic (and will never be run from a spreadsheet or checklist inside your building) the four steps of Customer Development are *designed to help entrepreneurs leverage the chaos* and turn it into actionable data:

- Customer *Discovery* is about the founders testing hypotheses and understanding customer problems and needs – in front of customers
- Customer *Validation* develops a sales model that can be replicated and scaled
- Customer *Creation* is creating and driving end user demand to scale sales
- Company *Building* transitions the organization from one designed for learning and discovery to a well-oiled machine engineered for execution.

Market Type

Integral to the Customer Development model is the notion that Market Type choices affect the way the company will deploy its sales, marketing and financial resources. Market Type changes how you evaluate customer needs, customer adoption rate, how the customer understands his needs and how you should position the product to the customer, etc. As a result, *different market types modify what you do in each step of* Customer Development.

Customer Development is Iterative

Learning and discovery versus linear execution is a major difference between this model and the traditional product development model. While the product development model is linear in one direction, the customer development model is a circular track with recursive arrows. The circles and arrows highlight the fact that each step in Customer Development is iterative. That's a polite way of saying, "Unlike product development, finding the right customers and market is unpredictable, and we will screw it up several times before we get it right." (Only in business school case studies does progress with customers happen in a nice linear fashion.) The nature of finding a market and customers guarantees that you will get it wrong several times.

The Customer Development model assumes that it will take several iterations of each of the four steps until you get it right. It's worth pondering this point for a moment because this philosophy of "It's OK to screw it up if you plan to learn from it" is the heart of the methodology.

The Facts Reside Outside Your Building

Customer Development starts by *testing your hypotheses outside the building*. Not in planning meetings, not in writing multiple pages of nicely formatted Marketing Requirements Documents, but by getting laughed at, ignored, thrown out and educated by potential customers as you listen to their needs and test the fundamental hypotheses of your business.

Failure *Is* an Option

Notice that the circle labeled Customer Validation in the diagram has an additional iterative loop going back to Customer Discovery. As you'll see later, Customer Validation is a key checkpoint in understanding whether you have a product that customers want to buy and a road map of how to sell it. If you can't find enough paying customers in the Customer Validation step, the model returns you to Customer Discovery to rediscover what you failed to hear or understand the first time through the loop.

Customer Development is Low Burn by Design

The Customer Development process keeps a startup at a low cash burn rate until the company has validated its business model by finding paying customers. In the first two steps of Customer Development, even an infinite amount of cash is useless because it can only obscure whether you have found a market. (Having raised lots of money tempts you to give products away, steeply discount to buy early business, etc., all while saying "we'll make it up later." It rarely happens that way.) Since the Customer Development model assumes that most startups cycle through these first two steps at least twice, it allows a well-managed company to carefully estimate and frugally husband its cash. The company doesn't build its non-product development teams (sales, marketing, business development) until it has proof in hand (a tested sales road map and valid purchase orders) that it has a business worth building. Once that proof is obtained, the company can go through the last two steps of Customer Creation and Company Building to capitalize on the opportunity it has found and validated.

Customer Development is For Winners and Warriors

The interesting thing about the Customer Development model is that the process represents the best practices of winning startups. Describe this model to entrepreneurs who have taken their companies all the way to a large profitable business, and you'll get heads nodding in recognition. It's just that until now, no one has ever explicitly mapped their journey to success.

Even more surprising, while the Customer Development model may sound like a new idea for entrepreneurs, it shares many features with a U.S. war fighting strategy known as the "OODA Loop" articulated by John Boyd and adopted by the U.S. armed forces in both Gulf Wars – and by others.

Customer Development In the Real World

Customer Development is Not a Focus Group

Posted on November 30, 2009 by steveblank |

On first description, hearing the "get out of the building and talk to customers" precept of Customer Development leads people to say, "Oh, I get it. Customer Development is all about gathering a list of what features customers want by talking to them, surveying them, or running "focus groups."

It's not.

One of the times I screwed this up it left a legacy of 25 years of questionable design in microprocessor architecture.

Little Indians and Big Indians

At MIPS Computers, my second semiconductor company, I was the VP of Marketing and defacto head of Sales. As the engineers were busy rearchitecting the original Stanford MIPS chip into a commercial product, one of my jobs was to find out what features customers wanted. Among other things our chip architects wanted to learn whether customers would want this chip to store data as big-endian or little-endian.

"Endianness" refers to the byte order of data stored in external memory. Data can be stored with the most significant byte at the lowest memory address – big-endian or it can be stored with the least significant byte at the lowest memory address – little-endian.

Different computers used different endianness. The leading minicomputer of the day, the DEC VAX, used little-endian as did microprocessors such as the Intel 8086 (used in the IBM PC) and the Mostek 6502 (used in the Apple II.) On the other hand, the Motorola 68000 microprocessor (used in the Sun and Apollo engineering workstations) and the IBM 360/370 mainframes were big-endian.

The term "endian" came from Jonathan Swift's *Gulliver's Travels*. In this story, the Lilliputians argue over how they should eat their hard boiled eggs. One group ate from the little end first – little-endians - while the other ate theirs from the big end – big-endians. This turned into a dispute over the "right way" and led to war – just like it did for generations of computer architects.

Just Add Every Feature

As I surveyed potential customers on which version of "endiannes" they wanted, prospects who had their data on VAX minicomputers or IBM PC's were unequivocal. "It has to be little-endian or we won't design your chip into our systems." And when I heard from those who had data on Sun or Apollo workstations or IBM mainframes, the answer was equally unambiguous. "It has to be big-endian or we'll never adopt your microprocessor." I still remember the day I talked to Ram Banin, the head of engineering of Daisy Systems (a maker of Electronic Design Automation workstations,) who told me, "Steve, you'll never make every potential customer happy. Why don't you tell your engineers to build both byte-orders into your new chip?"

What a great idea. Now I didn't have to decide or figure out whether one set of customers was more valuable than the other. I ran back to the company and said customers had told us, "We have to do both little and big endian." The reaction from the chip circuit design guys was, "OK, we could do that. We can put both little- and big-endian in the chip, and it won't cost us more than 1,000 gates." The reaction from our software guys was a little less kind. "Are you out of your !? *x! minds? Do you understand you are doubling the amount of work you are going to make for *generations* of software engineers?"

No, not really. I was just in marketing.

All I had done was proudly go out and get customer input. Isn't that what I was supposed to do?

No.

Customer Development is about Testing the Founder's Hypothesis

Any idiot can get outside the building and ask customers what they want, compile a feature list and hand it to engineering. Gathering feature requests from customers is not what marketing should be doing *in a startup*. And it's certainly not Customer Development.

In a startup the role of Customer Development is to:

- test the founder's hypothesis about the customer problem
- test if the product concept and minimum feature set solve that problem

This is a big idea and worth repeating. Customer Development is *about testing the founder's hypothesis* about what constitutes product/market fit with the minimum feature set. The goal is to answer the questions; "Does this product/service as spec'd solve a problem or a need customers have? Is our solution compelling enough that they want to buy it or use it today?" You know you have achieved product/market fit when you start getting orders (or users, eyeballs or whatever your criteria for success was in your business model.)

The time to start iterating the product is if and only if sufficient customers tell you your problem hypotheses are incorrect or point out features you missed that would cause them not to buy. If you're lucky, you'll find this out early in Customer Discovery or if not, when no one buys in Customer Validation.

The Jury is Still Out
At MIPS I was out collecting feature requests.

We put both byte orders into the MIPS chip. It's been there for 25 years.

Lessons Learned

> - Startups begin with hypotheses about a customer problem or need.
> - Founders talk to customers to discover and validate whether the total solution solves that problem or addresses that need.
> - If, and not only if, there are no "buy signs" from the customer or customers *repeatably* point out missing features, does the product change.
> - Collecting feature lists and holding focus groups are for established companies with existing customers looking to design product line extensions.

Lean Startups aren't Cheap Startups

Posted on November 2, 2009 by steveblank |

At an entrepreneurs panel last week, questions from the audience made me realize that the phrase "Lean Startup" was being confused with "Cheap Startup."

For those of you who have been following the discussion, a Lean Startup is Eric Ries's description of the intersection of Customer Development, Agile Development and if available, open platforms and open source.

Lean Startups aren't Cheap Startups

A Lean Startup is not about the total amount of money you may spend over the life of your startup. It is about *when in the life of your company you do the spending.*

Over its lifetime, a Lean Startup may spend less money than a traditional startup. It may end up spending the same amount of money as a traditional startup. And I can even imagine cases where it might burn more cash than a traditional startup.

Lets see why.

The Price of Mistakes are Inversely Proportional to Available Capital

In times of abundant venture capital, if you miss your revenue plan, additional funding from your investors is usually available to cover your mistakes – i.e. you get "do-overs" or iterations without onerous penalties (assuming your investors still believe in the technology and vision.) In times when venture capital is hard to get, investors extract high costs for failure (down-rounds, cram downs, new management teams, shut down the company.)

The key contributors to an out-of-control burn rate is: 1) hiring a sales force too early, 2) turning on the demand creation activities too early or 3) developing something other than the minimum feature set for first customer ship. Sales people cost money, and when they're not bringing in revenue, their wandering in the woods is time consuming, cash-draining and demoralizing. Marketing demand creation programs (Search Engine Marketing, Public Relations, Advertising, Lead Generation, Trade Shows, etc.) are all expensive and potentially fatal distractions if done *before you have found product/market fit and a repeatable sales model.* And *most startup code and features end up on the floor* as customers never really wanted them.

Therefore, when money is hard to come by, entrepreneurs (and their investors) look for ways to reduce cash burn rate and increase the chance of finding product/market fit before wasting a bunch of money. The Customer Development process (and the Lean Startup) help you to do that.

Repeatable and Scalable Sales Model

In Customer Development your goal is not to avoid spending money but to *preserve your cash as you search for a repeatable and scalable sales model and then spend like there is no tomorrow when you find one.*

This is the most important sentence in this post and worth deconstructing.

Preserve your cash: When you have unlimited cash (internet bubbles, frothy venture climate,) you can iterate on your mistakes by burning more dollars. When money is tight, when there aren't dollars to redo mistakes, you look for processes that allow you to minimize waste. The Customer Development process says preserve your cash by not hiring anyone in sales and marketing until *the founders* turn hypotheses into facts <u>and</u> you have found product/market fit.

As you search: Customer Development observes that when you start your company, all you and your business plan have are hypotheses, not facts –and that *the founders* are the ones who need to get out of the building to turn these hypotheses into customer data. This "get out of the building" activity is the Customer Discovery step of the Customer Development Model.

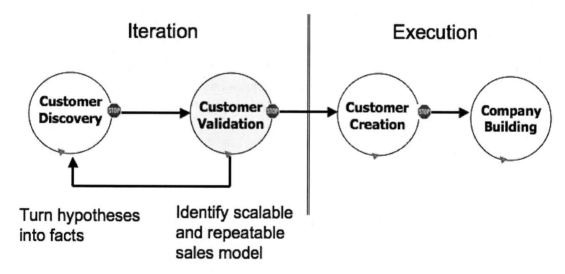

Repeatable: Startups may get orders that come from board members' customer relationships or heroic, single-shot efforts of the CEO. These are great, but they are not repeatable by a sales organization. What you are searching for is not the one-off revenue hits but rather a repeatable pattern that can be replicated by a sales organization selling off a pricelist or by customers coming to your web site.

Scalable: The goal is not to get one customer but many – and to get those customers so each additional customer adds incremental revenue *and* profit. The test is: If you add one more sales person or spend more marketing dollars, does your sales revenue go up by more than your expenses?

Sales model A sales model answers the basic questions involved in selling your product: Is this a revenue play or a freemium model going for users? Something else? Who's the customer? Who influences a sale? Who recommends a sale? Who is the decision maker? Who is the economic buyer? Where is the budget for purchasing the type of product you're selling? What's the customer acquisition cost? What's the lead and/or traffic generation strategy? How long does an average sale take from beginning to end? Etc." Finding out whether you have a *repeatable, scalable sales model* is the Customer Validation step of Customer Development. This is the most important phase in Customer Development. Have you learned how to sell your product to a target customer? Can you do this without running out of money?

Scale like there is no tomorrow The goal of an investor-backed startup is not to build a lifestyle business. The goal is to reach venture-scale (~10x return on investment.) When you and your board agree you've found a repeatable and scalable sales model (i.e. have product/market fit,) *then you invest the dollars to create end user demand and drive those customers into your sales channel.*

If you confuse Lean with Cheap when you do find a repeatable and scalable sales model, you will starve your company for resources needed to scale. Customer Development (and Lean) is about continuous customer contact/iteration *to find the right time for execution.*

Times Square Strategy Session – Web Startups and Customer Development

Posted on **November 16, 2009** by steveblank |

One of the benefits of teaching is that it forces me to get smarter. When I was in New York last week with my class at Columbia University, several events made me realize that the Customer Development model needs to better describe its fit with web-based businesses.

Dancing Around the Question

Union Square Ventures was kind enough to sponsor a meetup the night before my class. In it, I got asked a question I often hear: What if we have a web-based business that doesn't have revenue or paying customers? What metrics do we use to see if we learned enough in Customer Discovery? And without revenue how do we know if we achieved product/market fit to exit Customer Validation?

I gave my boilerplate answer: I'm a product guy and I tend to invest and look at deals that have measurable revenue metrics. However the Customer Development Model and the Lean Startup work equally well for startups on the web. Dave McClure has some great metrics. It was an honest but vaguely unsatisfying answer.

Union Square Ventures

The next morning I got to spend time with Brad Burnham, a partner at Union Square Ventures, talking about their investment strategy and insights about web-based businesses. Bill and his partner Fred Wilson have invested in ~30 or so companies with 27 still active.

They're putting money into web services/business – most without early revenue. It's an impressive portfolio. By the time the meeting was over, I left wondering whether the Customer Development model would help or hinder their companies.

Eric Ries in Times Square

For any model to be useful, it has to predict what happens in the real world – including the web. I realized the Customer Development model needed to be clearer in what exactly a startup is supposed to do, *regardless of the business model.*

Luckily, Eric Ries was spending a few days in New York so we sat down in the middle of Times Square and hashed this out.

What we concluded is that the Customer Development model needs an additional overlay.

103

Four Questions

Just as a reminder, the Customer Development has four simple steps: Discovery, Validation, Creation and Company Building. But it also requires you to ask a few questions about your startup before you use it.

The first question to ask is: Does your startup have market risk or is it dominated by technical risk? Lean Startup/Customer Development is used to find answers to the unknowns about customers and markets. Yet some startups such as Biotech don't have market risk. Instead they are dominated by *technical risk.* This class of startup needs to spend a decade or so proving that the product works, first in a test tube and then in FDA trials. Customer Development is unhelpful here.

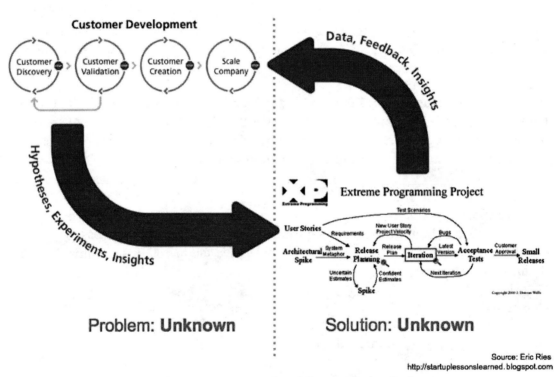

Use the Lean Startup When There's Market Risk

The second question is: What's the *Market Type* of your startup? Are you entering an existing market, resegmenting an existing market, or creating an entirely new market? Market Type affects your spending and sales ramp after you reach product/market fit. Startups who burn through their cash, usually fail by not understanding Market Type.

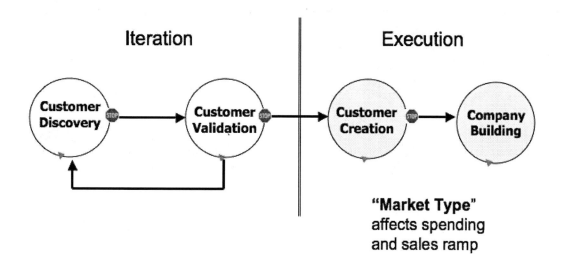

The *third question* (and the one Eric and I came up with watching the people stream by in Times Square): What is the *Business Model* of your startup? Your choice of *Business Model* affects the *metrics* you use in discovery and validation and the *exit criteria* for each step.

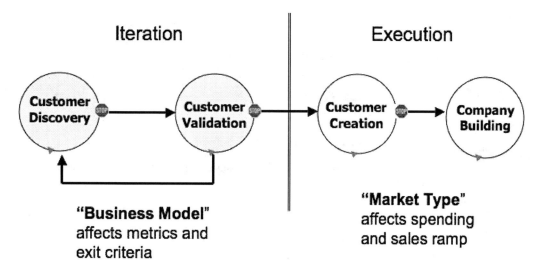

Web-based Business Model Exit Criteria
In a web-business model you're looking for traffic, users, conversion, virality, etc – not revenue. Dave McClure's AARRR metrics and Andrew Chen's specifics on freemium models, viral marketing, user acquisition and engagement both offer examples of exit criteria for Customer Discovery and Validation for startups on the web.

Eric Ries and I will be working on others.

Coffee With Startups

Posted on August 20, 2009 by steveblank |

I've just met four great startups in the last three days.

An Existing Market

All four were trying to resegment an *Existing Market*. An existing market is one where competitors have a profitable business selling to customers who can name the market and can tell you about the features that matter to them. Resegmentation means these startups are trying to lure some of the current or potential customers away from incumbents by either offering a lower cost product or by offering features that appealed to a specific niche or subset of the existing users.

Some of the conversations went like this:

Startup 1

Entrepreneur -"I'm competing against Company x and have been following the Customer Development process, and I've talked to lots of customers."

Me – "Have you used Company x's product? Do you know have they distribute their product? Do you know how they create demand? Do you know how many units they are selling? Do you know the archetype of their customers?

Entrepreneur -"Well no, but my product is much better than their product and I have this great idea."

Rule 1: In an existing market, Customer Development means not only understanding potential customers, but also *your competitors* in detail – their product features, their sales channels, their demand creation strategy, their business model, etc.

Startup 2

Entrepreneur -"I'm competing against Company x, and we are going to offer a lower-cost, web-based version. We're about to ship next week."

Me –"That's a great hypothesis. Do customers tell you that they'd buy your version if it was cheaper or on the web?

Entrepreneur -"Well no, but my product is much cheaper, and everyone's on the web, and I have this great idea."

Rule 2: In an existing market, Customer Development means understanding whether your hypothesis of why customers will buy matches reality. This is easy to test. Do this before you write code you may end up throwing away.

Startup 3

Entrepreneur -"I'm competing against Large Company x, and we solve problems for a set of customers. I've talked to many of them, and they would buy it."

Me – "So what's the problem?"

Entrepreneur – "We just started letting early customers access the product and adoption/sales isn't taking off the way we thought it would. We only have 20 customers, and Large Company x has millions."

Me – "How are you positioning your product?"

Entrepreneur – "We tell potential customers about all our features."

Rule 3: In an existing market, directly compare your product against the incumbent and specifically describe the problems you solve that Company x's products do not.

Startup 4

Entrepreneur -"I have something really, really new. No one has anything like it."

Me – "Isn't it kind of like Twitter but better?"

Entrepreneur – "You don't get it."

Rule 4: You may want to think twice positioning as a New Market. If customers immediately get an analogy for your product, don't dissuade them. Save the "New Billion Dollar Market" positioning for the investors, not customers.

Lessons Learned

- Deeply understand the incumbents that make up the Existing Market.
- The "hypotheses tested to lines of code written" ratio ought to be high.
- Position against the incumbents weaknesses – their customers will tell you what they are.
- Existing Markets adoption rates are measured in % market share gained, New Markets have adoption rates which may occur in your company's lifetime.

He's Only in Field Service

Posted on July 30, 2009 by steveblank |

The most important *early* customers for your startup usually turn out to be quite different from who you think they're going to be.

He's Only in Field Service
When I was at Zilog, the Z8000 peripheral chips included the new Serial Communications Controller (SCC). As the (very junior) product marketing manager, I got a call from our local salesman that someone at Apple wanted more technical information than just the spec sheets about our new (not yet shipping) chip. I vividly remember the sales guy saying, "It's only some kid in field service. I'm too busy so why don't you drive over there and talk to him." (My guess is that our salesman was busy trying to sell into the "official" projects of Apple, the Lisa and the Apple III.)

Zilog was also in Cupertino near Apple, and I remember driving to a small non-descript Apple building at the intersection of Stevens Creek and Sunnyvale/Saratoga. I had a pleasant meeting and was as convincing as a marketing type could be to a very earnest and quirky field service guy, mostly promising the moon for a versatile but then very buggy piece of silicon. We talked about some simple design rules, and I remember him thanking me for coming, saying we were the only chip company who cared enough to call on him (little did he know.)

I thought nothing about the meeting until years later. Long gone from Zilog, I saw the picture of the original Macintosh design team. The field service guy I had sold the chip to was Burrell Smith who had designed the Mac hardware.

The SCC had been designed into the Mac and became the hardware which drove all the serial communications as well as the AppleTalk network which allowed Macs to share printers and files.

Some sales guy who was too busy to take the meeting was probably retired in Maui on the commissions.

Your Customers are Not Who You Think
For years I thought this "million unit chip sale by accident" was a "one-off" funny story. That is until I saw that in startup after startup, *customers come from places you don't plan on.*

108

Unfortunately, most startups learn this by going through the "Fire the first Sales VP" drill: You start your company with a list of potential customers reading like a "who's who" of whatever vertical market you're in (or the Fortune 1000 list.) Your board nods sagely at your target customer list. A year goes by, you miss your revenue plan, and you've burned through your first VP of Sales. What happened?

What happened was that you didn't understand what "type of startup" you were and consequently you never had a chance to tailor your sales strategy to your *Market Type*. Most startups tend to think they are selling into an *Existing market* – a market exists, and your company has a faster and better product. If that's you, by all means hire a VP of Sales with a great Rolodex and call on established mainstream companies – and ignore the rest of this post.

Market Type
But most startups aren't in existing markets. Some are r*esegmenting an existing market*– directed at a niche that an incumbent isn't satisfying (like Dell and Compaq when they were startups) or providing a low cost alternative to an existing supplier (like Southwest Airlines when it first started.) And other startups are in a *New Market* — creating a market from scratch (like Apple with the iPhone or iPod/iTunes.)

(*Market Type* radically changes how you sell and market at each step in Customer Development. It's one of the subtle distinctions that at times gets lost in the process. I cover this in the *Four Steps to the Epiphany*.)

Five Signs You Can Sell to a Large Company
If you're resegmenting an existing market or creating a new market, the odds are low that your target list of market leaders will become your first customers. In fact having any large company buy from you will be difficult unless you know how to recognize the *five signs you can get a large company to buy from a startup:*

- They have a problem.
- They know they have a problem.
- They've been actively looking for a solution.
- They tried to solve the problem with piece parts or other vendors.
- They have or can acquire a budget to pay for your solution.

I advise startups to first *go after the companies that aren't the market leaders* in their industries, but are fighting hard to get there. (They usually fit the checklist above.) Then find the early adopter/internal evangelist inside that company who wants to gain a competitive advantage. These companies will look at innovative startups to help them gain market share from the incumbent.

Sell to the Skunk Works

The other place for a startup to go is the nooks and crannies of a market leader. *Look for some "skunk works" project where the product developers are actively seeking alternatives to their own engineering organization.* In Apple's case, Burrell Smith was designing a computer in a skunk works unbeknownst to the rest of Apple's engineering. He was looking for a communications chip that could cut parts cost to build an innovative new type of computer – which turned out to be the Mac.

Lessons Learned

- Early customers are usually not where you first think they are.
- Where they are depends on Market Type.
- Look for aggressive number 2's or 3's who are attacking a market leader.
- Look for a "skunk works" inside a market leader.

Let's Fire Our Customers

Posted on September 24, 2009 by steveblank |

As a board member, investor and consumer, I've encountered companies firing their customers. While this sounds inexplicable to an outside observer, sometimes it makes sense. Other times it's just plain dumb.

Pattern Recognition

One of the great things about being an entrepreneur is that *you are constantly running a pattern recognition algorithm against a continual collection of customer and market data.* For me this was one of the joys of entrepreneurship – constant learning and new insights. But at times it's why entrepreneurs can sink their own companies.

The Founder's New Insight

Smart founders are never satisfied with simply executing their current business model, they are constantly observing, orienting and deciding whether their current business model can be made better. This tendency is a two-edged sword: by iterating strategy, a startup can dramatically improve the size and trajectory of the company, but at times this process can be the bane of venture investors (and why they have prematurely grey hair.) When a startup finds a repeatable sales process and steadily increasing revenue, its investors wants to harvest the rewards and build a culture of "execution." However, if the founder is still running the company, the last thing he wants is a company complacent with day-to-day execution.

This disconnect – between a founder's endorphin rush from learning, discovery, insight and *acting* – versus investors' needs for stability, execution and liquidity – is the basis of lots of founder/board travails. (More on this in later posts.) But the purpose of this post is what happens when a founder (or large company CEO) finds a better business model.

Let's Fire Our Customers

Part of the DNA of great entrepreneurs is a bias towards decisive and immediate action. However, when a startup gets past its early days and has acquired a substantial customer base, an insight about a better path, if executed and *communicated* poorly, can lead to disaster.

I've seen startup CEO's realize that their company could be much more profitable if they only could get rid of some portion of their existing customers. (It's a natural part of learning about your customers and business model.) But instead of spending the time to move these unprofitable customers politely to some other company (hopefully a competitor,) founders tend to want to do it immediately. "Get it done, now. These customers are idiots and I don't want them anymore." The founder has seen the future and wants to get there immediately. And while technically correct, and *eventually the company ought to fire unprofitable customers,* the result when done by impatient founders is most often less than optimal.

While it is "just business," many customers form emotional bonds sometimes with products, other times with the company itself. In fact, if you're doing your job right as a startup, you're encouraging customers to be passionate about your company and products. When you abruptly break that connection, you can quickly generate hordes of hurt, disappointed and now disgruntled customers who feel jilted and badmouth the company to other potential or existing customers.

If you had taken the time to fire them politely with a bit more panache and patience, they're likely to break less furniture as they leave. Entrepreneurs overlook that the *customers you fire badly are ones who will do damage to your company for a long, long time (*even if the impact of their departure is an increase in profitability.)

The problem isn't about a founder's instinct to make a strategic shift. It's the "do it now" impatience and minimal communication once you have a sizeable customer base. Startups with a customer base need to maintain an *ongoing dialog with their customers –* not make a set of announcements when the founder thinks it's time for something new.

This is why entrepreneurship is an art. When you have a critical mass of customers, there's a fine line between sticking with the status quo too long and changing too abruptly.

You've Been an Idiot For Sticking With Us
This behavior is not just limited to startups. I've watched new CEO's brought into large existing consumer products companies to turn around a failing strategy. Their new strategy included a complete revamp and simplification of the product line. Yet instead of making their *existing customers feel like partners in the turnaround,* these smart CEO's *publicly* announce that the current product line is obsolete. ("Can't you see we're busy reinventing the company?")

Ok, that's a great strategy inside the boardroom, but what are you doing to transition your customers to your new strategy? Nothing? No trade-up program? No discount for existing users? No tools to transition your customers data to the new and improved but incompatible product(s)? Congratulations, you've just fired your existing customer base. Instead of having loyal customers willing to work with you, you've told them, "You own a product we no longer care about. You've been an idiot for sticking with us." The company now needs to acquire new customers rather than upgrade its existing ones. (Usually about 10x more expensive.)

(eBay's shift from a full range auction site to selling used and off-season goods is an example. Microsoft forcing users of Windows XP to have to format their disks to upgrade to Windows 7 seems to fit this pattern as well.)

The fact that this strategy seems to play out often seems to be symptomatic of turnaround CEO's transferring their impatience and disdain for the company's old strategy and products onto that of their loyal customers.

Customers who have been told they were idiots for being loyal tend to leave sadly and with regret. And they rarely come back.

Lessons Learned

- The art of firing customers is as important as the art of acquiring them.
- Don't confuse your impatience with getting to the new strategy with the damage badly fired customers can do.
- New strategic direction in companies with loyal customers have different consequences then when you had no customers.
- Acquiring new customers are a lot more expensive that converting existing ones.

Durant Versus Sloan

Posted on October 1, 2009 by steveblank |

The entrepreneur who built the largest startup in the United States is someone you probably never heard of. The guy who replaced him invented the idea of the modern corporation. Understanding the future of entrepreneurship may depend on understanding the contribution each of them made in the past.

Alfred P. Sloan

In the middle of the 20th century Alfred P. Sloan was one of the most famous businessmen in the world. Known as the "Inventor of the Modern Corporation," Sloan was president of General Motors from 1923 to 1956 when the U.S. automotive industry grew to become one of the drivers of the global economy.

If you look around the United States, it's hard to avoid Sloan. There's the Alfred P. Sloan Foundation, the Sloan School of Management at MIT, the Sloan program at Stanford, and the Sloan/Kettering Memorial Cancer Center in New York. Sloan's book <u>My Years with General Motors</u> written 40 years ago is still a business classic.

The Modern Corporation

Sloan is rightly credited with formalizing the idea of the modern U.S. corporation, and by extension, Sloan laid the foundation for America's economic leadership in the 20th century. One guy really did all of this.

Peter Drucker wrote that Sloan was "the first to work out how to systematically organize a big company. When Sloan became president of GM in 1923 he put in place planning and strategy, measurements, and most importantly, the principles of decentralization."

Sloan realized that the traditional centralized management structures (like General Motors had in 1920) were poor fits for the management of GM's already diverse product lines. Top management was trying to coordinate all of the operating details (sales, manufacturing, distribution and marketing) across all the divisions, and the company almost went bankrupt that year when poor planning led to excess inventory (with unsold cars piling up at dealers and the company running out of cash.)

Sloan transferred responsibility down from corporate into each of the operating divisions (Chevrolet, Pontiac, Oldsmobile, Buick and Cadillac). Each of these GM divisions each focused on its own day-to-day operations, with each division general manager responsible for the division's profit and loss. Sloan kept the corporate staff small and focused on policymaking, corporate finance and planning. Sloan had each of the divisions start systematic strategic planning.

Sloan put in place GM's management accounting system (borrowed from DuPont) that for the first time allowed the company to: 1) produce an annual operating forecast that compared each division's forecast (revenue, costs, capital requirements and return on investment) with the company's financial goals. 2) Provide corporate management with near real-time divisional sales reports and budgets that indicated when they deviated from plan. 3) Allowed management to allocate resources and compensation among divisions based on a standard set of corporate-wide performance criteria.

Finally, Sloan transformed corporate management into a real profession, establishing the standard that the professional manager is duty-bound to put the interests of the enterprise ahead of his own.

Modern Corporation Marketing

At the same time, General Motors also revolutionized automotive marketing by creating multiple *brands of cars,* each with its own identity targeted at a specific economic bracket of American customers. The company set the prices for each of these brands from lowest to highest (Chevrolet, Pontiac, Oldsmobile, Buick and Cadillac.) Within each brand, there were several models at different price points.

The idea was to keep customers coming back to General Motors over time to upgrade to a better brand as they became wealthier. Finally, GM created the notion of perpetual demand within brands by continually obsoleting their own products yearly with new models rolled out every year. (Think of the iPod family and its yearly new models.)

When Sloan took over as president of GM in 1923, Ford and its Model T was the dominant player in the U.S. auto market with 60% of the U.S. car market. General Motors had 20%. By 1931, with the combination of superior financial management and a astute brand and product line strategy, GM had 43% market share to Ford's 20% – a lead it never relinquished.

Thanks for the History Lesson – So What?

Well thanks for the history lesson, but why should you care?

If you're an entrepreneur you might be interested to know that when Sloan took over General Motors in 1923, it was already a $700 million dollar company (about $8.5 *billion* in sales in today's dollars.)

Yet you never hear who built that company. Who founded what would become General Motors 16 years earlier in 1904? Where are the charitable foundations, business schools and hospitals named after him? What happened to him? Who was he?

The founder of what became General Motors was William (Billy) Durant. His board (led by the DuPont family) tossed him out of General Motors (for the second time) in 1920 when GM sales were $567 million (about $6 billion in today's dollars.)

William Durant died managing a bowling alley in Flint Michigan in 1947.

From the day Durant was fired in 1920, and for the next half a century, American commerce would be led by an army of "Sloan-style managers."

But the spirit of Billy Durant would rise again, this time in what would become Silicon Valley.

Family – This Life Isn't Practice For the Next One

Lies Entrepreneurs Tell Themselves

Posted on June 15, 2009 by steveblank |

Watching my oldest daughter graduate high school this week made me think about what it was like raising a family and being an entrepreneur.

Convergent Technologies

When I was in my 20's, I worked at Convergent Technologies, a company that was proud to be known as the "Marine Corps of Silicon Valley." It was a brawling "take no prisoners," work hard, party hard, type of company. The founders came out of the DEC (Digital Equipment Corporation) and Intel culture of the 1960's and '70's. As an early employee, I worked all hours of the day, never hesitated to jump on a "red-eye" plane to see a customer at the drop of a hat, and did whatever was necessary to make the company a winner.

I learned a lot at Convergent, going from product marketing manager in a small startup to VP of Marketing of the Unix Division, as it became a public company. Two of my role models for my career were in this company. (And one would become my mentor and partner in later companies.) But this story is not about Convergent. It's about entrepreneurship and family.

Like most 20-somethings, I modeled my behavior on the CEO in the company. His marketing and sales instincts and skills seemed magical, and he built the company into a $400 million OEM supplier, ultimately selling the company to Unisys. But his work ethic was legendary. Convergent was a 6-day a week 12-hour day company. Not only didn't I mind, but I couldn't wait to go to work in the morning and would stay until I dropped at night. If I did go to social events, all I would talk about was my new company. My company became the most important thing in my life.

But the problem was that I was married.

Uh oh.

What's More Important – Me or Your Job?

If you're are a startup founder or an early employee, there may come a time in your relationship that your significant other/spouse will ask you the "*what's more important?*" question. It will come after you come home at 2 am in the morning after missing a dinner/movie date you promised to make. Or you'll hear it after announcing one morning that weekend trip isn't going to happen because you have a deadline at work. Or if you have kids, it will get asked when you've missed another one of their plays, soccer games or school events because you were too busy finishing that project or on yet another business trip. At some point your significant other/spouse's question will be,

"What's more important, me and your family or your job?"

I remember getting the question after missing yet another event my wife had counted on me attending. When she asked it, I had to stand there and actually think about it. And when I answered, it was "my job." We both then realized our marriage was over. Luckily we had no kids, minimal assets and actually held hands when we used the same lawyer for the divorce, but it was sad. If I had been older, wiser, or more honest with myself, I would have understood that my wife and family should have been the most important thing in my life.

Lies Entrepreneurs Tell Themselves

Part of my problem was that my reality distortion field encompassed my relationships. In hindsight I had convinced myself that throwing myself into work was the right thing to do because I succumbed to the four big lies entrepreneurs tell themselves about work and family:

- I'm only doing it for my family

- My spouse "understands"

- All I need is one startup to "hit" and then I can slow down or retire

- I'll make it up by spending "quality time" with my wife/kids

None of these were true. I had thrown myself into a startup because *work was an exciting technical challenge with a fixed set of end points and rewards.* In contrast, *relationships were messy, non deterministic* (i.e. emotional rather than technical) *and a lot harder to manage than a startup.*

The Reality

If it was up to my wife she wouldn't have had me working the hours I was working and would rather have me home. She didn't sign up for my startup, she had signed up for me.

While she stuck it out for seven years, she had no connection to the passion and excitement that was driving me; all she saw was a tired and stressed entrepreneur when I got home.

At this point in my career, I had hit a couple of successful startups as a low level exec, making enough to remodel our kitchen, but not the big "hit" that made us so much money I could slow down or retire. And even if it did, startups are like a gambling addiction – if I had been honest, I would have had to admit I would probably be doing many of them.

"Quality time" with the wife or kids is a phrase made up by guilty spouses. My relationship wasn't going to be saved by one great three-day weekend after 51 weekends at work. A great vacation with my wife wasn't going to make up for being AWOL from home the rest of the year.

Summary

For the next few years I licked my wounds and threw myself into two more startups. Over time I began to recognize and regret the tradeoffs I had made between work and relationships. I realized that if I ever wanted to get married again and raise a family that my life/work balance needed to radically change.

The next post describes what I have learned and observed in the following years about balancing my entrepreneurial drive with building a healthy relationship with my wife and kids.

Epitaph for an Entrepreneur

Posted on June 18, 2009 by steveblank |

Raising our kids and being an entrepreneur wasn't easy. Being in a startup and having a successful relationship and family was *very* hard work. But entrepreneurs *can be* great spouses and parents.

This post is not advice nor is it recommendation of what you should do. It's simply what my wife and I did to raise our kids in the middle of starting multiple companies. Our circumstances were unique, and your mileage will vary.

Biological Clocks

After Convergent and now single again, I was a co-founder of my next two startups; MIPS and Ardent. I threw myself into work and worked even more hours a day. And while I had great adventures by the time I was in my mid-30's I knew I wanted a family. (My friends noticed that I was picking up other people's babies a lot.) I didn't know if I was ready, but I finally could see myself as a father.

I met my wife on a blind-date, and we discovered that not only did we share the same interests but we were both ready for kids. My wife knew a bit about startups. Out of Stanford Business School she went to work for Apple as an evangelist and then joined Ansa Software, the developer of Paradox, a PC-database.

Product Launch

Our first daughter was born about four months after I started at SuperMac. We ended up sleeping in the hospital lounge for 5 days as she stayed in intensive care. Our second daughter followed 14½ months later.

Family Rules

My wife and I agreed to a few rules upfront and made up the rest as went along. We agreed I was still going to do startups, and probably more than most spouses she knew what that meant. To her credit she also understood that meant that child raising wasn't going to be a 50/50 split; I simply wasn't going to be home at 5 pm every night.

In hindsight this list looks pretty organized but in reality we made it up as we went along, accompanied with all the husband and wife struggles of being married and trying to raise a family in Silicon Valley. Here are the some of the rules that evolved that seemed to work for our family.

We would have a family dinner at home most nights of the week. Regardless of what I was doing, I had to be home by 7pm. (My kids still remember mom secretly feeding them when they were hungry at 5pm, but eating again with dad at 7pm.) But we would use dinnertime to talk about what they did at school, have family meetings etc.

Put the kids to bed. Since I was already home for dinner, it was fun to help give them their baths, read them stories and put them to bed. I never understood how important the continuity of time between dinner through bedtime was until my kids mentioned it as teenagers.

Act and be engaged. My kids and wife had better antenna than I thought. If I was home but my head was elsewhere and not mentally engaged, they would call me on it. So I figured out how to spit the flow of the day in half. I would work 10 hours a day in the office, come home and then

Back to work after the kids were in bed. What my kids never saw is that as soon as they were in bed, I was back on the computer and back at work for another 4 or 5 hours until the wee hours of the morning.

Weekends were with and for my kids. There was always some adventure on the weekends. I think we must have gone to the zoo, beach, museum, picnic, amusement park, etc. a 100 times.

Half a day work on Saturday. While weekends were for my kids, I did go to work on Saturday morning. But my kids would come with me. This had two unexpected consequences. First, my kids still remember that work was very cool. They liked going in with me, and they said it helped them understand what dad did at "work." Second, it set a cultural norm at my startups, first at Supermac as the VP of Marketing, then at Rocket Science as the CEO and at E.piphany as President. (Most Silicon Valley startups have great policies for having your dog at work but not your kids.)

Long vacations. We would take at least a 3-week vacation every summer. Since my wife and I liked to hike, we'd explore national parks around the U.S. (Alaska, Wyoming, Colorado, Washington, Oregon, Maine.) When the kids got older, our adventures took us to Mexico, Ecuador, India, Africa and Europe. The trips gave them a sense that the rest of the country and the world was not Silicon Valley and that their lives were not the norm.

Never miss an event. As my kids got older, there were class plays, soccer games, piano and dance performances, birthdays, etc. I never missed one if I was in town, sometimes even if it was in the middle of the day. (And I made sure I was in town for the major events.)

Engage your spouse. I asked my wife to read and critique every major presentation and document I wrote. Everything she touched was much better for it. What my investors never knew is that they were getting two of us for the price of one. (And one of us actually went to business school.) It helped her understand what I was working on and what I was trying to accomplish.

Have a Date-Night. We tried hard to set aside one evening a week when just the two of us went out to dinner and/or a movie.

Get your spouse help. Early on in our marriage we didn't have much money but we invested in childcare to help my wife. While it didn't make up for my absences, it offloaded a lot.

Traditions matter. Holidays, both religious and secular, weekly and yearly, were important to us. The kids looked forward to them, and we made them special.

Travel only if it needed me. As an executive, it was easy to think I had to get on a plane for every deal. But after I had kids, I definitely thought long and hard before I would jump on a plane. When I ran Rocket Science, our corporate partners were in Japan (Sega), Germany (Bertelsmann) and Italy (Mondadori,) and some travel was unavoidable. But I probably traveled 20% of what I did when I was single.

Document every step. Like most dads, I took thousands of photos. But I also filmed the girls once a week on the same couch, sitting in the same spot, for a few minutes – for 16 years. When my oldest graduated high school, I gave her a time-lapse movie of her life.

"Live to Work" or "Work to Live"?
When I was in my 20's the two concepts that mattered were "*me*" and "*right now.*" As I got older, I began to understand the concept of "*others*" and "*the future.*" I began to realize that working 24/7 wasn't my only goal in life.

As a single entrepreneur, I had a philosophy of "*I live to work*" – nothing was more exciting or important than my job. Now with kids it had become "*I work to live.*" I still loved what I did as an entrepreneur, but I wasn't working only for the sheer joy of it, I was also working to provide for my family and a longer-term goal of retirement and then doing something different. (The irony is when I was working insane hours it was to make someone else wealthy. When I moderated my behavior, it was when they were my startups.)

Work Smarter Not Harder
As I got older, I began to realize that how effective you are is not necessarily correlated with how many hours you work. My ideas about Customer Development started evolving around these concepts. Eric Ries's astute observations about engineering and

124

Lean Startups make the same point. I began to think how to be effective and strategic rather than just present and tactical.

Advice From Others
As my kids were growing up I got a piece of advice that stuck with me all these years.

The first was when our oldest daughter was 6 months old, and a friend was holding her. She looked at the baby then looked at me and asked, "Steve do you know what your most important job with this baby is?" I guessed, "Take care of her?" No. "Love her?" No. "OK, I give up, what is my most important job?" She answered, "Steve, your job is teaching her how to leave." This was one of the most unexpected things I ever heard. This baby could barely sit up, and I have to teach her how to leave?

My friend explained, "Your kids are only passing through. It will seem like forever, but it will be gone in a blink of an eye. Love them and care for them but remember they will be leaving. What will they remember that you taught them?"

For the next 18 years that thought was never far from my mind.

What Will Your Epitaph Say?
At some point I had heard two aphorisms which sounded very trite when I was single but took on a lot more meaning with a family.

This life isn't practice for the next one. I started to realize that some of the older guys who I had admired as role models at work had feet of clay at home. They had chosen their company over family and had kids who felt abandoned by their dads for work – and some of these kids have turned out less than optimally. I met lots of other dads going through the "could-have, would-have, should-have" regrets and reflections of the tradeoffs they had made between fatherhood and company building. Their regrets were lessons for me.

What will your epitaph say? When our kids were babies I was still struggling to try to put the work/life balance in perspective. Someone gave me a thought that I tried to live my live my life around. He asked me: When you're gone, would you rather have your gravestone say, "*He never missed a meeting*" or one that said, "*He was a great father?*" Holding my two kids on my lap, it was a pretty easy decision.

I hope I did it right.

Know When to Hold Them, Know When to Fold Them, Know When to Walk Away
When my last startup, E.piphany went public in the dot.com boom, I was faced with a choice; start company number nine, or retire.

I looked at my kids and never went back.

Thanks to my wife for being a great partner. It takes two.

Thanksgiving Day

Posted on November 26, 2009 by steveblank |

Thursday is Thanksgiving Day in the United States. Families gather from across the country to spend time with each other and feast on a traditional turkey dinner.

Since our kids were little, our Thanksgiving tradition was to head to Hawaii with friends and eat Thanksgiving dinner under the palm trees to the sound of the waves next to the warm ocean. This year, with the kids grown, their choice was to fly up from Southern California and spend the holidays at our ranch.

So today no post on entrepreneurship, Secret History of Silicon Valley, or Customer Development, just a reflection on my family and hopes for our children.

A Few Thoughts for Thanksgiving

On this day it's hard not to be grateful and give thanks for the things that matter – family, friends, our health, and feel blessed for all the things that have come to us. It's harder to remember that we have no perpetual rights to them, they aren't our due, but they're gifts. We try our best to give back to our community and country and always wonder – is it enough?

We've taken the kids to enough places in the world to realize the United States still remains a country of opportunity and hope. For all its flaws, America is still a beacon of liberty and justice. My parents were immigrants who came through Ellis Island with nothing but the clothes on their backs – but they believed in the American dream. They worked hard their entire lives so their children could have a better life. Each year I teach hundreds of students from around the world who come to America to pursue their version of this same dream.

This year as American families face economic hardships, (one out of eight Californian's are unemployed) we remember that as a nation we are still a generous people, willing to share and give to others less fortunate then ourselves – both at home and abroad. I hope we managed to teach our children compassion and charity for others. And as they find their own way in life, they will continue to give back to others.

I'm grateful to those who serve our country and remember that people sleep peaceably in their beds at night only because rough men stand ready to do violence on their behalf. I hope our children remember that freedom needs to be earned and that they too find their way to serve their country.

Happy Thanksgiving

The End of Innocence

Posted on August 24, 2009 by steveblank |

Discovering that your worldview is wrong or mistaken can be a life-changing event. It's part of growing up but can happen at any age. What you do when it happens shapes who you'll become.

Dinner in a Strange Land
When I was in my mid 20's working at ESL, I was sent overseas to a customer site where the customers were our three-letter intelligence agencies. All of us knew who they were, understood how important this site was for our country, and were proud of the work we were doing. (Their national technical means of verification made the world a safer place and hastened the end of the Soviet Union and the Cold War.)

As a single guy, I got to live in a motel-like room on the site while the married guys lived in town in houses and tried to blend in with the locals. When asked what they did, they said they worked at "the xxx research facility." (Of course the locals translated that to "oh do you work for the yyy or zzz intelligence agency?")

One warm summer evening I was invited over to the house of a married couple from my company for a BBQ and after-dinner entertainment – drinking mass quantities of the local beer. The quintessential California couple, they stood out in our crowd as the engineer (in his late 20's, respected by his peers and the customer) had hair down to his shoulders, sharply contrasting with the military crewcuts of the customers and most of the other contractors. His wife, about my age, could have been a poster child for the stereotypical California hippie surfer, with politics that matched her style – antiwar, anti government, antiestablishment.

One of the rules in the business was that you didn't tell your spouse, girlfriend, significant other who you worked for or what you worked on – ever. It was always a welcome change of pace to leave the brown of the unchanging desert and travel into town and have dinner with them and have a non-technical conversation about books, theater, politics, travel, etc. But it was a bit incongruous to hear her get wound up and rail against our government and the very people we were all working for. Her husband would look at me out the corner of his eye, and then we'd segue the conversation to some other topic.

That evening I was there with three other couples cooking over the barbeque in their backyard. After night fell we reconvened in their living room as we continued to go through the local beer. The conversation happened to hit on politics and culture, and my friend's' wife innocently offered up she had lived in a commune in California. Well that created a bit of alcohol-fueled cross-cultural disconnect and heated discussion.

Until one of the other wives changed a few lives *forever* with a slip of the tongue.

Tell Me it Isn't True

One of the other wives asked, "Well what would your friends in the commune think of you now that your husband is working for intelligence agencies x *and* y?"

As soon as the words came out of her mouth, I felt time slow down. The other couples laughed for about half a second expecting my friend's wife to do so as well. But instead the look on her face went from puzzlement in processing the question, to concentration, as she was thinking and correlating past questions she had about who exactly her husband had been working for. It seemed like forever before she asked with a look of confusion, "What do you mean agencies x and y?"

The laughter in the room stopped way too soon, and the room got deathly quiet. Her face slowly went from a look of puzzlement to betrayal to horror as she realized that that the drunken silence, the dirty looks from other husbands to the wife who made the agency comment, and the wives now staring at their shoes was an answer.

She had married someone who never told her who he was really working for. She was living in a lie with people she hated. In less than a minute her entire worldview had shattered and coming apart in front of us, she started screaming.

This probably took no more than 10 seconds, but watching her face, it felt like hours.

I don't remember how we all got out of the house or how I got back to the site, but to this day I still remember standing on her lawn staring at strange constellations in the night sky as she screamed at her husband, "Tell me it isn't true!"

The next day the site supervisor told me that my friend and his wife had been put on the next plane out of country and sent home (sedated) along with the other couple that made the comment. By the time I came back to the United States, he was gone from the company.

It's been thirty years, but every once in awhile I still wonder what happened to the rest of their lives.

The End of Innocence

In much smaller ways I've watched my children and now my students discover that their worldview is wrong, mistaken or naive. I've watched as they realize there's no Santa Claus and Tooth Fairy; the world has injustice, hypocrisy and inequality; capitalism and politics don't work like the textbooks and money moves the system; you can't opt out of dying, and without regulation people will try to "game" whatever system you put in place.

Learning to accept the things you can't change, finding the courage to change the things you can and acquiring the common sense to know the difference, is part of growing up.

Founders and dysfunctional families

Posted on May 18, 2009 by steveblank |

Startup CEO Traits

I was having lunch with a friend who is a retired venture capitalist, and we drifted into a discussion of the startups she funded. We agreed that all her founding CEOs seemed to have the same set of personality traits – tenacious, passionate, relentless, resilient, agile, and comfortable operating in chaos. I said, "Well for me you'd have to add coming from a dysfunctional family." Her response was surprising. "Steve, almost *all* my CEO's came from very tough childhoods. It was one of the characteristics I specifically looked for. It's why all of you operated so well in the unpredictable environment that all startups face."

I couldn't figure out if I was more perturbed about how casual the comment was or how insightful it was. What makes an individual a great startup founder (versus an employee) has been something I had been thinking about since I retired. My comfort in operating in chaos was something I first recognized when I was working in the Midwest.

The Rust Belt – (Skip this Section if I'm Boring You)

Out of the Air Force, my first job out of school was in Ann Arbor, Michigan, in the mid-1970's installing broadband process control systems in automotive and manufacturing plants throughout the Midwest. I got to travel and see almost every type of Rust Belt factory – at the time, the heart and muscle of American manufacturing – GM, American Motors, Ford, U.S. Steel, Whirlpool. Our equipment was installed in the manufacturing lines of these companies, and if it went down sometimes it brought the entire manufacturing line down.

I always made a habit of getting a tour of whatever manufacturing plant I was visiting. Most plant foremen were more than accommodating and flattered that someone actually was interested. I was fascinated to learn how everyday objects (cars, washing machines, structural steel, etc.) that ended up on our shelves or driveways were assembled.

My favorite factory was the massive U.S. Steel plant by Lake Erie. On my first visit the foreman walked through this enormous building, not much more than a giant steel shed, where they had an open-hearth furnace. We came in time to see the furnace being tapped, pouring steel out into giant buckets. (Years later I realized I watched the end of an era. The last open-hearth furnaces closed in the 1980's.)

We stood on a platform several stories up and light streamed diagonally through windows set high on top of the building cutting through the black soot particles created when the incandescent steel hit the bucket. It was too loud to talk so I just watched the steel pour through the clouds of soot backlit by the blinding bright liquid metal. It looked like an update of the iconic image of Penn Station writ large. And as I stared through the billowing clouds of soot flashing between black and white took on fantastical shapes as tiny figures on the factory floor scurried around the bucket. I could have stayed there all day.

Automobile plants were equally fascinating. They were like being inside a pinball machine. At the Ford plant in Milpitas the plant foreman proudly took me down the line. I remember stopping at one station a little confused about its purpose. All the other stations on the assembly line had swarms of workers with power tools adding something to the car.

This station just had one guy with a 2 x 4 piece of lumber, a large rubber mallet and a folded blanket. His spot was right after the station where they had dropped the hoods down on the cars, and had bolted them in. As I was watched, the next car rolled down the line, the station before attached the hood, and as the car approached this station, the worker took the 2 x 4, shoved it under one corner of the hood and put the blanket over the top of the hood and started pounding it with the rubber mallet while prying with the lumber. "It's our hood alignment station," the plant manager said proudly. These damn models weren't designed right so we're fixing them on the line."

I had a queasy feeling that perhaps this wasn't the way to solve the car quality problem. Little did I know that I was watching the demise of the auto industry in front of my eyes.

Operating in Chaos
Repairing our equipment could be time critical. One day, when I was at the Ford Wixom auto assembly plant training my replacement, I was at met at the door by an irate plant manager. He welcomed us by screaming, "Do you know how much it costs every minute this line is down?" As I'm troubleshooting our equipment scattered across the plant, (in the computer room, above the steel, in NEMA cabinets next to line, etc.) the manager followed us still yelling. My understudy looked at me and asked, "How can you deal with this chaos and still focus?" And until that moment I had never thought about it before. I realized that what others heard as chaos, I just shut out.

A Day in the Life of A Founder
For those of you who've never started a company, let me assure you that it never happens like the pleasant articles you read in business magazines or in case studies. Founding a company is a sheer act of will and tenacity in the face of immense skepticism from everyone – investors, customers, friends, etc. You literally have to take

your vision of the opportunity and against all rational odds assemble financing, and a team to help you execute. And that's just to get started.

Next, you have to deal with the daily crisis of product development and acquiring early customers. And here's where life gets really interesting, as the reality of product development and customer input collide, the facts change so rapidly that the original well-thought-out business plan becomes irrelevant.

If you can't manage chaos and uncertainty, if you can't bias yourself for action and if you wait around for someone else to tell you what to do, then your investors and competitors will make your decisions for you and you will run out of money and your company will die.

Great founders live for these moments.

Creating the Entrepreneurial Personality – A Thought Experiment

Fast forward three decades back to today. The lunch conversation was an interesting data point to add to a hypothesis I've had.

I've wondered, just as a thought experiment, how would we go about creating individuals who operate serenely in chaos, and have the skills we associate with one type of entrepreneurial founder/leader?

One possible path might be to raise children in an environment where parents struggling in their own lives create an environment where fighting, abusive or drug/alcohol related behavior is the norm.

In this household nothing would be the same from day to day, the parents would constantly bombard their kids with dogmatic parenting, (harsh and inflexible discipline) and they would control them by withholding love, praise, and attention. Finally we could make sure no child is allowed to express the "wrong" emotion. Children in these families would grow up thinking that this behavior is normal.

(If this seems unimaginably cruel to you, congratulations, you had a great set of parents. On the other hand, if the description is making you uncomfortable remembering some of how you were raised – welcome to a fairly wide club.)

Over the last 5 years I've asked over 500 of my students how many of them grew up in a dysfunctional family (participation was voluntary.) I've been surprised at the data. In this admittedly very unscientific survey I've found that between a quarter and half of the students I consider "hard-core" entrepreneurs/founders (working passionately to found a company,) self-identified as coming from a less than benign upbringing.

Founders as Survivors

My hypothesis is that most children are emotionally damaged by this upbringing. But a small percentage, whose brain chemistry and wiring is set for resilience, come out of this with a compulsive, relentless and tenacious drive to succeed. They have learned to function in a permanent state of chaos. And they have channeled all this into whatever activity they could find outside of their home – sports, business, or entrepreneurship.

Therefore, I'll posit *one* possible path for a startup founder – the dysfunctional family theory.

Throwing hand grenades in Your Own Company

One last thought. The dysfunctional family theory may explain why founders who excel in the chaotic early phases of a company throw organizational hand grenades into their own companies after they find a repeatable and scaleable business model and need to switch gears into execution.

The problem, I believe, is that repeatability represents the extreme discomfort zone of this class of entrepreneur. And I have seen entrepreneurs emotionally or organizationally try to create chaos — it's too calm around here — and actually self-destruct.

So What?

Lets be clear, in no way am I suggesting that growing up in a dysfunctional family is the only path to becoming a founder of a startup. Nor am I suggesting that everyone who does so turns out well. And in particular I'm not suggesting that every employee who joins a startup fits this profile. It just seems more prevalent in the founder(s).

And this hypothesis might be a good example of confusing cause and effect. Yet I am surprised given how much is written about the attributes of a startup founder, how little has been written about what "makes" a founder.

Unintended Lessons

Posted on September 28, 2009 by steveblank |

Last week I drove my daughter on an east coast college tour (1500 miles, 8 colleges in 6 days.) We started in North Carolina eating BBQ and enjoying the Southern culture, passed through Washington D.C checking out the shopping in Georgetown, enjoyed beautiful horse country in Pennsylvania and upstate NY and headed down into the bays and coves of Connecticut filled with sailboats.

We had some great conversations in the car, but one stuck in my mind. It was something I never thought about, and when I first heard it I thought it was a terrible thing to have taught her. She said, "Dad, one of the great things you and Mom did was never tell us how much things cost."

Whoa, when I first heard her say that, I thought she meant that we raised a spoiled kid who had and an unlimited sense of entitlement. For a minute it was a pretty depressing thought for a parent. But on further questioning what came out was a bit more interesting and rewarding.

She said, "Dad what I meant was that growing up we loved when we traveled. And I remember staying in everything from little cabins and small motels to big hotels and resorts, from national parks in Alaska to Hawaii every Thanksgiving and trips in India and Africa. And as kids we never had any idea which was cheap and which was expensive.

Now that I'm older, I'm starting to know what things cost. And I realize *you guys never told us we had to enjoy something any more or less because of the price.*

It made me realize that the goal is not to get the most expensive things, but to go and get what you enjoy."

It was a lesson we never intended to consciously teach.

It made me wonder how many other lessons we taught without knowing.

Ardent – Learning How To Get Out of the Building

Supercomputers Get Personal

Posted on October 5, 2009 by steveblank |

Last month on an east coast college tour with my daughter, I found myself in North Carolina for the first time in nearly 24 years.

I had last been in Chapel Hill on a winter's day in 1986, traveling with the VP of Sales of our new supercomputer startup, Ardent. We were on the University of North Carolina campus to meet with Fred Brooks and Henry Fuchs. As we entered campus we turned on the rental car radio and heard the mid day BBC news – the space shuttle Challenger had just exploded.

It was the best of times, it was the worst of times
Ardent would be my third technology company as a VP of Marketing (Convergent Technologies and MIPS Computers were the other two.) It would be the company where I actually earned the title.

A Phone Call
After I left MIPS Computers, I was in New York tagging along with a friend (a computer architect whose products at Apple a decade later would change the shape of personal computing) who was consulting for a voice recognition startup. We were sitting in our cheap hotel room when the phone rang. It was my ex boss from Convergent Technologies. "Steve we've all just resigned from Convergent, and we're starting a new company. I've convinced the team you'd be perfect. Come join us as the VP of Marketing." My ex-boss was going to be the VP of Engineering, and I would report to the CEO whose marketing acumen and sales instincts seemed at the time to be telepathic and whose sense of theater was legend. And so was his reputation for being verbally abusive to his direct reports. Gulp.

The culture and work ethic of Convergent had earned it the title "the Marine Corps of Silicon Valley". (Not until I was older and wiser did I realize that this was not always meant as a compliment.)

Working with my old boss sounded like a great idea. And in the course of the phone call, I put my friend on the phone and let him interview for a job. On the ride to the airport my friend asked me what our new company was going to do.

Only then did I realize we both forgot to ask.

Never mind
The first idea for our new company was a software product that looked something like Hypertext. With a bit of research, we learned that a professor at Brown University had

invented something close to what we had in mind. The VP of Sales and I flew to Providence to convince Andy van Dam at Brown to join our company or at a minimum lead our advisory board.

On a rainy day in Providence we tracked Andy down just as he was leaving for a trip to Europe. He agreed to talk to us as he packed his office, and we followed him down the street as he went to get a haircut. With me holding the umbrella our VP of Sales kept reminding him how wonderful it would be if his research could turn into commercial products- all as we all walked downtown to the barbershop. While van Dam sat in the chair getting his haircut, the VP of Sales and I flanked him on either side, with the barber trying to get his clippers in between us. We were painting a picture of hypertext on every desktop computer. I knew we almost had him convinced when our sales guy and Andy started talking to each other in Dutch.

As the conversation began to get down to how much stock and salary we could offer van Dam, we left the barber to finish his work and went to a payphone to call our CEO to confirm the deal. The response from across the country? "Glad you two called, we were trying to get a hold of you guys. Forget the Hypertext idea and come on back to California. We're building a supercomputer." Oops. We told Andy we'd talk further when he got back from Europe.

Supercomputers get Personal

Back in Sunnyvale my friend had not only been hired but had convinced the team that we should be building hardware – making a new class of computers not a software application. Our vision was that just as the PC was revolutionizing the business market, we were going to do the same for scientists and engineers. We were going to target scientists and researchers who were longing to do "interactive simulations," requiring both scientific computing and visualization of real-world phenomena. We were going to invent a new product and create an entirely new market by putting a personal graphics supercomputer on every desk.

By the mid 1980's microprocessor technology—specifically off-the-shelf RISC-based microprocessors like the one from MIPS, my previous startup– had evolved to support the speed needed to support a new class of computers for scientists and engineers. Unlike Intel chips, MIPS chip architecture also made it possible to plug in a math co-processor. By adding a vector unit to these RISC processors, we believed we could take some of the supercomputer market from Cray (at the time the maker of the most powerful scientific computers in the world) as well as from the emerging class of mini-supercomputers (Convex and Alliant.)

To do that we needed to build a supercomputer, but since the RISC processors weren't fast enough, we decided to build a multiprocessor supercomputer, (running up to 4 processors in parallel.) We had to write our own parallelizing and vectorizing compilers, build our own high-end graphics boards, and write our own 3d graphics subroutine language – and put in all in a box that could fit in an office. Oh, and since it was not code compatible with anything, we were going to have to port all the key scientific applications our customers needed (as soon as we figured out who they were.) Some of the other founders had sold minicomputers to scientists and engineers, but no one knew or understood the unique class of applications and customers of supercomputers. We were going to be guessing.

Personal supercomputers meant yet again learning something completely new, new computer architectures, new applications and customers, new markets.

I couldn't believe they were paying me to do this job. I would have gladly done it for free.

The Streets of Palo Alto

As our company was getting formed, I happened to bump into Gordon Bell – the ex VP of Engineering of DEC (the company that defined the minicomputer) on the streets of Palo Alto. (It was Gordon who had prodded John Hennessy and the MIPS team at Stanford to start a commercial chip company.) After telling Gordon what we were doing and who was doing it, he realized that he knew most of our founding team when they all had worked at DEC. I invited him to meet the team. A few days later Gordon became a founder. (Later he would leave for a few years to start the Computing Directorate at the National Science Foundation, help spec what became the Internet and then come back and run Ardent's engineering.)

I would learn a ton from Gordon over the next decade, not only about practical heuristics for managing complex engineering projects (i.e. the "schedule fantasy factor") or his eleven rules of supercomputer design but also a real appreciation for how a technical visionary thinks. (I tried my best to narrow the time that I went from believing that Gordon had yet another insane idea to when I realized it was a profound insight.) It was a challenge to keep up with him (I never did but it was fun to try.

At the same time Gordon was looking forward, he had a great appreciation of saving the past. He and his wife Gwen would found the Computer Museum, first in the lobby of DEC headquarters, then in Boston (and now as the Computer History Museum in Mountain View, California.) When our kids were little, they would play with the computer artifacts (Napier bones and Pascal engines) scattered across their living room and overflowing their shelves when we stayed at their condo in Boston. My first inkling that computing had a history (with deep military connections) was looking at the SAGE air defense computer at the Boston Computer Museum.

I would be lucky in my career to work with Gordon and three other people I consider as mentors. They would all work in this one company.

Get Out of Building

Our trip to North Carolina was part of a year long effort to get out of the building to understand our market, customers and their applications. How I learned to "get out of the building" is in the next post.

Lessons Learned:

- Ardent's personal supercomputer pushed at the edge of what was possible to build in technology.
- Our enthusiasm and passion for technology would soon intersect with our hypotheses about customers and market.

Get Out of My Building

Posted on October 8, 2009 by steveblank |

Some of the most important business lessons are learned in the most unlikely ways. At Ardent I learned many of them with a sharp smack on the side of the head from a brilliant but abusive boss. Not a process I recommend, but one in which the lessons stuck for a lifetime.

Lessons to Learn

By the time I joined Ardent I thought I was an experienced marketer, but I'll never forget my first real lesson in what it meant to understand customers and product/market fit.

We were sitting in our conference room in our first "system-planning meeting" trying to define the specifications of our new supercomputer and make the trade-offs between what was possible to build, and what customers in this new market would actually want and need. The conversation that day would become one of my professional watermarks.

Marketing is Heard From

Engineering was discussing how sophisticated the graphics portion of our computer should be, debating cost and time-to-market tradeoffs of arcane details such as double-buffering, 24 versus 32-bits of color, alpha channels, etc. I was pleased that not only did I understand the issues, but I also had an opinion about what we should build. All of a sudden I decided that I hadn't heard the sound of my own voice in a while so I piped up: "I think our customers will want 24-bits of double-buffered graphics."

Silence descended across the conference table. The CEO turned to me and asked, "What did you say?" Thinking he was impressed with my mastery of the subject as well as my brilliant observation, I repeated myself and embellished my initial observation with all the additional reasons why I thought our customers would want this feature. I was about to get an education that would last a lifetime.

Picture the scene: the entire company (all 15 of us) are present. For this startup we had assembled some of the best and brightest hardware and software engineers in the computer industry. My boss, the CEO, had just come from a string of successes at Convergent Technologies, Intel and Digital Equipment, names that at that time carried a lot of weight. Some of us had worked together in previous companies; some of us had just started working together for the first time. I thought I was bright, aggressive and could do no wrong as a marketer. I loved my job, and I was convinced I was God's gift to marketing. Now in a voice so quiet it could be barely heard across the conference table, our CEO turns to me and says, "That's what I thought you said. I just wanted to make sure I heard it correctly." It was the last sentence I heard before my career trajectory as a marketer was permanently changed.

Get Out of My Company

At the top of his lungs he screamed, "You don't know a damn thing about what these customers need! You've never talked to anyone in this market, you don't know who they are, you don't know what they need, and you have no right to speak in any of these planning meetings." I was mortified with the dressing down in front of my friends as well as new employees I barely knew. Later my friends told me my face went pale. He continued yelling, "We have a technical team assembled in this room that has more knowledge of scientific customers and scientific computers than any other startup has ever had. They've been talking to these customers since before you were born, and they have a right to have an opinion. You are a disgrace to the marketing profession and have made a fool of yourself and will continue to do so every time you open your mouth. Get out of this conference room, get out of this building and get out of my company; you are wasting all of our time."

I was stunned by the verbal onslaught. At that moment I felt so small I could have walked out of a room underneath the crack in a closed door.

Facts Not Opinions

The shock quickly wore off as I processed the gist of what he told me. He was right. I personally didn't have any facts, and if we were counting opinions, there were a bunch more educated opinions in that room than I had. All I had been doing was filling the air with marketing noises.

I was convinced that I had just been humiliatingly fired – 90 days into our new company.

Get Out of the Building

As I got up to leave the room, the CEO said, "I want you out of the building talking to customers; find out who they are, how they work, and what we need to do to sell them lots of these new computers." Motioning to our VP of Sales, he ordered: "Go with him and get him in front of customers, and both of you *don't come back until you can tell us something we don't know.*"

And he was smiling.

My career as a marketer had just begun.

Lessons learned:

- Corporate culture is either set by fiat, by default, or by consensus. But regardless of how it gets set, it gets set early.
- An intelligent opinion is still a guess.
- The dumbest person with a fact trumps anyone with an opinion.
- There are no facts inside the building so get the heck outside.

Supercomputer Porn

Posted on October 12, 2009 by steveblank |

As VP of Marketing at our new startup, the CEO literally threw me out of the building and told me not to return until I understood the market and could identify the key applications and customers for Ardent's new personal supercomputer.

Supercomputers

With the introduction in 1976 of the Cray-1, supercomputers were defined as the fastest vector-processing computer, one in which a single instruction performed operations on an array rather than a single number. Cray's first customers were the U.S. Nuclear Weapons Laboratories, which used supercomputers to run their hydrodynamics codes to simulate what went on in the first microseconds in a nuclear weapon and the National Security Agency (with Cray putting in a special population count hardware instruction) used to facilitate decryption of codes.

At first only the national laboratories and the largest companies could afford to buy supercomputers (the Cray-1 cost ~$9 million,) but over time scientists and researchers were also starting to use them. Companies wanted to run numerical simulations to model things that were too expensive, too dangerous or too time consuming to physically build. Because of the vagaries of how floating point units in computers were designed, your average IBM mainframe of the day would take forever to run a simulation application. A supercomputer could be a 100x faster.

What Markets?

At Ardent our hypothesis was that if we could build a desktop supercomputer powerful enough to run and display these numerical simulations, there were enough customers to make this a big business. My job was to figure out what markets Ardent should target, who were the key customers and what applications these customers had to have.

The problem was I didn't have a clue. And while others in our new startup came from companies like Digital Equipment Corporation (DEC) that had sold computers to automate scientific instrumentation and process control, the computers we were building at Ardent were targeted to different customers and markets.

The one thing I did know is that we were probably going to be running some of the same applications as the market leader Cray. I concluded that my first job was to understand Cray's markets, customers and applications. When I learned that Cray users would be giving papers at the Society of Petroleum Engineering conference in Denver the next day, I got on a plane to listen and learn.

Follow the Leader

At the conference I attended a bunch of technical sessions, and got lost as soon as the speaker got past, "My name is xxx." I could see that quite a few oil companies were buying or thinking of buying their own supercomputer. As I walked out of the conference hall, I ran into a small booth with salespeople from Cray. Since their computers were way too large to bring to a trade show, the Cray booth just had literature describing their machines. I grabbed one of each brochure, stuffed them into my bag, and wandered through the exhibit hall looking at other hardware and petroleum software companies.

Later I sat down for lunch and began to leaf through the bag of data sheets and brochures I had collected. Hmm - typical booth stuff - key chains, data sheets, pens- until I got to the material from Cray.

Intelligence

As I leafed through the Cray sales material, a glossy magazine with the headline *Cray Channels* jumped out of the pile. Skimming a few pages, I realized that this particular issue was all about computational fluid dynamics, one of Cray's key markets. The articles described the applications these users depended on and featured interviews with their most important customers. I went back and looked at the cover not quite believing what I was reading was real. *Cray Channels* was describing my market, applications and customers for me. Was it possible that *the existing market incumbent was handing my market research to me?*

I kept thinking; Could this be possible? Did Cray ever publish any more of these magazines? I looked at the cover of the magazine again and almost fell off my chair. It was Volume 7 issue 2. These magazines had been published for the last *seven years*. Could Cray have actually been describing their markets and users for that long?

I ran back to the Cray booth and as casually as I could, asked the salesman about the magazine. He assured me that each one profiled a different market, applications and users. I could order back issues from their publications department.

I don't remember how quickly I got to a payphone, but I'm pretty sure that every back issue of these magazines were on the way to Sunnyvale by the end of that day.

Supercomputer Porn

When the back issues of Cray Channels arrived at Ardent, I ripped open the package with the Cray return address and eagerly started to flip through them. I was excited about what I was going to learn, yet somehow felt guilty, as if I really shouldn't be looking at them. The pictures were great, but I was reading it for the articles. Breathing heavy, I felt like I was looking at supercomputer porn. The magazines got passed around to all the engineers until they were dog-eared and worn.

I spent the next few days building a table with three columns: markets, applications, key customers. At the same time I had found the Wall Street analyst who followed Cray (now a public company) who kept a list of where every one of Cray's machines was installed. I could now cross-correlate the markets by company that used supercomputers.

I started sharing what I had learned about potential target markets with our engineering team and my CEO. We agreed that now we had a roadmap, it was time to hit the road, talk to Cray customers and learn about supercomputer markets and applications in detail.

Lessons learned:

- If you are in an existing market or trying to resegment an existing market you need to understand the market leader.
- Market leaders tend to educate the market.
- Step one for a startup is know what the market leader knows.

You Know You're Getting Close to Your Customers When They Offer You a Job

Posted on October 15, 2009 by steveblank |

In 1985 Ardent Computer was determined to create a market niche for personal supercomputers. To understand our potential markets, we started by analyzing the marketing literature from Cray Research then crisscrossed the country talking to prospective customers – scientists and researchers in advanced corporate R&D centers and universities – to understand their needs.

A week might start with a visit to the MIT Media Lab, the next day at Princeton in the Aerospace Engineering department, then off to General Motors' advanced research group, across to the computer science department at the University of Illinois, up to Minneapolis to meet with ETA, Control Data and Cray, and across the country to Seattle to speak with Boeing's advanced propulsion group before returning to the geophysics department at Stanford.

Simulation applications

After six months, we hypothesized that our most likely customers were scientists and engineers who used one of five applications: computational fluid dynamics, finite element analysis, computational chemistry and seismic data processing and reservoir simulation.

At Boeing we had learned aircraft designers needed to calculate the airflow and turbulence around wings and engines. Instead of building a new wing to test designs, numerical simulation would allow them to use a supercomputer to build a virtual model of a wing on the screen and use an application called *computational fluid dynamics* to watch the resulting airflow without ever flying a plane. If they didn't like what they saw (say the wing had more drag than expected), they could change the design and rerun the simulation.

At General Motors we heard from mechanical engineers who needed to calculate the strength, breaking point and failure modes of structures – everything from piston rods to bumpers. Their interest was easy to understand. Before computer simulation, they would test real objects until they physically broke (or get sued when something important broke, blew up, or collapsed.) Now applications called *finite element analysis* could calculate these stresses and failure modes on a computer screen.

A third simulation market, this one new and just emerging, allowed biologists to examine how drugs would interact by simulating them on a computer. A precursor to today's biotech revolution, these *computational chemistry* applications allowed the active docking sites of potential drugs to be modeled and tested on a computer screen rather than in a test tube.

Finally, we could see that petroleum engineers at oil companies like Chevron and Exxon were using computers in exploration and extraction with *seismic data processing* and *reservoir simulation,* applications which were moving oil companies into the supercomputer age.

Traveling around the country had helped me begin to understand how these customers currently did their work, what journals they read, where they got their funding, what other software they ran on their machines, etc. I came back to the company and described the day-in-the-life of each type of customer.

This was one of the happiest times in my life as a marketer. I had known nothing about supercomputers and numerical simulation applications; now there wasn't a day that went by that I wasn't learning something new. As I traveled to some of the most arcane trade shows and conferences (AIAA, SPE, MSC, etc.), my hotel room was stacked with the journals and textbooks about each vertical market just to keep up with the people we were meeting. (I was a marketer, not an engineer and most of the fine points were way over my head – and probably not just the fine points. But reading their literature allowed me to discuss the problems and opportunities with customers.)

You're Getting Close to Your Customers When They Offer You a Job
I believed that good marketers used their own products. I got facile enough with a few of the applications that I could even run some of them myself. I could build simple finite element models with Patran and set up a run of the Nastran analysis codes.

Later on in the company's life, I went to give a lunchtime seminar to Chevron's La Habra research center on the use of graphics supercomputers in petroleum applications. I spoke about the state of the art in computational reservoir simulation and what could be accomplished using finite difference and finite element methods on the new class of machines that were coming from companies like ours. During the question and answer session my heart was in my throat since like any good marketer, my depth of knowledge was no more than one level away from being a complete idiot.

At the end of the talk, the head of the research facility came up to me and said, "That was a great talk. We're glad your company hired a real petroleum engineer to come speak to us. We hate when the sales and marketing types come down and try to get us to buy something."

For one of the few times in my life I was at a loss for words, and I was completely unprepared for what came next. "Here's my card, if you ever want to consider a career in Chevron research. We'd be happy to talk to you."

Marketing was really fun.

Lessons learned:

- To sell to customers you need to understand them: how they work, what they do and what problem you will solve for them.
- You can't understand customers from inside your building.

The Best Marketers Are Engineers

Posted on October 19, 2009 by steveblank |

While the last post was titled "You Know You're Getting Close to Your Customers When They Offer You a Job", this post should probably be titled, "You Know You're Getting Close to Your Customers When You Offer *Them* a Job."

I would discover that there was a more effective alternative in building a marketing department than hiring traditional marketers with MBA's.

Building an Advisory Board
In my travels outside the building, I kept my eyes out for articulate and visionary scientists and engineers who had expertise we lacked and were willing to help in an advisory capacity. I set up an advisory board as a vehicle to get these industry experts engaged with the company and product. Some of these advisors from the academic community would work with our VP of Engineering and help us solve specific technical problems.

Other advisors provided marketing with industry-specific advice in our initial vertical markets (computational fluid dynamics, computational chemistry, finite element analysis, and petroleum engineering). They gave us input on: 1) features our system needed, 2) what applications we needed to have, and 3) how to sell to people just like them. Of course we also hoped that in listening to their advice in how to build the perfect computer for customers just like them, they would actually buy one of the first computers. Since some of these advisory board members were leaders in their fields, we knew they would tell their peers about our company. Our company's stock was an inducement, but all of them were in it to help us build a better computer.

Engineers as Marketers
There was one other reason I was talent-spotting our advisors and potential customers. In most other companies a product-marketing department was responsible for the pricing, positioning and promotion of the product. Yet in our case the product, the machine as delivered from engineering, was a blank, featureless computer with just an operating system and compilers. The hardware held no interest for our target customers until it had become a "whole product," – that is not until the computer had the complete suite of applications appropriate for a scientist in their specific vertical market – i.e. all the applications to run computational fluid dynamics or finite element analysis.

While I had learned a lot about our target markets in the first few months, I would never know as much as people who had spent their careers in these fields. Since the universe of people who were great marketers who also understood these esoteric applications like finite element analysis could be counted on one hand, (and were all working at Cray, the market leader,) my choices were limited. I could either hire smart MBAs who were generalists and try to get them up to speed on these simulation applications or I could hire some of the most articulate domain experts and teach them how to be marketers.

I chose to hire engineers from within each of our target markets and set up "Steve's one month MBA course for engineers."

At the time this was a pretty controversial decision. These hires were definitely not your standard marketing types. We hired a PhD in computational fluid dynamics from Duke who had worked on helicopter design. (Years later he would become a venture capitalist at Sequoia Capital.)

Our head of finite element analysis came from General Motor's Chevy division, where he headed up one of their analysis groups. (He would go on to be a co-founder of two mechanical engineering software companies.) The rest of the vertical marketing recruits had similar backgrounds (and similar careers.) (I never could find one from the petroleum industry so I wore that hat along with the VP of Marketing title.)

Few of them had ever seen a data sheet or a price list let alone written one, but they were domain experts, they knew their fields, and they could communicate the benefits of owning a machine like ours to run their applications. They knew which applications were critical for their markets and which were nice-to-have. And they were responsible for helping our 3rd party software group reach the right application providers to port their software to our computer. Since these marketers knew what publications their peers read and what conferences and trade shows they attended, they led our presence at the right shows and conferences. They knew the technology trendsetters in their fields and got us in front of them. In short order they learned how to transition from being customers on the receiving end of a sales pitch to giving one. To a person they became passionate evangelists and effective marketers.

Technical Marketing

Years later in my career I would realize I had simply reinvented what the early pioneers in Silicon Valley knew and did – hiring engineers who were domain experts who could talk as peers to customers and communicate effectively with their own company's engineers. (Back in the 1960's and 70's no sane MBA's would work for a Silicon Valley startup.) While MBA's have a ton of useful skills, what they don't have is what most marketing departments lack – customer insight. I found that having a senior marketer responsible for business strategy surrounded by ex-engineers and domain experts makes one heck of a powerful marketing department.

A quick diagnostic I now use for marketing departments: if you are in a startup selling to a specific set of customers and/or industry and *your marketing department doesn't have any people from that industry, your tenure as a VP of Marketing has passed its half-life.*

Lessons learned:

- Advisory boards with domain experts get you connected quickly to customer needs.
- In specialized markets, hire domain experts, and teach them to be marketers.

Listen more, talk less

Posted on October 22, 2009 by steveblank |

At Ardent we assembled an amazing group of talented engineers to build personal supercomputers to sell to scientists and engineers. The company failed.

Getting Out of the Building Wasn't Entertainment – Discovery & Validation
Now that I was the master of the "facts" about customer needs in these specialized vertical markets, and with my team of vertical marketers, I thought I had achieved absolution and redemption. Opinions had been eliminated as part of marketing's dialog inside the company; we had achieved "fact nirvana." But there was one fatal flaw. As I enjoyed my post-graduate vertical marketing education, I had forgotten the real purpose of spending time in the field.

While understanding how customers do their work was one key part of Customer Discovery, I neglected the other key component – Customer Validation - to *understand whether there were sufficient number of customers who had a problem that needed to be solved – and would pay to solve it.* I had needed to ask customers four simple questions.

- Did the customers know they had a problem?

- If so, did they want to change the way they were doing things to solve that problem?

- If so, how much would they pay to solve the problem?

- Would they write us a Purchase Order now before our supercomputer was even complete, to be the first to solve their problems?

In hindsight, these questions seem blindingly apparent yet not asking them led to the ultimate demise of Ardent. I just assumed that since customers were talking to me and spending time with me, it must mean that they agreed with our new company's vision and would spend piles of money with us. At this point in my career I didn't understand that the goal of getting outside the building was not only finding markets with potential customers but also *confirming the company's vision, business model and product/market fit.*

I had done a good job of Customer Discovery but failed at Customer Validation.

Ignoring the Red Flags
While I had lots of people willing to talk to me, we never really pushed hard to see if any customers were willing to buy and pay for the product *before* it shipped.

Early startup customers are visionaries just like the founders selling to them. If your startup's vision is compelling enough, these early customers want to buy into the dream of what could be, and they want to get in early. They will put up with an unfinished system that barely works to get a competitive advantage outside their company (or sometimes a political one inside their company.) They will count on your startup to listen to their needs for subsequent releases or follow-on systems that actually deliver on the initial promise.

All industries, markets and segments have these visionary, early adopters. It is one of the wonderful intersections between human nature, capitalism, and startups. Not finding a *sufficient set of these early visionaries is the biggest red flag a company can encounter. Ignoring these warning signs is fatal.*

Product/Market Fit
Getting out of the building is *not to* collect feature lists from prospective customers nor run tons of focus groups (I had passed this test.) Instead, it was to validate the product/market fit by *discovering if there were enough customers who would buy our product as spec'd. This was where I had failed at Ardent.* Once we had found our target customers we spent our meetings describing our new personal supercomputer and what it could do for these researchers instead of listening and truly understanding whether what we were offering was a "nice to have it" or "got to have it."

If I had had actually been asking, Were we solving a problem these scientists and engineers felt they had? I would have gotten a half-hearted "maybe." If I had followed that up with a "If our personal supercomputer delivers as promised, would you write me a check now, before it ships?" I would have seen that no one was falling over themselves to be the first to buy our product. Another clue: lots of people said, "We'd try it if you give it to us." That answer is always a dead give-away that you don't yet have a product compelling enough to build a business.

As often happens in a startup, *we confused our own vision and passion with the passion of our potential customers.*

I had talked too much and listened too little.

What did the company do when we heard customer input that contradicted our business plan and assumptions? More in the next post.

Lessons learned:

- We had "discovered" Ardent's initial markets and customers.
- We spent too much time selling our vision and not enough time validating whether customers would actually buy.
- A lack of early, eager purchasers is a red-flag – time to revisit your business model.

Closure

Posted on November 19, 2009 by steveblank |

For those that know me, I'm kind of a "life is too short" kind of guy. I liked to fail fast, move on, and not look back.

However, in catching up with the VP of Sales of Ardent last night, I was reminded one of the few times I did return for closure.

National Supercomputer Centers

For a decade starting in 1985, the National Science Foundation (NSF) established and spent a pile of money (~$50 million/year) on four supercomputing centers in the U.S. – Cornell University; University of Illinois, Urbana-Champaign; the Pittsburgh Supercomputing Center at Carnegie Mellon University; and the San Diego Supercomputer Center at the University of California at San Diego. The ostensible goal of these centers was to allow scientists and researchers access to supercomputers to simulate commercial phenomena that were too expensive, too dangerous or too time consuming to physically build.

The reality was that the U.S. Nuclear Weapons Laboratories used supercomputers to run their hydrodynamics codes for nuclear weapon design and the National Security Agency used them to decrypt codes. But with the cold-war winding down, these agencies could no longer be counted on to provide Cray Research with enough business to sustain the company. Commercial applications needed to be found that could take advantage of this class of computers.

The search for commercial supercomputer applications was good news for Ardent, as this was our business as well. But bad news was that the supercomputing centers had concluded that they could justify their existence (and budget) only by buying the biggest and most expensive supercomputers Cray Research made.

We Lost the Deal

At Ardent we were building a personal supercomputer powerful enough to run and display numerical simulations just about the time the National Science Foundation was funding these centers. I remember that the Pittsburgh Supercomputing Center had put out a request for a proposal for a supercomputer to replace the Cray X-MP they installed in 1986. In reading it, there was no doubt that it was written only in a way that Cray could respond.

I realized that given the amount of money the Supercomputing Center wanted to spend on buying the new Cray Y-MP (list price $35 million,) we could put an Ardent personal supercomputer next to every scientist and researcher connected to the university. I responded to their RFP by proposing that Ardent build the Pittsburgh Supercomputing Center a distributed supercomputing environment with hundreds of Ardent personal supercomputers rather than a monolithic Cray supercomputer.

As one could imagine, this was the last thing the supercomputer center management wanted to hear. All their peers were buying a Cray, and they wanted one as well. We had support from the scientists and researchers who had bought one of our machines and were beginning to see that distributed computing would ultimately triumph, but bureaucracy marched on, and we lost the bid.

In my career I've been involved with lots of sales deals, and for some reason losing this was the one deal I never forgot. Maybe because a win here would have meant success rather than failure for the company, perhaps because I really believed we could make the impossible happen and win. For whatever reason, I hated that particular Cray that got installed in Pittsburg.

Closure

Fast forward 15 years. Retired for a year, I ran across an article that said, "$35 Million Dollar Supercomputer For Sale for Scrap." It was the Pittsburgh Supercomputing Center Cray Y-MP that had beaten me at Ardent.

It was for sale on EBay.

I bought the Cray.

It took two semi-trailers to deliver it.

It sat in my barn next to the tractors and manure for five years. I had the only farm capable of nuclear weapons design.

Cray called two years ago and bought it back for parts for an unnamed customer still running one.

Closure.

SuperMac – Learning How To Build A Startup Team

Joining SuperMac

Posted on **March 20, 2009** by steveblank |

After leaving Ardent in 1988, I consulted for Pixar, still a hardware company in San Rafael trying to make software and commercials. While there, I got a call from a recruiter for a company called SuperMac which made add-on graphics boards for the  Macintosh. One of the first companies to sell an external disk drive for the original Mac, SuperMac had the first "color paint programs" for the Mac; and when the Mac was just black and white they had the Mac's first color graphics boards and large screen color monitors. And with all of that they had gone broke, out of business and into Chapter 11.

Yet two smart VC firms, Sigma and Matrix Partners, realized that there was value somewhere in this mess. Their guess was that they would find value in the high margin graphics business. Now with a new infusion of $8 million dollars of venture capital, SuperMac had been resurrected from the dead and was attempting to restart. The first step was to recruit a new management team.

Why they were looking to me to run marketing wasn't clear. They sold their product through the computer retail channel, something I knew nothing about. They sold to a set of customers I knew nothing about. Yet somehow they thought that my prior experience in high-end computer graphics might be relevant. Why I was interested was equally obscure. The company was the laughing stock of the Mac market. The two other players in the add-on graphics business, Radius and RasterOps, had a combined 90% market share. After talking to its resellers and customers I realized that SuperMac was the only company that could be described as "fifth in a group of three."

In essence it was a "restart" with a mixed bag of assets and liabilities. The assets were a series of products already developed and on the market or in the development pipeline. The new products potentially looked to be industry leaders if and when they came to market. When I went through their financials as part of my due diligence, I realized that if they ditched their low margin disk drive products, it wouldn't take much to make them a profitable company. They had an existing distribution channel, and their dealers and customers knew who the company was and what it stood for.

The liabilities were equally clear: the existing distribution channel and their dealers and customers thought they knew who the company was – a failure – and what it stood for – a mixed bag of commodity products with low margins, no compelling reason to sell and a set of competitors with much better products. Worse, no one inside the company had a profound belief in who the company was and why they existed. They had no model of who their own customers were and what it would take to make those customers bang down their doors to buy their products.

Nothing I couldn't fix. I took the job.

Facts Exist Outside the Building, Opinions Reside Within – So Get the Hell Outside the Building

Posted on March 20, 2009 by steveblank |

A week before I started, I got inkling of really how deep in this I was. While I was waiting in the lobby to pick up my offer letter, the head of marketing communications (who was to be one of my direct reports) came up to me as I held my just signed employment agreement. She said, "Oh I'm glad you're coming, and I wanted to grab you before you started because we need to resolve the company's biggest marketing problem." I was impressed; this was something so important that she couldn't wait for my first day. Was she going to propose a coherent communications strategy? An in-depth reseller survey? Or offer some real insights into our customers? No. "We need to decide immediately which version of the new logo to use," she explained. Ignoring my dropping jaw, she pointed out the key differences in the Pantone colors between what appeared to me to be the two indistinguishable alternatives.

As her description receded to background noise, it dawned on me that the color of the logo seemed to be the size of the marketing communications department's universe. It wasn't a lack of competence or skill in her job, it was just that as far as she was concerned, her job had no connection to the rest of marketing, our customers or our ultimate success as a company. "We need your decision now because we are about to spend $50,000 on new collateral."

Coming out of the fog at the sound of serious dollars about to be spent, I politely suggested that the new collateral was on hold, and we were going to spend the first few weeks of my tenure trying to understand who our customers were, and what we wanted to say to them. And I hadn't even started work yet.

My first day at work, I found myself staring at a set of marketing faces, mostly holdovers from the previous version of the company that had gone belly up. Some were bright and eager, some clearly hostile. "OK, let's start with the basics, who does marketing think our customers are?" I asked them. We went around the room, and every one of them had an opinion. Unfortunately, all their answers were different.

By now, nothing surprised me. This was a company that had sold 15,000 graphics boards and monitors to consumers. A large number of these customers had mailed back their registration cards (this was pre-Internet) with their names, phone numbers, job titles, etc. So I asked the fatal question; "Has anyone ever looked at the customer registration cards? Has anyone ever spoken to a customer?" Silence. Most just stared at me like the question was incomprehensible. The one or two product mangers who should have known better glanced down at their shoes. Then someone asked, "Well, who do you think our customers are?" Ah, a leading question. I said, "I don't know. And if I tell you what I think, we'll just have one more uninformed opinion. But what we need right now is some facts. Does anyone know where to find the registration cards that the customers returned?"

Why did I ask these questions? *As a company with a past history, the company had a massive advantage over a typical startup – it had customers.* Normally in a startup, you spend an inordinate amount of time and energy in Customer Discovery and Customer Validation. Yet here was a "restart" with over 15,000 customers who by putting their money on the table had personally validated the market. Now I was cognizant I might find a customers who hated the products or company. Or I might find that the company was in a business that wasn't profitable with no way to get profitable (which I had concluded was the case with their commodity disk drive business.) But this was an opportunity that needed to start with customer facts, and I was going to get them.

Twenty minutes later, a cart rolled into my office with 10,000 unprocessed, untouched registration cards, all with names, addresses, phone numbers, job titles, all wonderful data longing for human contact.

Customer survey

Three hours later, I had composed a three-page customer questionnaire. I wanted to know some simple and not so simple things about our customers. The obvious ones: Who were they? What did they do that they needed an expensive color graphics card? If you believed the opinions in the marketing department, the customers were in science, engineering, color desktop publishing, and a variety of applications with no single industry or application dominating the list. I wanted to know the facts.

Within these user segments how did our customers spend their day? Were our products a small part of their life or large? And since the card was useless without any application software, what other software products did they use on it? How essential was the SuperMac card to getting their job done? What was the most important attribute about our graphics cards and monitors that made them buy these products? And by the way since we sold both the graphics card and a big screen color monitor, did they buy both from us? Did their choice of the card affect the choice of the monitor supplier from or vice versa?

I also wanted to know if the marketing our company had done to date was effective. So I asked a set of questions about how customers had heard about our company. Did they know anything about SuperMac? What did they think we stood for? What did they know about our products? If they had they heard anything about us, where did they hear it?

166

I also wanted to know who our existing customers were our competitors. While I could have told them, it was more valuable to learn their perspectives. Had they heard about our competitors and their products? If so, where? Who did they think were the leaders in the color graphics board and monitor market? Why? What did they think the leaders most important attributes were?

Since this was the marketing department, I planned to spend some advertising and public relations dollars. It would be great to know how these customers got news and information about new products and new companies. What magazines did they read? What reviews did they trust? Did they attend trade shows? Which ones? Had they seen any our ads? Did they understand them? Had they read any stories about us? I wanted to know if marketing was getting any bang-for-the-buck in spending its demand creation dollars.

I also wanted to understand how customers bought our products. I knew we were selling through a multi-level indirect sales channel. That's a mouthful to say that our sales people didn't sell our products directly to a customer. Instead, they managed rep firms (independent sales companies that carried multiple, non-competing products) who called on computer resellers who sold to the customers. Since we did not talk to our customers directly, I wanted to know if the message we gave our sales people were coming out the other end. Kind of like the game of telephone you played as a kid. You started a message on one side of a long line of people and passed it on, one-to-another until it came out the other end. The result is usually hilarious. The ending message sounds nothing like the one you started. Market messages to indirect sales channels are just like that. I wanted to know what kind of reseller they bought from? What product did they go into the store thinking they were going to buy? Was it the same one they left with?

Finally, I also wanted to understand the resellers themselves. These were the people who had the face-to-face interaction with our customers. What did they think about SuperMac? Our products? Was our compensation program good? Was it great? Were they making enough money with us? Who did they think were buying our products? Who did they think our competitors were?

Hypothesis to test
After writing up the questionnaire, and before I began to call our customers, I wrote a one page summary of who I thought SuperMac's customers were, what markets they were in, how and why they bought, etc. I was curious to see how close to my hypothesis the actual customer answers would be.

At the end I had a three-page questionnaire that I timed in a practice session with one of my marketing people. I could get it done in twenty minutes. Now the question was would anyone care to give me those twenty minutes.

With the questionnaire written, I stared at the cart full of registration cards, arranged in shoeboxes by month and year they were received. I figured that the newer ones were more relevant than those returned years ago. I took a deep breath and plunged in. I grabbed 500 of the most recent cards, from the last four months and started calling. Quite honestly since few customers ever get "How are you doing calls" directly from an executive at the company that sold them a product, I didn't know what to expect. Would anyone take my call? Would I get hung up on? Would they answer this long list of questions?

Three hours and ten customers later, I was beginning to feel like this would work. It had taken about two registration cards to get one customer on the line. And out of those, 9 out of 10 were happy to talk to me. Actually happy is the wrong word. Stunned was more like it. They had never had anyone from any company, let alone a computer company, call and ask them anything. When I told them I was actually the VP of Marketing, they were flabbergasted. They were happy to give me everything I asked for and more. Then to their surprise I offered them either a SuperMac coffee cup or T-shirt for their troubles. Now I had happy and surprised customers walking around with paid advertising for my company.

For the next three weeks, I spent 8 hours a day calling customers and another 6 hours a day managing my new department. I'm sure the CEO thought I was crazy. But after three weeks and three hundred customer calls, I was done. I had been to the mountaintop and had heard the message.

Here's what I found:

> **Market segment:** While the company did have customers in a wide range of industries and businesses, the actual users were in a (then) new and emerging segment called *color desktop publishing*.

> **80%:** In fact, over 80% of the customers who returned in their registration cards were in this group. This was a real eye-opener. No one in our company knew this. Now we could stop guessing about who our customers were. We could even go further and talk about how they worked, and what they needed to be successful in their jobs.

Key applications: At the time color desktop publishing customers used only four key applications: Page layout programs called Quark and PageMaker, a photo manipulation package called Photoshop, and a drawing program called Illustrator. These were big ungainly applications, and on the computers of the day, very slow in manipulating large color files. (The dependence on these applications was another new and important fact for our company.)

Performance: What these customers cared about more than anything was graphics performance in these four key applications. And by more than anything, I mean that the word performance came up time and again from these professionals. Waiting for images to move around the screen was not only driving them crazy, but it was costing them money.

Performance over price: In fact, for over half of these customers, performance was even more important than price! (If you haven't stopped reading, please do so. To find a customer who says anything is more important than price is the Holy Grail for a marketer. Few times in his/her life will you find such a market.)

Purchase driver: The color-publishing customers made their purchases based on the features of the graphics board, but they were buying the color monitor from whoever sold them the board. That is, none of the features of the monitor seemed to matter. It was the board that drove the monitor sale. (So much for all our efforts to promote our monitor features.) This meant that instead of dividing our marketing budget, dollars and resources, we could focus all our energy in promoting the graphics board and let its sale pull the monitor with it.

Three publications: In our market there were a myriad of magazines to read. Yet our customers said they got their company and product information from only three publications: <u>MacWorld</u>, <u>MacUser</u> and <u>MacWeek</u>. They reported that the product reviews in these publications were by far the biggest influence on which card they decided to buy. This made our PR problem manageable and focused. Now we knew what was a make-or-break publication and review and what we could pass on if we didn't have the time or resources.

Two trade shows: Customers who bought our products only went to two trade shows (if they went to any at all): MacWorld, the general Mac trade show, and if they were true publishing professionals, the Seybold Publishing conference. (Learning this meant that instead of attending every possible Macintosh tradeshow, we now knew we only had to look like the biggest and best in two.)

The bad news: That was the good news. The bad news was when I asked what they had heard about SuperMac, I got a litany of stories about the company going out of business, about how their dealers complained that they owed lots of money, and that our ads were incomprehensible. More importantly, no one knew what business the company was in. "Aren't you the cheap disk drive company?" This was coming from someone who had already bought our graphics boards. Gulp.

Worse news: Even worse: We learned that more than half of our customers had gone into their dealers to buy another brand of graphics board. And it had been the dealers who had convinced them to buy ours. (As we found out, when we interviewed our dealers, our sales department was using extra commission payments – called Spifs – to incent the channel to move our product.) The good news was that the Spif strategy worked; the bad news was that we were losing money on every board we sold.

The worst news: The worst news was what customers didn't say. Less than 10% of our existing customers bought because of some proactive marketing campaign. No one remembered our ads, saw our reviews or had read a positive article about us. Yet outside my office door was a mass of people who thought they were in the marketing department and had honestly believed they were contributing to the success of the company, spending $4 million dollars a year on marketing.

After three weeks, I stopped the customer survey when I started hearing the same stories again and again. Looking at the customer data, I realized there were some potential "gotchas":

- This was a survey of those who had already bought product from us. Those who didn't buy from us might have completely different characteristics

- This survey could only reach those who sent back their registration cards. Those who didn't might be different.

As it turned out, large companies that bought graphics card for their publishing departments didn't always send registration cards back so my survey was skewed to smaller groups.

Lessons Learned

- Organize questions about customers, channel and market.
- Build a series of your own hypothesis about each area.
- Test the hypothesis with real customers.

Customer Insight Is Everyone's Job

Posted on March 20, 2009 by steveblank |

After my first month of surveying customers we knew a lot, marketing knew more about our customers than anyone in the company. In this one month, we had learned more about desktop publishing on the Mac than any one of our competitors. Now the question was what to do with it. First I needed to make sure what we really learned was information on which we could base a company strategy on.

Our first question was: Did the total number of customers who had already bought products from our competitors and SuperMac represent a saturated market or the tip of the iceberg? In other words what was the Total Available Market (TAM) and how much of the market had been already served? Since our competitors were also small privately held companies, none of their data was readily available.

But we knew something they didn't. The total available market for color graphics boards was measurable by looking at an adjacent market, the color desktop publishing software market. As it happened, there were quite a few industry analysts following software companies like Adobe, Aldus, and Quark, the suppliers of the four key applications our customers used. These analysts not only told us that the market had plenty of room to grow, they took an interest in us since we were going to be a hardware company pursuing this growing market.

Since I was heading a marketing department, not an individual contributor, I needed to teach all of marketing the importance of customer data. First, I presented what I had learned. You could sense the skepticism in my staff meeting as I described what I found. But no one was prepared when I said, "These facts are now old, but since we are going to be changing customer perceptions, we need to get new customer data weekly. All of you are now part of the customer discovery collection team." Then I handed out the questionnaire to all the marketing staff and made two customer calls a week mandatory for everyone, including my secretary. At first people couldn't believe they were actually going to have to call a customer. Some took cajoling to make the calls, other took me sitting by their elbow, but eventually everyone began to dial. The first part of my weekly department staff meeting was dedicated to going around the room and hearing everyone report on their customer conversations.

Within a month, the change inside the marketing department was palpable. Customers were no longer some theoretical entities who existed only in data sheets, they were real people you talked to, understood, and connected with. Soon marketing was talking about the needs of our customers with first-hand knowledge, passion, and conviction. And without knowing it, the quality of the marketing department's work changed. Instead of specs and technical features, our literature and interaction with customers shifted to benefits and how SuperMac could solve their problems.

Within a year we had called over 1,000 customers, and every year after that another 1,000. Marketing, which had been unsure or unaware of what its job was now had weekly reinforcement of who the customer was we became a formidable force in the Macintosh graphics market.

Now we could execute a relentless come-from-behind strategy based the information we had learned and discovered from our customers. But what was the strategy?

Lessons Learned

- Facts are the rock on which you build your strategy and tactics.
- In a startup second-hand facts are almost as useless as opinions.
- Decision makers need to hear the facts first-hand.

Repositioning SuperMac – "Market Type" at Work

Posted on March 26, 2009 by steveblank |

With insight into our customers, we first needed to understand what kind of positioning problem we had. Was SuperMac attempting to introduce radically new products and create a new market? No, not really.

Was the company attempting to be a low cost provider by introducing cheaper products to an existing market? While we sometimes cut the price of graphics boards, it was only because we offered our customers no compelling reasons to buy one that was priced equivalently to the market share leaders. And we lost money when we did so. Therefore, no, we weren't really equipped to be the low cost provider.

Was the company attempting to introduce faster and better products to an existing market? On first glance, this was exactly what we were trying to do. But with a little bit of thought, it struck us that if we attempted to do that, our competitors had a pretty substantial advantage since they held nearly 90% of combined market share. If we tried to match them on their playing field. we'd never catch up. They had more than enough dollars to outspend and out-market us.

We knew from back-of-the-envelope calculations that we would need 3 times the combined marketing and sales budgets of the incumbents for a head-on assault. (I had found that the numbers 1.7x and 3x kept coming up time and again in attacker/defender ratios when I gamed out our market entry strategies. It wasn't until I found the extremely obscure Lanchester Strategy for market share that I realized that these ratios had their basis in operations research and the Lanchester's Laws.)

So if we couldn't be new, cheaper or attack our competitors head-on, what was left? The real answer seemed to lie in attempting something a bit more difficult. We needed to redefine or resegment the playing field (the existing graphics board market) so it favored us. We needed to negate our competitors' existing advantages and hopefully turn their strengths into weaknesses.

In the color graphics board market, our competitors had defined the market as one measured by technical metrics: screen resolution, number of bits of color, screen refresh rates, acceleration, etc. We had been attempting to compete by their rules with the same types of technology messages. I had a marketing department spending $4m a year trying to do so against competitors spending $20M year. The 3:1 Lanchester Laws said I would need $60M in marketing and sales spending to win.

I didn't have it, wasn't going to get it, and we needed to stop thinking that our path to success was just to "try harder."

Instead, we needed to create a playbook with completely new rules and then execute relentlessly and with urgently. Until now, all the graphics board companies supplied "technology", and it was up to the customers to figure out which of these arcane specs was best for their business. Our first radical move was to redefine the market from SuperMac, a company that sold graphics boards to SuperMac a company that provided desktop publishing professionals with better color-publishing tools. We were going to be the leading supplier of color publishing solutions for the Macintosh. Our strategy was to resegment a hardware business the graphics board and monitor market into a desktop color publishing market.

Types of Markets

- **Existing Market**
  - o Faster/Better – High End
- **Resegmenting** an Existing Market
  - o Niche = Marketing/Branding driven
  - o Cheaper = Low Cost/Low End
- **New Market**
  - o Never been done before

To say this was a radical notion was an understatement. I lost several very good product marketing people who couldn't/wouldn't get it or who couldn't/wouldn't move with the urgency I needed. But an 11% market share company wasn't one I wanted to work in. We were gearing up to go from status quo to relentless and continuous execution, and everyone needed to be on the same team.

Next, we needed to focus our messages away from technology and onto what the customers told us they needed – performance solutions for four key publishing applications. SuperMac's graphics boards were designed to speed up a key part of the Macintosh graphics operating system called QuickDraw. All the marketing materials, data sheets, advertising, press releases, trade shows, etc. focused on the technical fact that we accelerated this arcane piece of computer code. Technically, our positioning was correct, and with an infinite marketing budget (my back of the envelope calculations said $60M) and time, we might have made this technical fact (QuickDraw acceleration) something a customer understood and cared about. But we didn't have infinite cash. We had just emerged from bankruptcy, and unless we could get customers to quickly understand why our products were great, we were headed there again. Yet the customers not only had told us who they were – color desktop publishers – but also what they cared most about – graphics performance when running their four key software applications.

It didn't take much imagination to realize that we should tell our story around one key metric performance - performance for color publishing, performance on the applications that mattered. And paradoxically we had to raise our prices. Why? Because if we were going to be the high performance color graphics company, we were going to have to stop competing on price and start building a perception of a high-value, high performance color solutions company. Customers had already given us permission to do this when they said they were price-insensitive.

Now we needed to act.

Lessons Learned

- Deep and detailed understanding of the customer is the only way you can understand your "Market Type" choices.
- Market Type choice drives Positioning/differentiation strategy.
- Positioning/differentiation drives communications strategy.
- If you are resgementing into a niche in an existing market, make sure it's into a space that customers care passionately about so passionately they will pay for it.

Strategy versus Relentless Tactical Execution —
the Potrero Benchmarks

Posted on April 2, 2009 by steveblank |

A few months into my tenure as the VP of Marketing, we now understood who our customers were. We had thought really hard about "market type" and decided to reposition the company from a technology provider to a solutions provider. Now we needed to put the tactical programs in place to make this repositioning strategy happen.

Just as an aside, over my career I must have interviewed scores of business school graduates (some from the very fine universities where I now teach) who would say, "I want to do strategy." Well yes, I understand that, but this is a startup, what else do you want to do? "I just want to do strategy." Those were very short interviews. The "strategy" of learning who SuperMac's customers were, what solutions they needed and what our repositioning would be was a three-month effort.

The tactical execution took three years.

Note;if you want to do "strategy" (which is a fine endeavor) and nothing else, you have just defined your career as one in large corporation or in a consulting firm. Stay out of startups. Tactics mean tenacious and relentless execution measured over years.

Metrics – Mine is Bigger Than Yours

The first thing SuperMac needed to do was to change how our potential color desktop publishing customers viewed our products versus our competitors' products. Over the years, marketers have found that using numbers to compare yourself to other products works well. We've all seen ads that say, "Now 30% more" or "Marked down 50%" or "5 times faster." As hokey as it is, when confronted with uncertainty or unknowns, human beings like to be reassured by comparative metrics. But hardware metrics typically focused on raw speed and performance. The key insight we had was that it wasn't about raw speed, it was the speed of the applications that customers were using to get their work done.

Believe it or not, until that moment, there were no commonly agreed upon ways to measure the performance of graphics boards on real-world applications.

So I was going to give our customers metrics neither they nor anyone else had ever seen before.

First, by talking about solutions rather than hardware, we changed the way customers thought about graphics boards. Now we were going to change the metrics that customers and the press used to evaluate product performance.

Objects in Our Mirror are Larger than they Appear

Our first goal was to set up benchmarks which measured the performance of our own graphics boards on the real applications our customers used (Photoshop, Quark, Illustrator and PageMaker.) Then we were going to buy our competitors' boards (think "secret shopper") and compare them to ours.

Since no benchmarks existed, we enlisted our engineering department in a serious software development effort and wrote our own. And we made sure that instead of some artificial numbers, the benchmarks truly measured performance on these four key applications our customers told us were important. Then we ran the same benchmarks against our competitors' boards. When we found a subset of the tests on which we did worse than our competition, we used the data to make our boards perform better on the applications. The numbers were in. We won. Overwhelmingly. Any customer who used these four critical color publishing applications was going to be blown away by how much better the SuperMac boards performed.

Finally, since no one would believe a set of benchmarks named after our company, we needed a façade of independence so we named them after the street the company was headquartered on in Sunnyvale California – they became known as the Potrero Benchmarks.

Tell Me How to Find You

But having benchmarks in hand that showed us as the winner did us no good unless all our potential customers could see them. Our first thought was to spread the news ourselves, perhaps in a press release or a "white paper" (remember this was pre-Internet.) But upon reflection I remembered that in our interviews with our existing customers, *they had told us* how to get the news to them. That told us the three publications they relied on for news about graphics boards: MacWorld, MacUser and MacWeek became marketing's highest priority. Inside the covers of these publications our customers had said that it was the *product reviews that most influenced their buying decisions*. That by itself was a sobering challenge since our company had never come in first in any of the previous 14 reviews of graphics products that had been written to date.

Now this is worth stopping and thinking about for a second. We figured out how to reach our customers (through these three publications) because *they told us how to do so*. We figured out what were the most important criteria they used to evaluate which board to buy – product reviews – again *because they told us how to do so*. These were two of the questions I had intentionally asked when we did our initial customer surveys. Some of my staff had believed we were gathering extraneous customer data. "Hey, we can make these surveys shorter. We don't need to know all this stuff." Yes we do. You need to know the day-in-the-life of the customer. From top to bottom. If you're constantly correlating data and searching for patterns, all intelligence, if properly integrated, will give you insight.

The Chase

We began an educational blitz of these three critical publications. We set up a series of meetings with the editor-in chiefs and the key writers who reviewed graphics products. We had one story to tell and surprisingly, it wasn't about our company or our product. It was an educational mission to tell the story of who our customers were (and by inference who all the graphics board customers were) and why the current reviews of these graphics boards did not adequately measure what was important to this growing market.

(Now as VP of Marketing, I could have sat back and let my PR agency handle the press. Theoretically, that's why I hired them. But these meetings were life and death in our struggle for market share. You don't delegate life and death. The head of the PR agency agreed that we would work together as a team. We both met often and went to all of the press meetings together.)

Why did we believe that these magazines would care? At the time desktop publishing was one of the mainstays of the Macintosh market, and therefore the readership of these magazines reflected the demographics of the Mac. For these magazines to hear that they didn't truly understand what their customers cared about got their full attention.

I knew with a high probability before the meeting started what the end of the meeting would be like since there was no other way to go. My staff didn't believe it when I told them it would happen this way, but in meetings with all three magazines they said, "Ok, you convinced us these four applications are critical for the color publishing market, but how can we measure the performance of these applications?"

The Trojan Horse

"Well" I said hesitantly, "I'm not sure we should share this with you but we have a set of benchmarks that we use to measure performance." You can imagine the rest of the conversation. I sounded reluctant to let our own tests outside our building, the magazines begged us to let them have them, and finally we struck a deal to allow the benchmarks out to the test labs of these magazines under their own name "The Potrero Benchmark Suite" without attribution, of course, to us.

Our benchmark had just become the standard test suite for all magazine reviews that our potential customers would read. Our benchmarks, which were tuned for our boards, had just become the standard test suite for all our competitors' graphics boards.

Relentless Execution

Once the education and benchmarks were in place, we then worked with each magazine writer as their product review deadline approached. We provided customer references and testimonials supporting the key features we were promoting. Focused on winning these reviews, I left nothing to chance. My rule was no magazine could review our boards without us present. The magazines' rules were that no company could be in their labs when they reviewed the boards. So we would always wait to the last minute to provide our boards for testing and then "forget" to ship the cables to connect the board to a computer monitor. When the panicked manager of the magazine test lab would call under a last minute deadline, we would apologize profusely as we sent the cables over – with beer, pizza, and our product manager to help them through any testing "issues".

My PR agency, my head of marketing communications and I set up a wall-sized chart (in my office where I had to close my eyes not to see it) of the editorial calendars of these publications. We listed the editors, writers, what they had previously written, deadlines, what the competitive products were, how our benchmarks stacked up, what "upgrades" our boards needed from engineering to win, etc. This was upfront and center so that anyone who walked into my office could see what I thought was important.

In parallel, we educated the rest of our own company how essential winning these product reviews were to sales and our financial success. What used to be an exercise in teeth-pulling frustration to get help from our own manufacturing or engineering departments turned into a well-oiled process as everyone stopped what they were doing to help us win.

None of this was an accident. It was all part of a strategy. But its successful execution would take a focused set of tactics and a great group of marketers working with me. And I now had both.

From a company that never won a benchmark review with its graphics boards, we went on to win twenty-one in a row. It was two and a half years before our competitors even realized the connection between the Potrero benchmarks and SuperMac having its building on Potrero Street had any connection.

By then it was too late.

Our market share had started to climb.

And we were just getting started.

Lessons Learned

- Strategy points you to the goal.
- Relentless tactical execution gets you to the goal.
- Keep the tactics simple and focused.
- Tactical execution needs to be managed at the highest level – you can't delegate success in a startup.

Building The Killer Team – Mission, Intent and Values

Posted on April 9, 2009 by steveblank |

If you don't know where you're going, how will you know when you get there?

At the same time we were educating the press, we began to educate our own marketing department about what exactly we were supposed to be doing inside the company. During my first few weeks, I asked each of my department heads what they did for marketing and the company. When I asked our tradeshow manager, she looked at me like I was the house idiot and said, "Steve, don't you know that my job is to set up our trade show booth?" The other departments in marketing gave the same answers. The product-marketing department said their job was to write data sheets. But my favorite was when the public relations manager said, "We're here to write press releases and answer the phone in case the press calls."

If these sound like reasonable answers to you, and you are in a startup/small company, update your resume.

Titles are not your job

When I pressed my staff to explain why marketing did tradeshows or wrote press releases or penned data sheets, the best I could get was "why that's our job." It dawned on me that we had a department full of people who were confusing their titles with what contribution they were supposed to be making to the company. While their titles might be on their business cards, titles were not their job – at least in any marketing department I was running.

Titles are not the same as what your job is. This is a big idea.

Department Mission Statements – What am I Supposed to Do Today?

It wasn't that we somehow had inherited dumb employees. What I was actually hearing was a failure of management. No one had sat the marketing department down and defined what was our *department* Mission (with a capital "M".)

Most startups put together a corporate mission statement because the CEO remembered seeing one at their last job or the investors said they need one. Most companies spend an inordinate amount of time crafting a finely honed corporate mission statement for external consumption and then do nothing internally to actually make it happen. (And to this day I can't remember if we even had a corporate mission statement.) What I'm about to describe here is quite different.

What was missing in SuperMac marketing was anything in writing that gave the marketing staff daily guidance about what they should be doing. The first reaction from my CEO was, "That's why you're running the department." And yes, we could have built a top-down, command-and-control hierarchy. But what I wanted was an agile marketing team capable of operating independently without day-to-day direction.

So what we needed to do was to craft a *Departmental Mission statement* that told everyone *why they come to work, what they need to do, and how they will know they have succeeded.* And it was going to mention the two words that SuperMac marketing needed to live and breathe: revenue and profit.

Five Easy Pieces – The Marketing Mission

After a few months of talking to customers, listening to our channel and working with sales, we defined the marketing Mission (our job) as:

Help Sales deliver $25 million in sales with a 45% gross margin. To do that we will create end-user demand and drive it into the sales channel, educate the channel and customers about why our products are superior, and help Engineering understand customer needs and desires. We will accomplish this through demand-creation activities (advertising, PR, tradeshows, seminars, web sites, etc.), competitive analyses, channel and customer collateral (white papers, data sheets, product reviews), customer surveys, and market requirements documents.

This year, marketing need to provide sales with 40,000 active and accepted leads, company and product name recognition in over 65% in our target market, and five positive product reviews per quarter. We will reach 35% market share in year one of sales with a headcount of twenty people, spending less than $4,000,000.

- Generate end user demand (to match our revenue goals)
- Drive that demand into our sales channels
- Value price our products to achieve our high-value revenue and margin goals
- Educate our sales channel(s)
- Help engineering understand customer needs

That was it. Two paragraphs, Five bullets. It didn't take more.

Working to the Mission

Having the mission in place meant that our marketing team could see that what mattered was not what their business card said, but how much closer did their work move our department to completing the mission. Period.

It wasn't an easy concept for everyone to understand.

Building the Team

My new Director of Marketing Communications turned the Marcom departments into a mission-focused organization. Her new tradeshow manager quickly came to understand that her job was not to set up booths. We hired union laborers to do that. A trade show was where our company went to create awareness and/or leads. If you ran the tradeshow department, you owned the responsibility of awareness and leads. The booth was incidental. I couldn't care less if we had a booth or if we could generate the same number of leads by skydiving naked into a coffee cup.

The same was true for PR. My new head of Public Relations quickly learned that my admin could answer calls from the press. The job of Public Relations at SuperMac wasn't a passive "write a press release and wait for something to happen" activity. It wasn't measured by how busy you were. It was measured by results. And the results weren't the traditional PR metrics of number of articles or inches of ink. I couldn't care less about those. I wanted our PR department to get close and personal with the press and use it to generate end user demand and then drive that demand into our sales channel. (The Potrero benchmark strategy was one component of this creating end user demand through PR.) We were constantly creating metrics to see the effects of different PR messages, channels and audiences on end-user purchases.

The same was true for the Product Marketing group. I hired a Director of Product Marketing who in his last company had ran its marketing and then went out into the field and became its national sales director. He got the job when I asked him how much of his own marketing material his sales team actually used in the field. When he said, "about ten percent," I knew by the embarrassed look on his face I had found the right guy. And our Director of Technical Marketing was superb at understanding customer needs and communicating them to engineering.

Teaching Mission Intent – What's Really Important

With a great team in place, the next step was recognizing that our Mission statement might change on the fly. "Hey, we just all bought into this Mission idea and now you're telling us it can change?!"

We introduced the notion of *Mission intent*. What is the company goal behind the mission. In our case it was to sell $25 million in graphics boards with 45% gross margin. The idea of *intention* is that if employees understand the thinking behind the mission, they can work collaboratively to achieve it.

But we recognized that there would be time marketing would screw up, making the mission obsolete (i.e. we might fail to deliver 40,000 leads.) Think of intention as the answer to the adage, "When you are up to your neck in alligators, it's hard to remember you were supposed to drain the swamp." For example; our mission said that the reason why marketing needed to deliver 40,000 leads and 35% market share, etc, was so that the company could sell $25 million in graphics boards at 45% gross margin.

What we taught everyone is that *the intention is more enduring then the mission*. Let's see, the company is trying to sell $25 million in graphics boards with 45% gross margin. If marketing can't deliver the 40,000 leads what else can we do for sales to still achieve our revenue and profitability?" T*he mission was our goal*, but based on circumstances, it may change, but *the Intent was immovable.*

When faced with the time pressures of a startup, too many demands and too few people, we began to teach our staff to refer back to the five Mission goals and the Intent of the department. When stuff started piling up on their desks, they learned to ask, "Is what I'm working on furthering these goals? If so, which one? If not, why am I doing it?"

They understood the mission intent was our corporate revenue and profit goals.

Core Values

Even after we had Mission and Intent down pat, one of the things that still drove me crazy was when we failed to deliver a project for sales on time or we missed a media deadline. Everyone in my department had an excuse. (Since a large part of marketing was as a service organization to sales, our inability to deliver on time meant we weren't holding up our end of the mission.) I realized that this was a broken part of our culture, but couldn't figure out why. One day it hit me that when deadlines slipped, there were no consequences.

With no consequences we acted as if schedules and commitments really didn't matter. I heard a constant refrain of, "The channel sales brochure was late because the vendor got busy, and they couldn't meet the original deadline." Or, "The January ad had to be moved into February because my graphic artist was sick, but I didn't tell you assuming it was OK." Or "We're going to slip our product launch because the team thought they couldn't get ready in time." We had a culture that had no accountability, and no consequences. Instead there were simply shrugged shoulders and a litany of excuses.

This had to change. I wanted a department that could be counted on delivering. One day I simply put up a sign on my door that said, "*No excuses accepted.*" And I let the department know what I meant was we were all going to be "accountable."

What I didn't mean was "deliver or else." By accountable, I meant: We agreed on a delivery date, and between now and the delivery date, *it's OK if you ask for help because you're stuck, or something happened outside of your control.* But do not walk into my office the day something was due and give me an excuse. It will cost you your job. That kind of accountable.

And, "Since I won't accept those kind of excuses, you are no longer authorized to accept them from your staff or vendors either." *The goal wasn't inflexible dates and deadlines, it was no surprises and collective problem solving.* After that, we spent a lot more time working together to solve problems and remove obstacles to getting things done on time.

Over time, accountability, execution, honesty and integrity became the cornerstones of our communication with each other, other departments and vendors.

- We wouldn't give excuses for failures, just facts and requests for help
- We wouldn't accept excuses for failures, just facts, and offer help
- Relentless execution
- Individual honesty and integrity

That was it. Four bullets. It defined our culture.

Why Do It?

By the end of the first year, our marketing team had jelled. We were a department willing to exercise initiative with the judgment to act wisely and the eagerness to accept responsibility.

I remember at the end of a hard week, my direct reports came into my office just to talk about the week's little victories. As they shared their stories, they all began to realize that our company that had just come off of life support was beginning to kick the rear of our better-funded and bigger competitors.

We all marveled in the moment.

Lessons Learned

- Push independent execution of tasks down to the lowest possible level.
- Give everyone a shared Mission Statement: why they come to work, what they need to do, and how they will know they have succeeded.
- Share Mission Intent for the big picture for the Mission Statement.
- Build a team comfortable with independent Mission execution.
- Agree on Core Values to define your culture.

Rabbits Out of the Hat – Product Line Extensions

Posted on April 16, 2009 by steveblank |

A year after we started repositioning the company, Engineering, which had been working on a family of new products literally for years, came to deliver some good news and bad news.

First the bad news

The new family of eight high performance graphics cards we were counting on couldn't be delivered. The plug-in co-processor architecture was too complex and couldn't be made to work reliably. Instead of the family of eight products we were expecting, *only one could be delivered.* Nothing else was in the development pipeline for the next 12 months.

I couldn't believe what I heard. One of the reasons I had joined SuperMac was seeing these boards as hope for the future. Now we were faced with the fact that even though we were gaining market share daily, there was nothing coming out of Engineering.

Well not quite nothing. There was the good news.

Instead of eight boards, Engineering was going to be able to deliver one new graphics board. Just one. *But it was going to be the fastest graphics board ever made.* In fact, according to our Potrero benchmark suite, this new board ran our customer applications ten times faster than our current products.

I went home to think about this. Instead of a product family, we had a single point product. Each of my competitors each had 5-10 graphics boards covering a range of prices with performance to match. Even our current product line had four graphics boards in it. Now our new product line would only have one board?!. What could we do?

Marketing Gets into the Engineering Business

The next day I walked in uninvited to the VP of Engineering's office and asked if he had a minute. I said, "I realize you're trying to get the one board out to market, but I have a question – can you slow our new board down?" It doesn't take much imagination to see the look he gave me when I asked that question. "Steve, this hasn't been a good week. What do you really want?" I felt sorry for him. He was working really hard to dig out of this mess. I replied, "No joke. Can you make it slower? I think he wanted to strangle me as he barely replied, "We worked for years to deliver a product that's ten times faster than anything that exists and you want to make it slower?" Well, not exactly. "What I want to know is if the board would work if you slowed it down by 10%?" Yes, was the answer. "How about if you slowed it down 20%?" Yes, was still the answer. "By 30%?" The change in his demeanor – from trying to kill me – to laughing, as it dawned on him where I was going, could only be described as hysterical relief. "40%?" Yes, yes and yes.

We were about to be partners in building a new product family.

Rabbits Out of the Hat – Branding and Line Extensions
First, what we proposed is that we take our world class, ten-times-faster-than-anyone board and build an entire product family around it, by slowing it down. We wanted nine boards, each differing in performance by 10%. The only real difference between them would be the addition of "wait states" or "slow down" instructions on a chip. Our entire new product family would be an identical board.

Next, we were going to create three separate product families, making each its own unique brand. And within each brand we would have a "good", "better", and "best" graphic board, all tailored to our color publishing market.

Finally, these product families would be priced to bracket (box in) everyone of our competitors' products with better price and performance. We were going to price the products from $699 to $3,999. Our calculations had us losing money on the two lowest cost boards, breaking even on the third and making great margins on the other six. We calculated our blended gross margin for the company by estimating the number of units we would sell of each board times the gross margin of each individual board (then I crossed my fingers and prayed we were right.)

In essence we proposed that we ship the same board in 9 different colored boxes and charge from $699 to $3,999 depending on the color of the box and the speed of the board. (This turned out to give our customers immense value. We would have charged $3,999 for the high-end board. Now we could give customers lower price boards without Engineering spending 12 months to design new ones.)

You're Going to Do What?!
The reaction inside our company could not be described as polite. At first most people thought we were joking. No one believed it would work. Some engineers were insulted that we were going to slow down their board, and sales was convinced that within days of the board hitting the street we would have a black market in chips to speed up the $699 boards and turn them into $3,999 ones. My own marketing department was convinced that the same industry magazines, which we had managed so well, would turn on us when they saw that the boards were physically identical.

Yet I believed that this was the only alternative to slowly going out of business. (While our engineering department was close to the customer, seven of those eight products they were going to ship to those customers weren't going to see the light of day.) Now it was up to marketing to take the technology as delivered by Engineering and shape it to the needs of the customers and market. By creating these new families of products, we could provide real value to our color desktop publishing customers by giving them performance at a price they couldn't get anywhere else.

188

A Big Idea - Marketing Adds Value.

This notion of Marketing taking what Engineering builds as a starting point, not an end point, is the difference between being a marcom department or a value-added Marketing department. If all you're doing is shipping and launching the product as spec'd by Engineering, you're not adding much value. The job of Marketing is to help Engineering figure out how to deliver product(s) that customers need and will pay for. It starts with a deep understanding of what customers need (and making sure Engineering is getting continuous customer feedback and interaction.) We did that when we surveyed our customers. Next, we had a good understanding of the capabilities of the product that Engineering was building. And in this very unique case, we figured out how to maximize revenue and profit by branding and product line extensions.

We would use this same idea 10 years later at E.piphany.

Relentless Execution

If we were right, this line extension and branding strategy would allow us to catch up to our competitors and overtake them.

Luckily, marketing had built a reservoir of credibility with our peers and our CEO. After the VP of Engineering described the alternatives (no new products for a year), *desperation became the mother of innovation,* and we launched our new family of nine new graphics boards. As far as manufacturing was concerned, they were the identical graphics board. As customers saw them, they were a new family of products *aimed directly at the color desktop publishing market* with astonishing performance and a low-cost entry price.

The results spoke for themselves: Not one black-market board ever appeared, and the press was satisfied with our "customer value and product family" explanation. Our new graphics boards became the market leader of the industry. In three and a half years SuperMac's market share went from 11% to 68% as the company went from bankruptcy to $150 million in sales.

Years later, as I was having coffee with the VP of Sales and Marketing from one our competitors he said, "We would have beat you guys, but we just couldn't keep up with the tidal wave of products coming from your engineering department. They came up with exactly the right products at the right price." I took a long sip of coffee as I thought of all the things I could say. Instead I smiled, nodded and said, "Yep, it was amazing. Ghey just kept pulling rabbits out of the hat."

Lessons Learned

- At times, what Engineering delivers is the raw material.
- Marketings job is to take engineering products and use them to maximize revenue and profit.
- In an existing or resegmented market, this may include branding and product line extensions.
- This requires deep customer and competitive knowledge.
- In most markets, "first mover advantage" is illusorily; fast followers often win.

Cats and Dogs – Admitting a Mistake

Posted on April 23, 2009 by steveblank |

At SuperMac, I thought I was good VP of marketing; aggressive, relentless and would take no prisoners – even with my peers inside the company. But a series of Zen-like moments helped me move to a different level that changed how I operated. It didn't make my marketing skills any worse or better, but moved me to play forever on a different field.

Zen moment #1- Admitting a mistake and asking for help

Up until this point in my career, I had one response anytime I screwed something up: blame someone else. The only variable was how big the screw-up was – that made a difference in whom I blamed. If it was a very big mistake, I blamed the VP of Sales. "This marketing campaign didn't work? It was a brilliant strategy but Sales screwed it up." (My own lame defense here for this behavior is that sales and marketing are always cats and dogs in startups. Historically, these were two guys with high testosterone. They hit each other with baseball bats until one of them dropped.)

This first Zen moment happened at a SuperMac exec staff meeting. I was asked to explain why a marketing program that cost $150,000 bucks literally generated nothing in revenue for the company. I still remember that I was gearing up to go into my 'I'm going to blame the sales guy' routine. Since our sales guy was a good street fighter, I knew the ensuing melee would create enough of a distraction that no one would talk about my marketing debacle. My brain had queued up the standard, "It's all Sales' fault," but instead, what came out of my mouth was, "You know, I really screwed this marketing campaign up. Making it successful is important for the company, and I need all your help to fix it." You could have heard a pin drop. It was so out of character, people were shocked. Some stammered out, "Can you say that again?"

Our president picked up on the momentum and asked me what I needed from the rest of the exec team to fix this debacle. I replied: "This is really important for our success as a company and I'm really at a loss why customers didn't respond the way we expected. Anybody else got some other ideas?"

From there, the conversation took a different trajectory. It was uncomfortable for some people because it was new ground. I was asking for help to do what was right for the company.

It was definitely a "Zen moment" for me in terms of my career. From then on when I screwed up, not only did I own up to it, I asked for help. This behavior had an unintended consequence I couldn't have predicted: when others started volunteering to help me solve a problem, finding a solution became their goal as well.

Soon one or two others execs tested the waters by making a small tentative "ask." When they discovered that the sky didn't fall and they still had their jobs, our corporate culture took one more step toward a more effective and cohesive company.

Lessons Learned

- Admitting mistakes and asking for help sets the culture in a startup.
- The culture becomes solution-oriented not blame-oriented.
- The goal is ownership and teamwork not turf.

Sales, Not Awards

Posted on April 30, 2009 by steveblank |

While this story is about my experience in packaging for computer retail channels, if you substitute the word "web site" for retail, you'll get the idea why these lessons were timeless for me.

SuperMac sold our graphic boards for the Macintosh through multiple distribution channels: direct sales to major accounts, national chains, independent rep firms, etc. But the computer retail channel was a large part of our sales. That meant that our boards were packaged in boxes sold to retailers and were displayed on shelves in their computer stores. Customers went into the store either looking for the SuperMac product by name (if our demand creation activities had been effective) or unsure of which brand of board to buy. If they were in the store but teetering on the edge of a purchasing decision, there were only two ways to influence them: incent the sales staff (give the salespeople a special bonus to sell your product) and/or have box packaging sell itself by screaming "Buy me!"

Maybe It's Me

When I got to the SuperMac, our Marketing Communications group told me about the "award-winning" retail packaging for our graphics boards. Yet when I saw our retail package, I was confused. Confused because while I knew absolutely nothing about retail packaging, as a consumer, I knew this box was not something I would pay attention to. It was black with absolutely no compelling reason to buy – no awards, no why-to-buy message, nothing.

While I wasn't an expert in retail packaging, even as a consumer, I knew that when I was in a store, I scanned four or five products on a shelf, grabbed the most interesting one, read what was on the box and picked one. And the product that "talked to me" the loudest and most seductively was the one I took home.

"Black Hole of Packaging" Strategy

Since we had no facts other than my opinion that something wasn't right, I took our staff on a field trip. (*You can't do marketing from inside the building.*) We visited a few retail stores to look at how other companies were packaging their products and how ours looked next to theirs. Standing in the aisles, we collectively got a sinking feeling. Our choice of black had made our retail box invisible on the shelf.

But worse, we had been relegated to the bottom shelf (death valley, since very few people look at their feet when shopping.) We were down on the bottom because no one had done any "shelf merchandizing" – that is we did not employ "rack jobbers" or

193

the retail stores themselves to put our boxes at eye level in the right place on the shelf.

(These are basic practices for companies selling through retail stores.)

We were on the bottom row – with an invisible box. We labeled this our "Black Hole of Packaging" strategy. The package had won awards all right – for the ad agency. The design was actually a negative drag on selling anything off a retail shelf.

Getting Smarter

While we all had opinions about what we should do, we realized we needed some facts from someone with retail packaging expertise. Luckily (or maybe because we were in Silicon Valley where there was a domain expert for everything,) there was a very smart consultant in the retail computer space, Seymour Merrin, who preached about the importance of packaging. He had teamed up with a former product manager at P&G to deliver seminars on just this subject. We learned the basics of retail packaging: make the box eye-catching, ensure there was a "why-to-buy" message, include just enough information to close the sale, fight and pay for eye-level shelf space, etc. Her packaging class was so good that we sent every new marketer at SuperMac to take it. From grumbling skeptics, they all became packaging design converts.

We realized that we needed to take all these lessons and redesign our packaging.

You May Hate It, But You Won't Ignore It

The results of our package redesigns were packages like "SuperMac Thunder II". They were bright, they were loud, and they had lots of reasons to buy front and back. And for sure they were never going to win any design awards.

To check how effective our new packaging was, we ran tests at our local computer retailer. We would run in and put test versions of dummy boxes on the shelf and just watch what happened – we wanted to see if people picked up the box, and when they did what they looked at and what they read. (We would interview them after they put the box back on the shelf. And we had to convince a few of them the box was really empty.) The most interesting thing we learned was that people felt more comfortable about a product when there were words of encouragement on the package. So we started putting stickers on the packaging every time we'd win an award. People would go, "Oh, this one won the "Best of MacUser Magazine Benchmark" a confirmation that this was a safe purchase choice.

Owning Marketing for our Entire Channel

In thinking about the packaging story, it would have been easy to blame the agency that designed the box for poor package design. Or blame my MarCom department who approved it. But that wasn't the root cause of the problem. *It was a management problem.* We had been outsourcing an important part of our demand creation strategy – packaging – to an outside agency *without having the expertise to judge or manage the results*. We hadn't taken the time to learn the basics of packaging ourselves. And the final lesson was that we were keeping score on our packaging with the wrong metrics – *it wasn't about awards, it was about <u>sales</u> in the retail channel.*

So we not only sent everyone through packaging school, we also brought the packaging design in-house. From now on we would design the retail boxes ourselves, not because we could do a better design job, but because *using packaging to increase retail sales* was a critical skill that our company and department needed to learn. When we had mastered the art, then I was ready to outsource it again, but not before this became a core competency of my department.

Oh yes, and retail sales doubled with the new product packaging.

New Century, New Channels

For many of you reading this, boxes sitting on a retail shelf may seem hopelessly outdated, but the same marketing lessons hold for "award winning" web sites or social media. Your design or ad agencies can impress you with their awards, but if you're not moving product or creating demand, you've missed the point.

Worry about the sales results.

Lessons Learned

- The only "award" in marketing that matters is sales revenue.
- Marketing needs to own all the marketing in a channel.
- Core competencies cannot be outsourced until they're learned.

The Video Spigot

Posted on **May 11, 2009** by steveblank |

I was lucky to have been standing in the right place when video became part of the Macintosh. And I got to experience a type of customer buying behavior I had never seen before – the *Novelty Effect.*

Present at the Creation

It was early 1991 and Apple's software development team was hard at work on QuickTime, the first multimedia framework for a computer. At the time, still pre-Internet, no one (including Apple) knew exactly what consumers were going to do with multimedia. Still the SuperMac team believed that adding video as an integral part of an operating system and user experience (where there had only been text and still images) would be transformative.

But Apple had planned to announce and demo QuickTime without a way to get video into the Mac. They had this great architecture, and Apple had figured out to get movies into their own computers for a demo, but for the rest of us, there was no physical device that allowed an average consumer to plug a video camera or VCR into and get video into a Mac.

A month or two before the QuickTime public announcement in May, the SuperMac hardware engineers who had a great relationship with the QuickTime team at Apple started a "skunk works" project. In less than a month, they designed a low-cost video-capture board which plugged into the Mac and allowed you to connect a video camera and VCR. But to get video to fit and playback on the computers of the era, they needed to compress it. So SuperMac engineering also developed video compression software called Cinepak. The software was idiot proof. There was nothing for the consumer to do. No settings, no buttons – plug your camera or VCR in and it just worked seamlessly. (The Cinepak codec was written by the engineer who would become my cofounder at Rocket Science Games.) It worked great on the slow CPUs at the time.

Something Profound

Engineering gave us a demo of the prototype board and software and asked, "Do you guys think we can sell a few of these boards?" Remember, this is the first time anyone outside of Apple or the broadcast industry had seen moving images on a Macintosh computer. (A company called Avid had introduced a $50,000 Mac-based professional broadcast video editing for two years earlier. But here was a $499 product that could let everyone use video.) Our engineers connected a VCR, pushed a button and poured in the video of the Apple 1984 commercial. We watched as it started playing video at 30 frames/second in a 320 x 240 window.

Up until that moment, QuickTime had been an abstract software concept to me. But now, standing there, I realized how people felt when they saw the first flickering images in a movie theater. We must have made them play the demo twenty times. There were a few times in my career I knew at that moment I was watching something profound – Holding the glass masks of the Z80 microprocessor, first IPO at Convergent, first silicon of the MIPS RISC processor. I stood there believing that video on computers was another – and equally as memorable.

Lets Sell it Like There's No Tomorrow

When we all regained the power of speech, our reaction was unanimous. What are you talking about – can we sell it? This is the first way to get video into a computer, we're going to sell and market this board like there's no tomorrow. Even though we won't make a ton of money, it will be an ambassador for the rest of our product family. People who aren't current customers of our graphics boards will get to know our company and brand. If we're smart, we'll cross-sell them one of our other products. We might even sell a few thousand of these.

Everyone laughed at such an absurd number.

The Video Spigot

"What are we going to call it?" Lets see, it's video input, how about we call it the Video Spigot?"

Now, in hindsight, with a spigot, you're actually pouring stuff out, and, in fact, the ad actually shows you stuff pouring stuff out, but into your Mac. It made no logical sense (a fact engineering reminded us about several times.) But it made the point that this device could pour video into your Mac and consumers instinctually got it.

Our CEO and our VP of manufacturing were incredibly nervous about manufacturing more than a few hundred of these boards. There's nothing to do with this product once you get the video in. You can't manipulate it, you can't do anything other than playback the video in QuickTime. And they were right. (Remember there were no video applications available at all. None. This was day zero of consumer video on the Mac.)

Our answer was, "People will love this thing, as long as we don't oversell the product." We knew something our CEO didn't. We had seen the reactions of people playing with the prototypes in our lab and when we demo'd it to our sales force. When we saw our salespeople actually trying to steal the early boards to take home and show their kids, we knew we had a winner. All we had to do was tell customers they could get video into their computer – and not promise anything else.

But the rest of the management team really skeptical. We kept saying, "Don't worry, we're going to sell thousands of these." Little did we know.

We launched the product with an ad that said: Video Spigot. Now pour video into your computer. This just hit a nerve.

We sold 50,000 Video Spigots in six months.

(As an aside, we saved money by putting my daughter in the ad. (That's every marketers' excuse for putting their kids in an ad.) She's in the little car on the monitor, and she's also, if you look very carefully, in the water. We had that little car around the house for a while.)

They're All Coming Back

So manufacturing ramped up our factory, and as we're selling 10,000 Video Spigots a month, our CEO is now concerned that maybe all these boards were all going to be returned to us because they didn't really do anything once you got video into your computer. (A rational fear, as the sum of all of our other graphics boards shipped was about 7,500/month.)

Marketing knew who the Spigot customers were. We had all the registration cards and all the data. So we turned to our customers, surveying a few hundred people who had bought the product and asked:

> *Question:* Were you the person who bought the board?
> *Answer:* Yes.
>
> *Question* Are you happy with the board?
> *Answer:* Oh, it's great.
>
> *Question* Are you using the board?
> *Answer:* <u>No</u>.
>
> *Question* And - wait a minute, you're not using it anymore?
> *Answer:* No.
>
> *Question* So do you want a refund?
> *Answer:* No, no.
>
> *Question* Why not?
> *Answer:* It did everything you said. We loved this product.

It didn't do anything else. People loved it, they used it, and they put it in their desk drawer.

We accidently had a product with *the Novelty Effect.*

The Novelty effect

I didn't recognize the behavior at the time, but anyone who loves technology and gadgets has at one time or another has bought a technology toy – USB memory sticks, iPod Shuffles, umbrellas with LED lights, alarm clocks that talked, Flip Video Cameras, etc. – used them for a while and then stuck them in the drawer. The product does what it said it would, and amuses you for a while. You don't regret the purchase price because you were entertained and then you lose interest - the *Novelty Effect.*

Unintended Consequences – Video Editing

As these boards are flying out the door, one of the software engineers at SuperMac got to thinking about what did you do with video once you did get it into a computer – so he wrote the first QuickTime-based video editor which we called ReelTime.

You probably never heard of ReelTime, but you may know it by its final name.

Since we had left the software business when we came out of Chapter 11, and our sales channel didn't know what to do with software, we licensed ReelTime to Adobe. And, of course, Adobe said, "Oh, by the way, you don't mind if the software engineer comes with us, do you?"

Adobe renamed ReelTime to Adobe Premiere. And Randy Ubillos, its author, went on to author Mac-based video editing software for the next 18 years. His team wrote what became FinalCut Pro at Macromedia which was bought by Apple. Now he's at Apple doing new versions of iMovie.

So an unintended consequence of the VideoSpigot, and to the benefit of video editors everywhere, video editing for the masses was invented at SuperMac.

Thanks to Bruce Leak and the Apple QuickTime team, Peter Barrett for Cinepak and Randy Ubillos for giving us video editing on the Mac. It was fun watching it happen.

The Curse of a New Building

Posted on **May 15, 2009** by steveblank |

Pondering how/why startups morph from agile, "can do" companies into ones that have lost their edge. I don't need to look much further than the "new building" debacle at SuperMac.

Signs of Success

One of the things you do right in a startup is to move from one cheap and cramped building to another as you grow with desks, cubicles and engineers piled cheek to jowl.

A real sign of success is when you outgrow your last cramped quarters and can afford a "real" building. This happened at SuperMac when our sales skyrocketed.

That's when things went south.

Let's Fix Everything that Was Broken

We were excited to finally get out of the crummy building we had occupied since the company emerged from bankruptcy. Now with cash in hand, we wanted to fix everything that seemed broken and annoying about our office environment. We made what seemed to be a series of logical and rational decisions about what to do with our next office building.

- *Engineers were packed in cubicles or desks right on top of each other?*
  Now every engineer can have their own office.
- *We can't bring customers to this rundown building.*
  The new building needs to reflect that we're a successful and established company.
- *The lobby of the last building didn't "represent" the company in a professional manner.*
  Let's "do it right" and have a lobby and reception area that projects a professional image.
- *We had used, crummy and uncomfortable furniture.*
  Let's get comfortable chairs and great new desks for everyone. None of this used stuff.
- *The last building had stained carpets and walls that haven't been painted in years.*
  Now we can pick out carpets that look good and feel good, and we can have clean walls with great artwork and murals.
- *We didn't have enough conference rooms.*
  Let's make sure that we have plenty of conference rooms.
- *Everyone left the building for lunch.*
  We need our own cafeteria so employees don't have to leave the building.

Designing the Perfect Building

Once the commitment to fix everything wrong was in place, we were off and running on the design phase. We hired an interior designer and a great facilities person to manage the process. At meetings, the exec staff focused on = the design of the new building.

The company decided that now engineers can have their own offices rather than cramped cubes. The staff got involved about what color the carpet and walls would be. And there was lots of discussion of what style of furniture was appropriate.

Our exec staff spent time worrying about who had the corner office, and which departments had the "prime" location. (I was great at "office wars.") There was lots of talk about the importance of natural lighting and how maybe we needed our own cafeteria. And even better, marketing got to design the graphics for the lobby and hallway (bright and colorful neon) to better represent the color graphics business we were in.

We kept the board informed, but they didn't have much to say since business was going so well, and a new building was needed to accommodate the growing company.

None of This is Good News

This is when things started to go downhill for SuperMac. The most obvious problem: the time we spent planning the building distracted the company from running the business. But there were three more insidious problems.

While offices for everyone sound good on paper, moving everyone out of cubicles destroyed a culture of tight-knit interaction and communication. Individuals within departments were isolated, and the size and scale of the building isolated departments from each other.

The new building telegraphed to our employees: We've arrived. We're no longer a small struggling startup. You can stop working like a startup and start working like a big company.

We started to believe that the new building was a reflection of the company's (and our own) success. We took our eye off the business. We thought that since we in such a fine building, we were geniuses, and the business would take care of itself.

While our competitors furiously worked on regaining market share, we were arguing about whether the carpets should be wool or nylon. The result was not pretty.

The Curse of a New Building

If this were just a sad story about a single company, it would be interesting, but not instructive. However, I've seen this story repeated time and again, and not just in Silicon Valley. There's a mindset that says, "By the dint of our hard work, we are "entitled" to a building upgrade, and this is our just reward." On an emotional level, it makes sense. But if you are lucky, you have a board of directors who have seen this before. (And they'll take the CEO out for a trip to the woodshed.)

An upgraded new building is a premature transition away from a startup culture.

It's a tipping point to a big company culture.

This is a culture and values issue worth fighting over.

Letting this happen is a failure of a board. If the management team is thinking they've made it, *the new building is just symptomatic of a company heading for a crash.* It's a company that's lost sight of the values that got it there.

Don't let it happen to you.

Stay hungry, stay lean.

Lessons Learned

- New buildings are a distraction. You should avoid them at all costs.
- Building upgrades can destroy a culture.

Rocket Science Games – Hubris and the Fall

Drinking the Kool-Aid

Posted on July 2, 2009 by steveblank |

Sometimes faith-based decisions can be based on too much faith.

Entrepreneur-in-Residence

After SuperMac I had been approached by one of our venture investors to be an *entrepreneur-i- residence (EIR),* a Silicon Valley phrase that says one thing but means another.

To an entrepreneur, being asked to join a venture firm with an Entrepreneur-in-Residence title means you have been tapped on the shoulder by the VC gods. It means you get to sit at a venture capital firm (some even pay you for the privilege) and stay until you have come up with an idea for your next company or have joined a company you've met as they passed through the VC's offices. Depending on the size of the venture firm, they may have one to three EIR's who stay an average of a year or so. It really means that the VC's would like to own a piece of you.

To a VC it's a cheap investment, and if they somehow don't bind you to their firm, someone else will. In reality an EIR is a set of wonderful golden handcuffs. Of course no VC firm will come right out and say, "If you're an EIR for us, you can't do your next deal with any other firm." Hmm- you've taken their money, eaten their food, sat in their meetings, and you are going to take money from someone else? They have your soul. It sounded like a great deal. I had no idea what I wanted to do next and would get paid to think about it? How could it go wrong? Little did I know.

Video Games

At SuperMac, Peter Barrett was the witty and creative 24-year old Australian engineer who had designed several of our most successful products, culminating with the software for the Video Spigot. Now he wanted to go off to start his own company. I offered to introduce him to the firm whose Entrepreneur-in-Residence offer I had just accepted. I asked Peter what kind of company he had in mind and was surprised and dismayed by the answer, "I want to make video games." I remember thinking, "What a disappointment, one of the smartest engineers I know, and he is going to waste his time making games." I didn't give his video game idea another thought. I set up the meeting for him, and at the request of the VC who was going to see him, agreed to sit in when they met.

It was a Friday when we showed up at the VC offices on Sand Hill road. Peter had no slides, and I had absolutely no idea what he was about to say. All I knew is that he wanted to talk about something I was utterly uninterested in – video games.

Henry the Vth

To this day, the VC and I still believe either Peter made what was the single most compelling speech we have ever heard or he had slipped something funny into our water. As Peter began to speak extemporaneously, our mouths slowly fell open as he described the video game market, its size, its demographics, the state of the technology, and the state of games. He took us through a day (and a night) of a hardcore gamer and told us about the new class of CD-ROM based game machines about to hit the market.

Peter described the first company in which "Hollywood meets Silicon Valley" and we were enthralled. When he elaborated how CD-ROMs were going to change both the nature of gaming and the economics of the content business, we were certain he had a brilliant idea. By the end of the meeting we were convinced that this was a company would make a ton of money.

By the end of the meeting, the seasoned venture capitalist and I had signed up.

While this all might sound farcical now, a little historical context is in order. The CD-ROM content business in the early 1990's was one of the many of the long line of venture capital fads. If you were a "with it" VC, you needed to have a "Content" or "Multimedia" company in your portfolio to impress your limited partners – educational software companies, game companies or anything that could be described as content and/or Multimedia.

There Ought to be a Law

Nowadays there are laws that allow you to back out of a time-share condo contract or used car purchase after seven days because even the government believes there are times when grown adults lose their minds and stand up and yell, "Yes I believe, sign me up!" There are still no laws like that in the venture capital business.

A month later, after raising $4 million dollars (we literally had VC's fighting over who else would fund us), Peter and I started our video game company, Rocket Science Games.

In reality I had been hired as CEO and the adult supervision and administrative overseer of one of the most creative talents in the valley. And I would get to use my marketing skills at generating an industry-wide reality distortion field to make this company look like the second coming.

I was going to find out why this wasn't a good idea.

Lessons learned

- Your level of due diligence should be commensurate with your position in the company and proportional to the reality distortion field of the presenter.
- Never join (or start) a company whose business model you can't draw.
- Subjects in which you are not a domain expert always sound exciting.
- Sleep on any major decision.

Hollywood Meets Silicon Valley

Posted on July 9, 2009 by steveblank |

What do you mean you don't want to hear about features?

I was now a CEO of Rocket Science, and having a great time building the company

(more about that in future posts.) Unfortunately, while I had gone through phases of video game addiction in my life, in no way could I be described as even a "moderate hard-core gamer" which ruled me out as a domain expert. So I got out of the building to meet and understand our customers and distribution partners. I remember after a month or two of talking to 14-22 year old male gamers (our potential target market) I realized that for the first time in my career, I had no emotional connection to my customers or channel partners.

I was about 90 days into the company when I began to realize there was something very different about this business. In previous companies, I could talk about technology details and how the product features could solve a customers problem. But people didn't buy video games on features, and they weren't looking to solve a problem. I was in a very, very different business.

I was in the entertainment business.

There couldn't have been a worse choice for CEO in Silicon Valley.

Alarm bell one should have started ringing – for me and my board.

Hollywood Meets Silicon Valley was an Oxymoron

A key premise of our new company was that our video compression and authoring technology would revolutionize how games were made and played. We believed that by putting full motion video (i.e. movies) into video games, we could tell stories, build characters, have narratives and bring all the 100 years of craft and cinematic experience of Hollywood to the sterile "shoot and die" twitch games that were currently in vogue. (This wasn't just some random Silicon Valley fantasy. My partner had convinced several major Hollywood names that this was the inevitable consequence of the merger of Hollywood and Silicon Valley. And at the time it was a plausible scenario.)

But in reality, our passionate belief that video would transform gaming *was just our hypothesis*. There was zero proof in the marketplace that was the case. And we weren't going to be bothered to go out and prove ourselves wrong with facts. (Why should we –

our VC's had already told us what geniuses we were by fighting to even get into the deal to fund us. Never mind that no one on our board was in the game business or even played games.)

Alarm bell two should have started ringing – for me and my board.

Swing For the Fences

Since we were so smart, we were going to ramp up and build not one game, but an entire game studio based on this hypothesis. Why shouldn't we? Doing one game and seeing customer reaction meant a) acknowledging that some of our assumptions might be wrong, and 2) wasting time. We were all about scale and swinging for the fences. That's what VC funded companies do, don't they?

Alarm bell three should have started ringing – for my partner and me.

Tools Are the Not the Product

We were going to build an easy-to-use authoring system that would revolutionize how games were made. (My partner had convinced several of the key members of the Apple QuickTime team to join us.) Our tools group became as important as our content group. Unfortunately, the market was going to remind us that *games are about game play*.

Customers don't care about your tools regardless of what business you're in. Customers of software applications don't say, "wow, elegant code base." In movies theater-goers don't leave talking about your cameras, just whether they were entertained, and in restaurants, diners don't care about your cooking implements. What matters is what the food tasted like. The tools may provide efficiencies, but what customers care about is your final *product*. (Later on, way too late, we'd remind ourselves *it's the game stupid*.)

Alarm bell four should have started ringing louder for me.

Lessons learned

- Never, ever, start a company when you're not passionate about the company, product and customers.
- Always validate your key assumptions on what makes your company tick.
- Swing for the fences is your VC's strategy. Make sure it is yours.
- Don't confuse your passion for your tools with why your customers will buy your product.

The Press is Our Best Product

Posted on July 13, 2009 by steveblank |

At Rocket Science while my partner Peter was managing the tools and game development, I was managing everything else. Which at this stage of the company was marketing and financing.

Our "Hollywood meets Silicon Valley" story played great in Silicon Valley, they ate it up in Hollywood, and the business press tripped over themselves to talk to us. The story had universal appeal, and we spun the tale and kept the buzz going. It worked.

Judging by the ink we had received, we were the hottest company in the game business, with stories in *Fortune, Forbes, Variety, The Hollywood Reporter,* and the cover of *Wired* magazine. Yet we hadn't shipped a single product.

While it felt wonderful at the time, this was a *very* bad idea.

Everyone Else is an Idiot

The theme of our press blitz was all about how we were going to show the old tired game companies the right way to make video games. Our press infuriated the established companies that had spent years building games that sold well, but had zero press recognition. (They all accurately predicted our demise because of our lack of game expertise.) Ah, the arrogance of inexperience. Fortunately, I've never been good at lying. To be effective in communicating a story I truly had to believe in what I was saying. At the time I was a true believer that Rocket Science was going to change the gaming world. The tidal wave of press opened doors for us to raise money from corporate partners. Companies in the entertainment business around the world knew who we were and wanted to meet us, if only to see what the hype was about. Our VP of Business Development had no problems getting meetings, and fund raising was easy.

The Digital Dream Team

Way before the Internet phenomenon, we had created "Rocket Science *the brand*" that was much bigger in size and importance than Rocket Science the company. One magazine called us the "Digital Dream Team", young, edgy and hip, and by the looks of the company (great building, nice furniture, and well dressed 20-year olds,) we were trying to live up to the reputation. All this activity occurring before we actually shipped a product. We were larger than life, but as one potential investor told us, "You guys are all hat and no cattle."

Believing Your Own BS is Toxic

Lots of noise and smoke before a product ships seems to be a toxic byproduct of enthusiastic entrepreneurs. Every generation of new technology seems to find a willing audience in naïve journalists and eager readers. However, when the smoke clears, *the surviving companies are more than likely the ones that focused on execution, not on creating a cacophony of press releases.* If Rocket Science wasn't a clear enough lesson in the danger of premature enthusiasm, the dot-com bubble that followed should have been. The only difference between us and the Internet bubble that would follow was that we did branding on the cheap by creating our image with public relations while the dot-bomb era did it by spending enormous sums on advertising (those large venture rounds had to get spent somewhere.)

Hindsight is wonderful. For years the one solace I was able to take from the Rocket Science debacle was that I had got the branding right. Then I watched the criminally expensive dot-bomb-bust branding activities to see how futile and wasteful it was to brand a company before it has shipped products.

To a Hammer Everything Looks Like a Nail

In hindsight my failure was that I executed to my strength – telling a compelling story – without actually listening to customer feedback.

It wasn't that I didn't know how to listen to customers. It wasn't that I didn't have a smart VP of Marketing who was getting early feedback from customers and screaming that the games didn't match the hype. It's that as CEO I was too busy talking to the press and raising money to hear customer comments directly.

I had outsourced customer feedback and ignored the input. In fact, hearing input that contradicted the story I was telling created cognitive dissonance. So while the words may have passed through my ears, I couldn't "hear" it. Not being able to hear negative customer input is an *extremely* bad idea.

Out of the Ashes

A few of the key tenets of Customer Development came from the ashes. The Customer Discovery lessons of "get outside the building and test your hypothesis with customers," and "the founders need to hear the results" came from the Rocket Science debacle.

The Customer Validation lesson of "no formal launch until you have early sales validating the product and sales process" was also born here. Given the lukewarm feedback we were getting from potential customers and channel buyers, we should have dramatically dialed back the hype until the follow-on games could match it. Given the talented people we had, there's no doubt they would have done so. Instead, the huge mismatch between expectations and the reality of our first games diminished the brand and demoralized the company – we never recovered.

Lessons Learned

- PR is not a product- it is a demand creation activity to fill a sales channel.
- The product needs to come close to the hype.
- Fire the CEO who insists on press and PR *before* they understand customer feedback.
- Branding is a process that should happen *after* you have customers.

Who Needs Domain Experts

Posted on July 16, 2009 by steveblank |

What Business Are We In?

While the Rocket Science press juggernaut moved inexorably forward, a few troubling facts kept trying to bubble up into my consciousness. The company was founded to build games with embedded video to bring Hollywood stories, characters, and narratives to a market where "shoot and die" twitch games were in vogue. But underlying the company's existence was a fundamental hypothesis we refused to see or test - *customers would care if we did.*

In the game business of the early 1990's, video was at best a brief narrative, a distraction you maybe watched once, not the core of the game. Our potential customers didn't seem to be calling for Hollywood stories, characters and narrative. That's OK, because we knew better. We thought we had figured out what the next generation of games was going to be. We thought we were in the movie business, but video games were more akin to pinball; both pinball and movies are entertainment, but you would never confuse them with each other. Successful pinball companies didn't hire Hollywood talent.

Meanwhile, our company was pouring an enormous amount of dollars into building tools and video compression technology while also hiring a lot of high-priced Hollywood talent like art directors, and script and story editors.

We Don't Need Domain Experts

When I looked around at our executive staff, there wasn't a single founder who had built a game. Worse, there wasn't a single person on our executive team who had come from a game company. Nor was there anyone with game experience on our board. As the company grew, a sense of unease started gnawing at the outer fringes of the "you're in trouble" part of my brain. Meanwhile, my partner was in heaven working with his newly hired group of game designers, directing and producing our first games. When I pointed out my rising apprehension, his response was, "I've been playing games since I was 10. I know what's great and what's not. We agreed this part of the company was my responsibility. Don't worry. The games are going to be great." Given my fiduciary responsibility to my board and my investors did his blasé answer force me to grab him by the collar and scream, "Snap out of it! We're in trouble!"

Nah. Instead I said, "Oh, OK, glad it's all under control." Then I went back to raising more money and getting more press for our soon to be spectacular games.

Hire the Best Advice I Can Ignore

But the nagging little voice in the back of my head that said, "This doesn't feel right," wouldn't go away. So I hired a VP of Marketing from Sega, one of the video game platforms on which our games would run. After only two weeks on the job, he came into my office and said, "Have you've seen the games we are building?" What kind of question was that? Of course I had seen pieces of video and beautiful storyboards. "No," he insisted, "Have you seen the game play, the part that supposed to keep players addictively glued to the game console for hours?" Hmm. "No, not really, but my partner owns the studio and tells me it's spectacular and everyone will love it. Don't bother him; he knows what he's doing. Go spend some time outside the building talking to potential distribution partners. Tell them how great it's going to be and see how many pre-orders we can get."

A month later, the VP of Marketing appeared in my office again. "Steve I have to tell you some bad news, I just showed our potential channel partners and customers a few completed pieces of the games we had. *They think the games stink*."

Now I know I heard his words because years later I can still remember them well enough to write them down. But somehow the translation between my ears and what I was supposed to do with what I was hearing shut down. Was my response to stop development of the games? Bring in some outside professionals to review our progress? Call a board meeting and say we may have a serious problem? Nah. I said, "That can't be true! The press is saying we are the hottest super group around. Look, we're on the cover of *Wired* magazine. They think we're brilliant. Our VCs think we are visionary. Stop annoying our game designers and start working on selling and marketing the games."

Hindsight
In hindsight, it's easy to laugh. Saying you knew how to build great games because you played them all your life was like saying, "Hey I eat out a lot so why don't I open a restaurant." Or "I've seen a lot of movies so let's start a movie studio." Only in Silicon Valley could we have got funded with this idea, and not surprisingly, it was our technology that had the VC's confused. It was more like we had invented the world's best new kitchen utensils and wanted to open a restaurant or had built the world's finest movie cameras and wanted to start a movie studio. Our venture backers and our executive team confused our technology and our tools – and our passion for the games business – with any practical experience in the real business we were in. We were an *entertainment* business – and not a very subtle entertainment business. As we were

216

about to find out, if video game players wanted a cinematic experience, they went to the movies, they didn't buy a video game. Our customers wanted to kill, shoot or hunt for something. Fancy video narratives and plots were not video games.

Interest Alignment

Why VC's invested in companies like ours is what's great and bad about entrepreneurship. A venture capitalist I respect reminded me that he thought about investment risk as either:

- Investing $1 million in 10 companies and have all ten succeed, with each of those ten companies returning 2x their money for $20 million. Or

- Investing in 10 companies and having 8 fail - but the remaining two companies returning 20x their money for $40 million.

His point was that it was in the VC's interest to have entrepreneurs swing for the fences.

However, the *VC's are managing a portfolio while you, the entrepreneur, are managing one company – yours.* While VC's might love you and your firm, a 2x return isn't why they're in business. It's nothing personal, but your interests and your VC's may not be aligned. (More on this in future posts.)

The Search for the Black Swan

What keeps founders and their investors going is the dream/belief that your startup will be the Black Swan – a company that breaks all the obvious rules, ignores tradition and does something unique and spectacular, with a result that is unpredicted and financial returns that are breathtaking.

Think of the Microprocessor, Personal Computer, Internet, Twitter, YouTube, Facebook, Google, the iPhone. Creating those technologies and companies required entrepreneurs willing to follow their own vision and convincing others that the path is worth following.

The mistake isn't having a vision and taking risks. The mistake is assuming you are a Black Swan and continuing to ignore the facts as they pile up in front of you.

Customer Development

There was nothing wrong about Rocket Science having a vision radically different than the conventional wisdom. We could have been right and invented a new form of gaming and entertainment. What went awry was continuing to execute on the vision when all the evidence in front of us told us our hypothesis was wrong. We compounded the problem when we failed to have an honest discussion about why it made sense to ignore the evidence. (A tip-off is when you start saying, "They just don't get it yet.")

At Rocket Science, hubris took over and was about to lead to the fall.

Customer Development says having a vision, faith and a set of hypotheses are a normal part of the startup experience. But it is critical to build in a process for testing those hypotheses outside the building and listening to the responses – or you might as well throw your money in the street.

Lessons learned?

- While a lack of relevant domain expertise is not always fatal, believing you don't need any is.
- Founders need to validate their vision in front of customers early and often.
- Your goals and your VC's goals may not be aligned. Make sure they are.

Rocks in the Rocket Science Lobby

Posted on June 1, 2009 by steveblank |

In 1994 Rocket Science Games was the only video game company with a rock in its lobby.

We had moved our game development facilities from Berkeley and Palo Alto and consolidated into one building on Townsend Street in the South of Market neighborhood in San Francisco. (We were just around the corner from the future home of SF Giants AT&T Baseball Park, which then was just a rubble-strewn parking lot in a sketchy neighborhood.)

Since we were the hip, new, edgy "Hollywood meets Silicon Valley" video game company (more about "big hat, no cattle" startups in subsequent posts) our office obviously had to match the image.

Our receptionists' desk was built on the wing of a WWII P-51 fighter plane, and the rest of the office décor matched. All that is, except for our lobby, as our offices were on the 4th floor. When you got off the elevator, you faced a non descript corporate-looking set of walls.

This was about the time Christies and Sotheby's were starting to auction Soviet space program artifacts, and I thought that perhaps a spacesuit in the lobby would be appropriate given our name.

One day, out for a walk at lunch, enjoying one of my favorite activities – watching them tear down the Embarcadero freeway (San Francisco urban upgrade post 1989 earthquake,) – I realized I was looking at the answer.

And it was much, much better than a space suit.

A week later, as our employees came up the elevator, there was a Lucite case on a pedestal with a single grey rock, lit with a single spotlight, on a velvet pillow. In front was a brass plaque that read:

"Moon rock, Apollo 18, July 1973 – Copernicus Crater."

For the next few years, people from all around South of Market would come by the Rocket Science Games lobby to see our moon rock. It added to the mystique of the company – which helped with raising money and getting press ink. Everyone agreed that having our own moon rock was way cool.

Postscript. In all that time, not a single person who admired the moon rock questioned its provenance or authenticity, a bit surprising considering the intersection between geekdom and space. Maybe it was just too much ancient history.

NASA's moon missions ended at Apollo 17.

The rock was a piece of rubble from the Embarcadero Freeway.

Only over time would I realize it augured the future of the company.

The Secret History of Silicon Valley

The Story Behind the Story

If I Told You I'd Have to Kill You

Posted on March 23, 2009 by steveblank

About a month ago, I had one of the strangest phones call of my life. "Steve my name is Donald xx, and I'm the head of external affairs of the CIA's venture capital firm and we'd like you to keynote our conference." CIA? "Do you mean the Culinary Institute of America? And you'd like me to do my talk on Customer Development and startups?" "No, we're the other CIA."

So I gave my "The Secret History of Silicon Valley" talk as the keynote to the CIA's venture capital conference. (See the video at http://bit.ly/SecHistory and the slides at http://bit.ly/secretslides). Their VC firm, In-Q-Tel, has been in business for 10 years, and like most VC firms, they have an annual event where they show off their new portfolio companies to their limited partners and other VC partners. Except at this VC conference, 100 or so of the 300 attendees had badges with their first name and only the last initial of their last name. (And I could have sworn they all had the same badge.) They were all from somewhere in the intelligence community.

As I was leaving, someone asked me, "You must have been working on this story for awhile?" Until then, I had never thought about how long I had been thinking about this. But as I got into my car, I realized that this talk was the result of my never-ending asking "How come?" for 36 years. So this post is how I came to write "The Secret History of Silicon Valley". (I'll post more about the history itself later.)

So here it is in multiple parts.

Part I. Thailand: Bats, Moths and John Scoggins
In 1973 I was 19 and in Thailand in the Air Force repairing electronic warfare equipment on fighter planes, gunships and Wild Weasels, at the tail end of the Vietnam War. I remember asking out of the blue one day: "Where does our equipment come from? What is exactly that we're doing?"

My sergeant looked at me like the dog just talked: "What do you mean, what are we doing? We're fixing this equipment; that's your job. When the pilots say it doesn't work, we take the stuff out of the plane, bring it to the shop, make sure it really is broken, you know, and unbreak it." And I went, "No, no, no, but why are we doing this?"

I wanted to understand more about the North Vietnamese and their surface to air missiles and radar guided AAA they got from the Russians, and how we were trying to out-smart them with receivers to pick up their radar and jammers to jam the acquisition radars and missile guidance uplink signals — a little of which I had learned in my one year of training at Keesler Air Force Base in Biloxi Mississippi. Since it was the military and I was a lowly airman (I was outranked by the rest of the entire air force), the answer I got was, "Don't you know there's a war on? Shut up and keep fixing that equipment."

But I kept on asking enough questions until finally, I got the attention again of the guy who had brought me off of the very hot and humid flight line into the shop in the first place, John Scoggins. John said, "You're really interested in this stuff, aren't you?" I said, "Yeah, you know, like where did it come from? I mean, how long have the Russians had this stuff? Why did they build it? How did we figure out how to build jammers?" There was no public history about surface to air missiles, though I'm sure there were probably some good classified histories, which I didn't have access to.

John said, "Well, Steve, it's been going on for tens of millions of years." I said, "What are you talking about? I'm asking about electronic warfare and countermeasures." He said, "Tens of millions of years." And I said, "What?" And he said, "Meet me at the tennis courts tonight."

John was a lifer, who I guess in hindsight was a nerd and was in his element as an enlisted guy, but a master sergeant. He must have been in his 30s, so a real "old" guy to a 19 year old.

So, he said, "tennis courts, 8:00 PM tonight." You're on an airbase with 180 fighter planes, but we had a tennis court and gym and all kinds of accoutrements to give thousands of airmen in the middle of a war zone an alternative to almost free drugs and women (note to military: nice try, but it didn't work.)

The tennis courts had these very bright lights which attracted all kinds of bizarre tropical insects, including these large flying water beetles. I don't know their actual genus, but they were called "Baht Bugs" because the Thai locals would capture them and sell them for a nickel each since they were a delicacy, and the Thais would take the raw bugs and literally slurp out their insides in real time. So, they would be running around the tennis courts collecting Baht Bugs.

Baht Bugs
There were also these large moths that attracted bats.

So, I met John Scoggins at the tennis court. It's night, and no one played tennis at night, even though they lit the tennis court. But there's a pile of electronic equipment under one of the lights with a parabolic dish antenna, kind of a miniature setup of stuff we had in the labs and our shop.

"What on earth is this?" I asked. John put on headphones, and he gave me a set of headphones, and all of a sudden I could hear this chirping sound. I said, "What are we listening to?" He said, "Bats." "What?" "Bats."

John explained that bats have the equivalent of radar. Not radar in terms of microwave radar frequencies, but they use ultrasonic frequencies to locate their prey at night, essentially radar to locate bugs. And since they fly at night, they don't use vision; their ultrasonic's are essentially their eyes. They've build up a mental map – just like our vision – with echolocation. They send out these chirps, and when one bounces off an object, it comes back. Then they would go after the moths.

We're listening to the radar signals of a bat and it's very cool. John recorded the flight of the bats as they were going after bugs on a reel-to-reel tape recorder. Every couple of minutes he'd say, "Now listen to this one," and you'd hear the bat chirp. Every once in a while, you'd hear even a higher frequency but lower volume sound.

John said, "Listen, you can hear the jammer." The what? "The jammer," he said, "Watch the moths." It turns out the moths, through evolution, had developed their own electronic countermeasures to jam the bat radar. They had developed ultrasonic receivers and ultrasonic jammers and physical countermeasures. When they picked up the bat radar illuminating them by sensitive hairs on their antennas, they would send out their own little squirt of ultrasonics by rubbing their legs together to jam the bat radar, and then they would immediately take evasive action and dive to the left and right.

Through Darwinian selection over millions of years, these moths had developed an entire electronic intelligence and electronic countermeasures suite, and here was a guy in 1973 in Thailand who was figuring this stuff out. To be honest, it was my first insight that there was really a bigger picture in life and in war.

John's point was: "I keep trying to tell officers way above me that there's probably a ton we could learn from watching these natural systems. What we're doing in the air war over the North is just nothing more than something that's been going on in nature for millions of years, but I can't seem to get anybody's attention." (Thirty years later MIT would develop the Insect Lab and work on swarm behaviors for UAV's and robotics.)

Years later, I searched Google for anything written on moth/bat radar and countermeasures, and while now there are quite a few papers, John had never published anything on the subject. If he had he would have been 20 years ahead of everyone else. But I always had thought the bat and moth thing was incredibly cool, and it answered a question I had never even asked: where is all this coming from?

In exchange for helping John with his bats and bugs, I learned about the big picture – about the North Vietnamese air defense radar network and SAMs and what systems our equipment were trying to shut down, what the Wild Weasels were doing, and what John had heard from friends in Utapao and Guam about why we lost all those B-52's in Linebacker II, what worked and didn't over the north, almost all which was classified way past my pay level (and his.)

I was always a sponge for new data and curious about where it came from, and what the history was, and what we were trying to do. Most of it went in one ear and out the other. But some of it was sticking. And all of it was interesting. It gave me a sense of purpose for the rest of the war. Under John's tutelage, I ended up running a small shift and part a very large shop and was sent to other bases in Thailand to train others how to repair the new equipment.

Thanks John, wherever you are.

I had just turned 20.

Gravity Will be Turned Off

Posted on May 13, 2009 by steveblank |

Part of marketing is the ability to communicate a message to thousands of people and convince them to believe your version of reality. When I was 19, I accidentally had a test run of my ability to do so. I created havoc at an air force base by convincing thousands of airman that *gravity would be turned off* so the Air Force could make repairs under their buildings.

Two Million Students

First some background. Ever since WWII, U.S. Air Force aircraft have carried sophisticated avionics equipment – radar, navigation, electronic warfare, etc. While the sharp end of the stick were the pilot and/or crew, each of these systems required a cadre of technicians to maintain and repair the equipment. Keesler Air Force Base in Biloxi Mississippi was the Training Center responsible for teaching 10's of thousands of students a year how to repair radar, communications, and electronics. Some 2 million students have trained there since it opened in 1942. Think of it as the ultimate vocational training school.

Trade School

At the height of the Vietnam War, I was at Keesler learning how to repair electronic warfare equipment, a skill which had gone from *theory* (our B-52 bombers might one day have to use this stuff –once – penetrating the Soviet Air Defense system) to *practice* (our fighter/bombers were encountering the murderously effective North Vietnamese air defense system every day.)

In hindsight, the USAF did a damn good job. We spent the first five months learning basic electronics theory and the next months getting our hands dirty with the theory and practice of electronic warfare receivers and jammers. As it was a vocational school, I think the most math we had to do was to figure out whether we got a passing grade. No one was in any danger of actually designing new equipment, but I left with an excellent education in troubleshooting and solving complex problems in real-time.

Duality – Student Life – in the Military

Here we were, thousands of students with an average age of 19 going to school and living in barracks on the airbase. The barracks were like college dorms except we had to polish the brass doorknobs, wax and buff the hallway floors and make our beds. We attended classes from 6am to noon – five days a week. And we had to march to class (I'm convinced it was the only way they figured they were going to get us up and out of bed at that hour).

There was a duality to our existence. On one hand, we were in a rigid command and control system where we had to follow orders, salute officers and understand the military hierarchy. Yet on the other we were in an educational institution where we were encouraged to ask all the questions we wanted. And we had afternoons and weekends off. We could go off base and do anything a group of 19-year olds wanted to, like skydiving, but that's another story.

Library Hours

Ever since I was a kid I loved libraries. Growing up in New York, the library was the only calm and stable place in my life, a refuge from home. I read my way through our small neighborhood library.

My fondness for libraries and my reading habit carried through to the Air Force, and this technical school had an awesome technology library. One day I opened up a Scientific American magazine and read an article on a prank that had been pulled at CalTech the year before. And something about the story clicked for me. I thought that this practical joke would be even funnier in a military organization than it was at Caltech. (I'll describe the actual prank in a bit.)

Alone with Letterhead

Every evening someone in the barracks had to serve as the "fire warden" for the night. In hindsight, fire warden meant you were a manual smoke alarm. You walked around the barracks and made sure the building wasn't on fire. (Anytime you put 10,000 19-year olds on a base, you can bet one of them will go to sleep with a cigarette and burn his mattress, if not the building.)

The other minor duty of the fire warden was to update the squadron bulletin board. This was the one place you had to go daily to read all the official notices, and orders. Reading official military notices and memos always seemed funny to me as they had the most verbose and obtuse ways of saying even the simplest things. You usually had to read two pages to realize the memo said, "No Smoking Indoors," or "Mandatory meeting on Thursday."

Following Orders

One night it was my turn on fire warden duty, and with way too much time on my hands, I was mulling over the philosophical contradictions of the literal interpretation that my fellow military students placed on even the most trivial orders. Orders didn't have to make sense, we were told "An order is an order. Don't think, just follow it." I wondered how far that would really go.

Then I thought of the Caltech prank. If it worked on a college campus, I wonder what would happen on a military base?

So working into the wee hours of the morning, I typed up a version of the Cal Tech prank on official base letterhead, translating it into military phraseology. I typed 30 copies, and using the master key, I went into every squadron building and posted these orders from the base commander on all 30 bulletin boards. The memo I posted looked something like this:

KEESLER AIR FORCE BASE
81ST TRAINING WING
OFFICE OF THE BASE COMMANDER
228-377-2179: DSN 597-2179

To: All Kessler Base Occupants
Subject: Civil Engineering AFS Standard 72-47c-31d
      Compliance Work Commencing 0900 12 September

On 0900 12 September the 81st Civil Engineering Squadron
will be instituting structural renovations to all barracks
to ensure their compliance with AFS standard 72-47c-31d.
These renovations will require lifting all Unaccompanied
Enlisted Personnel Housing off of their foundations and
reinforcing structural cross members to ensure their
compliance with above cited AFS standard. The attached
base map lists the affected barracks.

To expedite this process Civil Engineering will temporarily
interrupt gravity for construction access to these
barracks. It is expected that gravity will be off for a
period of 8 hours on 12 September 1973, from 0900 to 1700.
Only the campus areas south and west of Base Drive will be
affected.

Civil Engineering has advised that the interruption will
undoubtedly create non-causal gravitational singularities
along the boundaries of the region affected. Therefore
Hurricane Drive and Base Drive will be closed to traffic
throughout the day.

All personnel are advised that from 0900 to 1700 the
following precautions must be taken:

1. Officers with families and those in Bachelor Officer
   Quarters may leave the base before 0845. Please take
   all pets including waterborne animals.

2. Due to danger of walking outside, all enlisted
   personnel are confined to quarters 0845 to 1715.
   Barracks leaders will sound the All Clear when normal
   activities can resume.

3. All heavy objects (stereos, televisions, etc.) must be tied down and secured. (Refer to AF Regulation 5845 for securing heavy objects.) Each squadron commander will hold a "tie-down" barracks inspection at 0700 to ensure compliance.

4. As each building is raised and gravity is reduced, enlisted personnel must remain seated in beds or chairs. Footprints on walls or ceilings are a violation of the UCMJ article 12 and will be treated as such.

5. Change in the pressure differential in pipes may trigger fire alarms and sprinklers. Please do not leave the buildings.

6. Cars driven south of Hurricane Drive and Base Drive may be subject to gravitational distortion.

7. Electricity will continue to be supplied to these buildings during the day. However, the use of water if available, may have unpredictable results. Do not flush toliets when gravity is turned off.

81st Civil Engineering Squadron AFS Standard 72-47c-31d Compliance Work

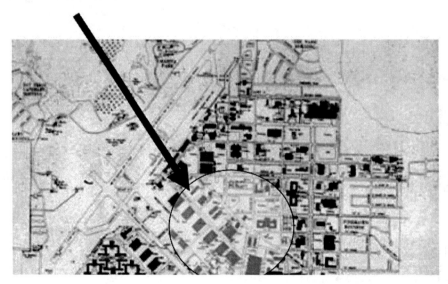

Friday Formation

I had posted my memo on Wednesday, got a good chuckle over it and promptly forget all about it. I thought it was very funny, a good one-time joke, and people would laugh and then remove it from the bulletin board. But a few days had passed, and I hadn't heard anything so I assumed the joke had fallen flat on its face.

Every building/squadron had an officer in charge of us, and all 300 hundred or so would gather in the courtyard every Friday for our squadron meeting, where our lieutenant would give us orders for the weekend, (usually have a good time) and answer any questions.

At that Friday's squadron formation the lieutenant, (who is all of 22 years old,) comes out. As the sergeant calls, "Squadron a-ten hut," we all snap to attention. The lieutenant reads the orders of the weekend, blah, blah, blah, and then says, "Okay, any questions?" Usually there weren't any questions because everyone wants to be dismissed for the weekend. But today was going to be a bit different.

I'm ready to run for the gate, but wait, there's a raised hand.

"Sir, about the gravity being turned off, what if we have fish? Should we cover their bowls?" I almost burst out laughing, surprised there was at least one person in the squadron who believed the memo. The lieutenant is silent for a long minute, staring at the airman who asked the question, and calculating whether he heard it correctly or was being made fun of. But before he could respond, someone else raised his hand and said, "Sir, what if we have small children and they're crawling, and we can't get them off base, will they affected by the gravity?"

Ok, I think, maybe there were two.

But that was the cue for 10 more people simultaneously to burst out with questions; "How about motorcycles will they be OK? Can we go to the bathroom when the gravity is turned off?" And I started to panic as it dawned on me that this conversation is occurring 30 times the 300 people in each of the 30 squadrons on this airbase.

The lieutenant looks stunned. Were we all on drugs? What on earth were we talking about? He sent the sergeant to get the memo from the bulletin board, reads it and he looks really confused. It can't be real, but yet it does look like an official order from the base commander.

The lieutenant leaves to call the base commander,(about the same time 29 other lieutenants were doing the same.) "But sir, the order came from you." An hour and a half later we finally get dismissed with a, "Ignore that order, it wasn't really an order."

Years later at different air bases, at the most unexpected times, I'd hear someone bring up, "Hey, were you at Keesler when they had those orders about the gravity being turned off?" And I always say, "No, never heard of it. Tell me about it." The story was even better when someone else told it.

Getting B-52s through the Soviet Air Defense System

Posted on March 29, 2009 by steveblank

1974. The Vietnam War was winding down. After been stationed at three fighter bases in Thailand (Ubon, Udorn and Korat) and working on Electronic Warfare suites on F-4's, A-7's, F-105's and AC-130's, I got orders to report to a Strategic Air Command (SAC) B-52 bomber base in Alpena, Michigan.

Imagine how hot, humid and unbearable the weather was in Thailand. Now I was on an airbase that issued some very 'cool' gear – bunny boots and arctic parkas. The downside was that the average winter temperature was about 10 degrees. I remember the few times I had to go out to the flight line, it was usually 15 below zero (Fahrenheit.)

The B-52 – When it Absolutely Had to Get There the Next Day

During the Cold War, the B-52 bomber was one-third of what was called our strategic triad – meaning, it made up one-third of the U.S.'s strategic weapons: ICBMs, nuclear submarines, and manned bombers. The notion was that while the Soviets could knock any one or any two of those out, we still had a retaliatory capability. (That was our strategic posture from the '50s, '60s, and '70s, the '80s, and I think maybe even through the '90s. Now we have ditched the cold war triad in the 21st century since the Soviet Union became Russia again and discovered its own style of capitalism.)

Think of a plane the length of a 767 airliner (but with 30 foot longer wings and 8 engines rather than 2) whose only mission was to FedEx 70,000 pounds of nuclear weapons to the Soviet Union.

Soviet Air Defense – PVO Strany

The B-52s had to get through a massive Soviet air defense system which had been built and evolved over two decades and was designed to shoot down manned bombers. Not only did Soviet Air Defense have the same SA-2 missiles the North Vietnamese had (since they had given it to them), but the Soviet air defense environment was much denser with a layered defensive system of radars, Surface to Air Missiles (old SA-1's and newer SA-3s, SA-5s) and a huge manned 1000+ plane fighter interceptor fleet. In fact, the Soviet Air Defense Forces, PVO Strany, was so important in the defense of the Motherland, it was a separate branch of their military.

And just to make the problem harder, the North Vietnamese had shot down B-52s in December 1972 and given the Soviets the captured electronic countermeasures equipment. Even though the bombers we lost over North Vietnam were older versions, B-52 D-models, they ironically had more modern electronic warfare systems. Now the Soviets had first hand knowledge of how their air defense systems would work against our nuclear-armed B-52G and H models in an operational environment.

Ann Arbor to Alpena – 180 Miles and a Major Culture Gap

While I never got tired of looking at the planes, one my fondest memories of this base was driving down U.S. 23 to Ann Arbor when the leaves turned in the fall. Late September to mid-October, the riot of the colors was so intense I pulled the car off to the side of the road to just stare for awhile. Each week as I would head down south, I could track the progress of the trees putting on their electric reds and yellows fall colors as their shifting color also headed south. I'd spend a weekend in a college town, without a uniform, in a world as far away from nuclear weapons and the Strategic Air Command in politics and culture as you could get. While it seemed a bit incongruous, it was fun listening to my friends in graduate school worrying over dinner about grades and jobs. Then I would return back north to the much drabber green palette of bombers and uniforms and continue to defend democracy.

I had plenty of time in those three-hour drives to ponder the value of universal National Service.

The Electronic Warfare Officer (EWO) and the Nielsen Ratings

The largest payload next to the nuclear weapons on B-52s was the electronic warfare equipment, designed to help the bomber jam its way through the radar environment in the Soviet Union. The bombers had wideband panoramic receivers and displays, chaff, and kilowatts of jammers up and down the frequency band. One of the six-crew members was dedicated solely to get the plane to the target through the gauntlet of the Soviet air defense system: the EWO or Electronic Warfare Officer.

When I first got to this B-52 base, I began to ask: "What are we working on?" Again, just like in Thailand, the answer was, "Just fix the damn boxes." I'd always be the one in the shop going, well, "Why? What are we jamming? How many Soviet radar types are there? What does each one of them they do? How do we know about them? How did someone know to build these jammers to these specifications? How do these bombers penetrate Soviet airspace? How, when and where did the EWO use his equipment?" People used to just look at me: why are you asking these questions?

But now I was running the part of the electronic warfare shop that repaired the receivers and could get some of my questions answered. The receiver I worked on, the ALR-20, when turned off looked like nothing more than a big orange TV display. But it was the main display for the EWO on the B-52 for situational awareness. When it was on, the EWO could see every signal from one end of the electromagnetic spectrum to the other and for a long way out around the aircraft. Think of the most amazing spectrum analyzer you could build with 1960s technology. Then think some more.

In time of war, the B-52's would be piloted into Soviet territory at 500mph at 500 feet above the ground (by eyeball and by using some pretty sophisticated low-light TV and infrared cameras.) Sitting behind the pilots, the EWO was also steering the plane, but he was taking it through the hostile electromagnetic spectrum. He was constantly looking at the multiple lines on the ALR-20 display and could see the Soviet radar order of battle: ground to air communications, what radars were around (search, acquisition, tracking, etc.), were they about to get locked on the bomber and whether they were going to get a SAM up their rear or was it going to be an air-to-air missile from a fighter. And because of his training, an EWO could identify and prioritize the threats.

The signals displayed by the ALR-20 were used to control the jammers of the rest of electronic countermeasures systems – putting out enormous number of kilowatts using brute force noise jamming and later on some much more sophisticated jamming techniques. All of this was designed to make the plane if not invisible to Soviet radar, at least really difficult to lock onto and shoot down.

Just to rank how difficult it was to protect a B-52 in a dense defensive radar environment, our current B-2 stealth bomber has a radar signature of about an aluminum marble, while the B-52 designed in 1950 has the radar signature of a 170-foot sphere. It was like trying to fly a whale through a fish tank and not get noticed.

(I remember a few times when the bombers were flying practice missions over their test ranges. On the way home the Electronic Warfare Officer would "accidentally" turn on the communications jammers over populated parts of the U.S. and shut down television and FM radio stations for hundreds of miles. This stuff was so powerful it probably could affect the Nielsen ratings. When they landed, the EWOs would write it up as an "equipment malfunction." I could never tell if they had a sense of humor or just wanted to see if the equipment would work in the real world.)

Peace Is Our Profession – Is It a Drill?

In front of the entrance to every Strategic Air Command air base was a sign that said, "Peace is our Profession." No joke. Really. Yet every time I came back to base, I kept thinking about whether this was the day for the alert drills.

At this time in the cold war, several B-52s at every Strategic Air Command base were on ground alert – they were loaded with nuclear weapons, had their orders and targets and were cocked and ready to take off to execute their mission – to destroy some part of the Soviet Union with large nuclear weapons. All as an integral part of the Strategic Integrated Operating Plan – our war-fighting plan to destroy the Soviet Union. When the alert sirens sounded, the bomber crews and the ground crews raced for their planes and they and their KC-135 refueling tankers would practice like they were about to take off, hoping to miss the incoming Soviet ICBMs and SLBMs intended to destroy the bombers, the base and a good chunk of Michigan.

The problem for the rest of us on the base was that when the alert sirens went off, you did not know it was a drill. I would always look at my watch and count down 10 minutes to see if we would be vaporized by a submarine-launched attack, and then hold my breath for another 15 minutes to see if there were ICBMs coming across the pole to take us out. I wondered if I would actually see the flash or feel anything. At these times, you never forgot that peace was the last profession we were in.

I never got used to it.

Stay Hungry, Stay Curious

When these bombers got their first modern Electronic Countermeasures suite (the ALQ-117 with automatic wide-band receivers and jammers,) I was sent back to school for three months (to scenic Biloxi Mississippi again) to learn how to repair them. This equipment was modern in the sense that it used integrated circuits rather than transistors, and it responded to threats "automagically" rather than requiring the EWO to do something. Learning about integrated circuits in the mid 1970s was fun as it meant learning a whole new language of digital versus analog computing and learning how to use a logic analyzer instead of just an oscilloscope. Little did I know that these integrated circuits were coming from a place I would one day call home, and I'd be working at the companies who were designing them.

But once again, learning about the new electronic warfare equipment meant learning more about the Soviet threat environment and what we knew about the latest Soviet radar order of battle.

So now with a bit more "need to know" and a lot more "I want to know," I started reading all the technical manuals I could get my hands on. One of the wonderful things about a classified location is once you are inside, you have access to everything and can read anything and I did. I not only knew about my equipment but also everyone else's in the shop. And I began to understand a bit about the Soviet radar order of battle at the height of the cold war from reverse engineering what our jammers were designed to counter and what frequencies our receivers were looking at and how the EWOs were trained to use our equipment.

I was always kind of curious. I was always curious about, and asking about, the big picture.

I was 22

The Most Important Company You Never Heard Of

Posted on April 6, 2009 by steveblank |

1978. Two years out of the Air Force, serendipity (which would be my lifelong form of career planning) found me in Silicon Valley working for my first company: ESL. If you're an entrepreneur, ESL is the most important company you've never heard of. If you are a practitioner of Customer Development, ESL was doing it before most us were born. If you think the Cold War turned out the right side up (i.e. Communism being a bad science experiment,) ESL's founder Bill Perry was moving the chess pieces. And no one who really knew could tell you.

Bill Perry's public life as Secretary of Defense and his subsequent work in preventing nuclear proliferation and nuclear terrorism is public knowledge. But part of his life that that doesn't even merit a Wikipedia entry is that Bill Perry used Silicon Valley to help end the cold war.

Fred Terman Sent Us

In 1953 the U.S. Army needed to build missile and proximity fuse jammers and Quick Reaction Capability (QRC) systems (translation: the other side just came up with something that's killing us in a shooting war. Get us a fix quick.) The Army offered Fred Terman, the Dean of Engineering at Stanford, a $5M contract to build an electronics countermeasures lab. When Terman said no, Sylvania, a tube company which built proximity fuse tubes in WWII, won the contract and set up its Electronic Defense Lab (EDL) in Mountain View California in the middle of an orchard. Terman became a consultant to the company.

In ten years, Sylvania EDL grew to be one the largest companies in the valley with 1300 people working on electronic countermeasures and electronic intelligence. By 1961, its customers now included our intelligence agencies. (BTW, when the customers were "three-letter" intelligence agencies, contractors used an oblique way of talking about who they were working for: they were all referred to as simply the "customer.")

In 1964, Bill Perry, the head of the lab, frustrated with GTE's management, quit (GTE, a phone company had bought Sylvania in 1959.) And in the tradition of great startups, on the way out Perry took 6 of his best managers with him.

240

At ESL Military Intelligence Was No Longer an Oxymoron

Perry not only took his best managers, but he also took his customers, and his desire to build a company culture that was the antithesis of working for a phone company. In building ESL, Perry made a conscious choice to emulate Hewlett Packard (then considered the "gold standard" of a great technology company.) HP had an ethical culture, entrepreneurial spirit, and deep Stanford engineering department connections. One key difference: unlike HP, which had restricted stock ownership to the founders and top management, Perry made sure everyone at ESL had stock. There were no venture investors. The "customers'" contracts funded the company. Seven years later, in 1971, ESL went public.

Not surprising with a CEO with a PhD in Math, at ESL the engineers ran the company, pursuing bleeding-edge designs in antennas, receivers and microwaves – at times hand in hand with Stanford's engineering department. (Some of this stuff was so advanced that the rumors were that we got it from the alien spacecraft hidden at Wright-Patterson Air Force base.)

ESL was unique among the "we do microwaves" that the Valley specialized in before it was Silicon Valley. ESL was a systems company that used computers, and in the mid-1960's, using computers for electronic intelligence was considered revolutionary. ESL specialized in embedding minicomputers in electronic intelligence systems, turning a tedious manual process into one that looked like magic. The "customers" in Washington had never seen anything like it.

While those computer-based systems paid the bills, Perry's even more profound insight would change the outcome of the Cold War. Up until ESL, radio and radar signals had always been received by analog receivers. ESL realized that by turning these radio waves into computer bits, ones and zeros, they could be processed in ways that had been considered theoretically impossible. ESL's systems allowed signal extraction and correlation against targets the Soviet Union thought were undetectable and impenetrable. But this digital world required new theories, and new devices – two items provided by Silicon Valley in the form of Stanford's engineering department and the emerging/booming semiconductor business.

ESL and "the Customer" – No Such Agency

ESL kept getting business and growing mostly through unsolicited bids. Because they were extremely good at what they did, most of the contracts they won were "sole source." However, it didn't hurt that Perry several allies at the "customer." One of them, Bud Wheelon, had been a classmate of Perry's at Stanford, and they both had worked on the electronic intelligence collection problem, Perry at Sylvania EDL and Wheelon at the Space Technology Lab at Ramo Woolridge. In 1962, Wheelon left for a new job as the first director of the CIA's Directorate of Science and Technology where he was responsible for development of OXCART, the A-12 Spyplane, and three major satellite reconnaissance systems. These would become the heart of ESL's business.

ESL found other ways to stay very close to its customers. Forty years before Agile Development methodologies became popular, ESL had analysts from its "customer" sitting side-by-side with ESL engineers designing new equipment together. And in the 1960s, ESL's customers asked the company to analyze and interpret telemetry data even though this was a traditional function of the "customer." In five years, ESL went from a plucky startup to the market leader in Sigint and telemetry intercepts. While it was a for-profit company, Perry believed ESL's goal was to serve the national interest instead of just the stockholders. He identified with their customers, not shareholders. If there was a conflict between profits and doing the right thing, at ESL the goal was to "think of the country first." Yet ESL was just act one for Bill Perry.

Yes We Can – Dumping Detente – Bill Perry and "the Revolution in Military Affairs"

After 20 years of an escalating arms race, the Nixon administration decided to take a new approach to dealing with the Soviet Union: Détente. Kissenger's thinking was: history may be tilting to the Communists, and we may not be able to win the struggle with the Soviet Union so let's settle for parity. Yet while the U.S. had been engaged in the Vietnam War, and had agreed to parity in nuclear weapons, Soviet forces in Europe had built a 3 to 1 advantage in tanks, artillery, armored personnel carriers, and soldiers, all under Détente.

In response, the U.S. dumped Détente and embraced a new strategy to counter the Warsaw Pact by not matching them tank for tank or solider to solider. The new insight was that we could change the game completely and take advantage of a lead we had that was getting longer every day by using *our computer and chip technology to aggressively build a new generation of weapons that the Soviet Union could not build.*

At the heart of this idea was something called "precision strike," what we would today call smart bombs or precision guided munitions. But this new strategy was more than making the bombs smarter. It involved building stealth aircraft to deliver these precision weapons unseen by any enemy radar, and designing intelligence and reconnaissance systems that would target for them. *Smart weapons, smart sensors, and stealth*. And the heart of all of this were microwaves, silicon chips, electronics and computers that only the U.S. could design and produce, and a good part of it was coming from Silicon Valley.

The Arms Factories that Won the Cold War Were Semiconductor Factories

Who was the government official pushing all of this? It was none other than Bill Perry, who had become the head of Research and Engineering for the Defense Department. From 1977 to 1981 Perry cranked up spending for research and development on a massive scale. The budget for the Defense Advanced Research Projects Agency (DARPA) doubled, and huge "smart weapons" defense programs were funded: the F-117 stealth ground attack plane and the B-2 stealth bomber; precision guided munitions; JSTARS, a surveillance system; and the satellite Global Positioning System (GPS); MX missile; Trident submarine; and Tomahawk cruise missiles.

These changes in American defense policy spooked the Soviets. The Chief of Staff of the Red Army said that this "Offset Strategy" was revolutionizing contemporary warfare and posed a military threat that the Red Army could not match. "We cannot equal the quality of US arms for a generation or two. . . . We will never be able to catch up with you in modern arms until we have an economic revolution. And the question is whether we can have an economic revolution without a political revolution."

The U.S. Cold War strategy had gone from a "let's be friends" to a "yes we can win" strategy. By the mid 1980s Ronald Reagan was cranking U.S. defense spending even higher. Gorbachev, now the Soviet Premier, had to grapple with the spiraling cost of military systems that weren't amortized by consumer purchases. Arms control with the U.S. and massive cuts in weapons and the military seemed like the only way out. And the rest is history.

Bill Perry put us on the path to use Silicon Valley as a weapon in the cold war.

My small part as a foot solider in this adventure is in the next post.

Library Hours at an Undisclosed Location

Posted on April 13, 2009 by steveblank |

All You Can Read Without a Library Card

It was 1978. Here I was, a very junior employee of ESL, a company with its hands in the heart of our Cold War strategy. Clueless about the chess game being played in Washington, I was just a minion in a corporate halfway house in between my military career and entrepreneurship.

ESL sent me overseas to a secret site run by one of the company's "customers." It was so secret the entire site could have qualified as one of Dick Cheney's "undisclosed locations." As a going away gift, my roommates got me a joke disguise kit with a fake nose, glasses and mustache.

The ESL equipment were racks of the latest semiconductors designed into a system so complicated that the mean-time-between-failure was measured in days. Before leaving California, the engineers gave me a course in this specialized receiver design. Since I had spent the last four years working on advanced Air Force electronic intelligence receivers, I thought there wouldn't be anything new. The reality was pretty humbling. Here was a real-world example of the Cold War "offset strategy." Taking concepts that had been only abstract PhD theses, ESL had built receivers so sensitive they seemed like science fiction. For the first time we were able to process analog signals (think radio waves) and manipulate them in the digital domain. We were combining Stanford Engineering theory with ESL design engineers and implementing it with chips so new we were debugging the silicon as we were debugging the entire system. And we were using thousands of chips in a configuration no rational commercial customer could imagine or afford. The concepts were so radically different that I spent weeks dreaming about the system theory and waking up with headaches. Nothing I would work on in the next 30 years was as bleeding edge.

Now half a world away on the customer site, my very small role was to keep our equipment running and train the "customer." As complex as it was, our subsystem was only maybe one-twentieth of what was contained in that entire site. Since this was a location that worked 24/7, I was on the night shift (my favorite time of the day.) Because I could get through what I needed to do quickly, there wasn't much else to do except to read. As the sun came up, I'd step out of the chilled buildings and go for an early morning run outside the perimeter fence to beat the desert heat. As I ran, if I looked at the base behind the fence I was staring at the most advanced technology of the 20th century. Yet if turned my head the other way, I'd stare out at a landscape that was untouched by humans.

(At the end of a run, I used to lay out and relax on the rocks to rest – at least I did, until

244

the guards asked if I knew that there were more poisonous things per square foot here than anywhere in the world.)

I was in one of the most isolated places on earth yet here I was wired into everywhere on earth. Coming to work I would walk down the very long, silent, empty corridors, open a non-descript door and enter the operations floor (which looked like a miniature NASA Mission Control), plug a headset into the networked audio that connected all the console operators – and hear the Rolling Stones "Sympathy for the Devil." (With no apparent irony.) But when the targets lit up, the music and chatter would stop, and the communications would get very professional.

Before long I realized that down the hall sat all the manuals for all the equipment at the entire site - twenty times more technical reading than just my equipment. Although all the manuals were in safes, the whole site was so secure that anybody who had access to that site had access to everything – including other compartmentalized systems that had nothing to do with me – and that I wasn't cleared for. Back home at ESL control of compartmentalized documents were incredibly strict. As a contractor handling the "customer's" information, ESL went by the book with librarians inside the vaults and had strict document access and control procedures. In contrast, this site belonged to the "customer." They set their own rules about how documents were handled, and the safes were open to everyone.

I was now inside the firewall with access to everything. It never dawned on me that this might not be a good idea.

Starting on the safe on the left side, moving to the safe on the right side, I planned to read my way through every technical manual of every customer system. We're talking about a row of 20 or so safes each with five drawers, and each drawer full of manuals. Because I kept finding interesting connections and new facts, I kept notes, and since the whole place was classified, I thought, "Oh, I'll keep the notes in one of these safes." So I started a notebook, dutifully noting the classification of each of the manuals I had read on the top and bottom of each page. As I ran into more systems I added the additional code words that on the classification headers. Soon each page of my notes had a header and footer that read something like this: Top Secret / codeword / codeword / codeword / codeword / codeword / codeword.

Nine months into my year tour, and seven months into my reading program, I was learning something interesting every day. (We could do what!? From where??) Then one day I got a call from the head of security to say, "Hey, Steve can you stop into my office when you get a chance?"

Are These Yours?

Now this was a small site, about 200-300 people, and here was the head of security asking me over for coffee. How nice, I thought, he just wants to get to know me better. (Duh.) When I got to his office, we made small talk and then he opened a small envelope, tapped it on a white sheet of paper, and low and behold, three or four long black curly hairs fell out. "Are these yours?" he asked me.

This was one of the very few times I've been, really, really impressed. I said, "Why yes they are, where did you get them?" He replied, 'They were found in the 'name of system I should have absolutely no knowledge or access to' manuals. Were you reading those?" I said, "Absolutely." When he asked me, "Were you reading anything else?" I explained, "Well I started on the safe on the left, and have been reading my way through and I'm about three quarters of the way done."

Now it was his turn to be surprised. He just stared at me for a while. "Why on earth are you doing that?" he said in a real quiet voice. I blurted out, "Oh, it's really interesting, I never knew all this stuff, and I've been making all these notes, and . . ." I never quite understood the word "startled" before this moment. He did a double-take out of the movies and interrupted me, "You've been making notes?" I said, "Yeah, it's like a puzzle," I explained. "I found out all this great stuff and kept notes and stored in the safe on the bottom right under all the. . ." He literally ran out of the office to the safes and got my notebook and started reading it in front of me.

And the joke (now) was that even though this was the secret, secret, secret, secret site, the document I had created was more secret than the site.

While the manuals described technical equipment, I was reading about all the equipment and making connections and seeing patterns across 20 systems. And when I wasn't reading, I was also teaching operations, which gave me a pretty good understanding of what we were looking for on the other side. At times we got the end product reports from the "customer" back at the site which these allowed me to understand how our system was cued by other sensors collecting other parts of the electromagnetic spectrum, and to start looking for them, then figuring out what their capabilities were.

Pattern Recognition

As I acquired a new piece of data a new set of my neurons would light up, and I would correlate it, write it down and go back through reams of manuals remembering that there was a mention elsewhere of something connected. By the time the security chief and I were having our 'curly hairs in the envelope' conversation not only did I know what every single part of our site did, but what scared the security guy is that I had also put together a pretty good guesstimate of what other systems we had in place worldwide.

246

For one small moment in time, I may have assembled a picture of the sum of the state of U.S. signals intelligence in 1978, the breadth and depth of the integrated system of technical assets we had in space, air, land, and other places all focused on collection. (If you're a techie, you'd be blown away even 30 years later.) And the document that the head of security had in his hand and was reading, as he told me later, he wasn't cleared to read – and I wasn't cleared to write or see. I'm sure I knew just a very small fraction of what was going on, but still it was much more than I was cleared for.

At the time this seemed quite funny to me probably because I was completely clueless about what I had done, and thought that no one could believe there was another intent. But in hindsight, rather than the career I did have, I could now just be getting out of federal prison. It still sends shivers up my back. After what I assume were a few phone calls back to Washington, the rules said they couldn't destroy my notebook, but they couldn't keep it at the site either. Instead my notebook was couriered to Washington – back to the "customer." (I picture it still sitting in some secure warehouse.) The head of security and I agreed my library hours were over, and I would take up another hobby until I went home.

Thank you to the security people who could tell the difference between an idiot and a spy.

When I got back to Sunnyvale, my biggest surprise was that I didn't get into trouble. Instead someone realized that the knowledge I had accumulated could provide the big picture to brief new guys "read in" to this compartmentalized program. Of course I had to work with the customer to scrub the information to get its classification back down to our compartmental clearance. (My officemate who would replace me on the site, Richard Farley, would go on to a more tragic career.) I continued to give these briefings as a consultant to ESL even after I had joined my first chip startup; Zilog.

Two Roads Diverged in a Wood and I took the Road Less Traveled By, And That Has Made All the Difference

Extraordinary times bring extraordinary people to the front. Bill Perry, the founder of ESL, is now acknowledged as one of the founders of the entire field of National Reconnaissance, working the NSA and the CIA in programs to intercept and evaluate Soviet missile telemetry and communications intelligence.

ESL had no marketing people. It had no PR agency. It shunned publicity. It was the model for almost every military startup that followed, and its alumni who lived through its engineering and customer-centric culture had a profound effect on the rest of the valley, the intelligence community and the country. And during the Cold War it sat side by side with commercial firms in Silicon Valley, with its nondescript sign on the front lawn. It had Hidden in Plain Sight.

As for me, after a few years, I decided that into was time to turn swords into plowshares. I left ESL and the black world for a career in startups; semiconductors, supercomputers, consumer electronics, video games and enterprise software.

I never looked back.

It would be decades before I understood what an extraordinary company I had worked for.

Thank you Bill Perry for one hell of a start in Silicon Valley.

I was 24.

My first class of students at ESL: Guardrail V Training Class (note the long black curly hairs)

Happy 100th Birthday Silicon Valley

Posted on **April 20, 2009** by steveblank |

When the legend becomes fact, print the legend. - The Man Who Shot Liberty Valance

I always had been curious about how Silicon Valley, a place I had lived and worked in, came to be. Throughout my career as an entrepreneur, I kept asking questions of my VC investors and friends; where did entrepreneurship come from? How did Silicon Valley start? Why here? Why now? How did this culture of "make it happen" emerge? etc. And the answer came back much as it did in my past jobs; "Who cares, get back to work."

After I retired, Jerry Engel, director of the Lester Center on Entrepreneurship, at U.C. Berkeley Haas Business School, was courageous enough to give me a forum to teach the Customer Development Methodology. As I was researching my class text, I thought it would be simple enough to read up on a few histories of the valley and finally get my questions about the genesis of entrepreneurship answered.

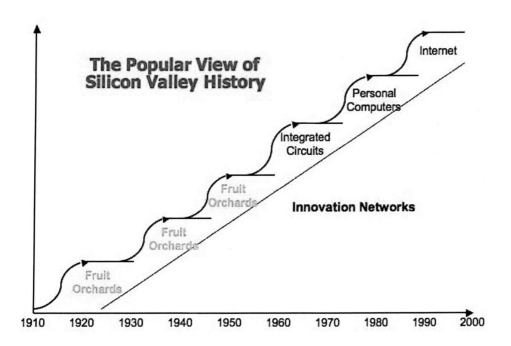

The Legend: HP, Intel and Apple

I read all the popular books about the valley, which all told a variant of the same story: entrepreneurs as heroes building the semiconductor and personal computer companies; Bill Hewlett and David Packard at HP, Bob Taylor and the team at Xerox PARC, Steve Jobs and Wozniak at Apple, Gordon Moore and Bob Noyce at Intel, etc. These were inspiring stories, but I realized that, no surprise, the popular press were writing books that had mass appeal. They were all fun reads about plucky entrepreneurs who start from nothing and against all odds, build a successful company.

But no one was writing about where the valley's entrepreneurial culture had come from. Where were the books explaining why were all these chip and computer companies started here? Why not elsewhere in the country or the world? With the exception of Anna Lee Saxenian's great book *Regional Advantage*, no one wrote about what made this part of the country unique. Was t because entrepreneurs keep moving forward and rarely look back? I needed to dig deeper.

The Facts: Vacuum Tube Valley – Our 100th Anniversary

To my surprise, I discovered that yes, Silicon Valley did start in a garage in Palo Alto, but *it didn't start in the Hewlett Packard garage.* The first electronics company in Silicon Valley was Federal Telegraph, a tube company started in 1909 in Palo Alto as Poulsen Wireless. (October 2009 is the 100th anniversary of Silicon Valley, unnoticed and unmentioned by anyone.) By 1912, Lee Deforest working at Federal Telegraph would invent the Triode, (a tube amplifier) and would go on to become the Steve Jobs of his day – visionary, charismatic and controversial.

* Federal Telegraph and Lee Deforest in Palo Alto are the first major events in what would become Silicon Valley. We need to reset our Silicon Valley birthday calendars to here.

By 1937, when Bill Hewlett and David Packard left Stanford to start HP, the agricultural fields outside of Stanford had already become "Vacuum Tube Valley." HP was a supplier of electronic test equipment and joined a small but thriving valley electronics industry with companies like Litton and Eitel and McCollough.

* By the late 1930's when HP started, a small group (measured in hundreds) of engineers who made radio tubes were building the valley" ecosystem for electronics manufacturing, product engineering and technology management.

Who would have known?

250

Microwave Valley – the 1950's and '60's

There isn't much written about Silicon Valley during and after World War II. The story of the valley post war, through the 1950's, is mostly about the growth of the tube companies and the rise of Hewlett Packard. The popular literature has the valley springing to life in the 1960's with the semiconductor revolution started by Shockley, Fairchild, Signetics, National and Intel, followed by the emergence of the personal computer in the mid 1970's.

But the more I read, the more I realized that the public histories of the valley in the 1950's and '60's *were incomplete and just plain wrong.* The truth was that huge dollars had been spent on a large number of companies that never made the press or into the history books. Companies specializing in components and systems that operated in the microwave portion of the electromagnetic spectrum sprouted faster than fruit trees in the valley orchards. In ten years, from the early 1950's to the early 1960's, the valley went through a hiring frenzy as jobs in microwave companies grew from 700 to 7,000.

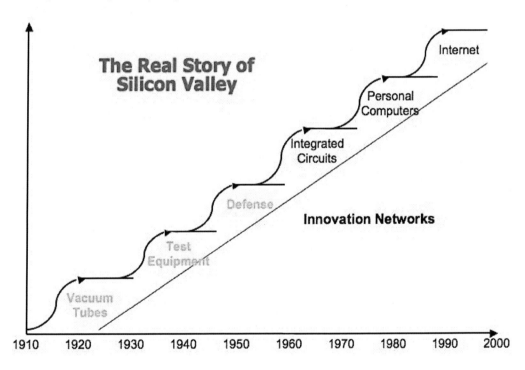

This wave of 1950's/'60's startups (Watkins-Johnson, Varian, Huggins Labs, MEC, Stewart Engineering, etc.) were making a dizzying array of new microwave components: power grid tubes, klystrons, magnetrons, backward wave oscillators, traveling wave tubes (TWT's), cross-field amplifiers, gyrotrons, and on, on. And literally across the valley, these microwave devices were being built into complete systems for the U.S. military by other new startups; Sylvania Electronics Defense Laboratory, Granger Associates, Philco, Dalmo Victor, ESL and Argosystems. In the 1950's and

'60's, more money was pouring into these companies than on the fledgling chip and computer companies.

The 10x expansion in the number of engineers in the valley in the 1950's came from the military and microwaves – before the semiconductor boom. And these microwave engineers were working at startups – not large companies. You never heard of them because their work was secret.

When I read the funny names of these microwaves devices: Backward wave oscillators, TWT's, Magnetrons, long silent memories came back. These components were the heart of the electronic warfare equipment I have worked on; including fighters in Thailand and on B-52 bombers. After 20 years, the story started coming home for me.

The Revolution Wasn't Televised

What the heck happened here to create this burst of innovation? What created this microwave startup culture in the 1950's? And since there was no venture capital in the 1950's/'60's, where was the money coming from? This startup boom seemed to come out of nowhere. Why was it occurring here? And why on earth the sudden military interest in microwaves?

Part of the answer was that these companies and the military had forged some type of relationship. And it appeared that Stanford University's engineering department was in middle of all this. The formation of the military/industrial/university relationships during the Cold War and the relationship between Stanford and the intelligence community in particular went on untold and out of sight.

While nothing I read described the actual products being worked on, or what specifically was Stanford's contribution, there were some really tantalizing pointers to who the real customers were (hint, it wasn't just the "military,") or why was this work was being done at Stanford.

No one knew that it all pointed to just one guy at the center of it all - *Fred Terman of Stanford* University.

Stanford, the military and our intelligence agencies started the wave of entrepreneurial culture that today's Silicon Valley takes for granted.

Every World War II Movie was Wrong

Posted on April 27, 2009 by steveblank |

The next piece of the Secret History of Silicon Valley puzzle came together when Tom Byers, Tina Selig and Kathy Eisenhardt invited me to teach entrepreneurship in the Stanford Technology Ventures Program (STVP) in Stanford's School of Engineering. My office is in the Terman Engineering Building.

Fred Terman – the Cover Story

I'd heard of Terman, but I didn't really know what he did. His biography reported that he was one of the preeminent radio engineers in the 1930's literally writing the textbooks. He was the professor who helped his students Bill Hewlett and David Packard start a company in 1939. In World War II, he headed up something called the Harvard Radio Research Lab. There was plenty in his biography about his post WWII activities: chair of electrical engineering in 1937, dean of engineering in 1946, provost in 1955. In 1954 he started the Stanford Honors Co-op which allowed companies in the valley to send their engineers to Stanford graduate engineering programs.

Since I was interested in the history of Silicon Valley, Entrepreneurship, and now Terman, I began to understand that Terman had a lot to do with the proliferation of microwave companies in Silicon Valley in the 1950's and '60's. But how? And why? So I started to read all I could find on the development of microwaves. That led me back to the history of radar in World War II – and a story you may not know.

What Does WWII Have to Do with Silicon Valley?

Just a quick history refresher. In December 1941, the Japanese attack Pearl Harbor, and Germany declares war on the United States. And while the Soviets are fighting the Germans in massive land battles in eastern Europe, until the allies invade Western Europe in June 1944, the only way the U.S. and Britain can affect German war-fighting capability is by mounting a Strategic Bombing campaign, from England. Their goal was to destroy the German capability to wage war by aerial bombing the critical infrastructure of the German war machine.

The allies bombed every important component of German infrastructure: petroleum, aircraft manufacturing, chemical, and transportation. The Americans and British split up the air campaign: the British bombed at night, the Americans during the day.

The Odds Weren't Good

These bombers flew for 7+ hours from England and over occupied Europe, through a gauntlet of intense antiaircraft fire and continuous attack by German fighter planes. And they got it coming and going to the target.

But what the bomber crews didn't know was that the antiaircraft fire and German fighters they encountered were controlled via a sophisticated radar-guided electronic air defense system covering all of occupied Europe and Germany.

The German electronic air defense system was designed to detect the allied bomber raids, target and aim the German radar-guided weapons, and destroy the American and British bombers. The German air defense system had 100's of early warning radars, *and thousands* of radar controlled anti-aircraft guns and Ground Controlled Intercept radars to guide the fighters into the bombers.

And the German night fighters had their own on-board radar. In all the Germans had over *7,500 radars* dedicated to tracking and killing the allied bombers.

Each allied bombing mission lost 2-20% of their planes. Bomber crews had to fly 25 missions to go home. The German objective was to make strategic bombing too costly for the Allies to continue.

By 1942 the Allied Air Command recognized they needed to reduce allied losses to fighters and flak. We needed a way to shut down the German Air Defense system. (Bear with me as this history takes you from the skies of Europe to Fred Terman.)

The Electronic Shield

To shut down the German air defense system, the Allies first needed to understand the German "Radar Order of Battle." What radars did the Germans have and what were their technical characteristics? How effective they were? What weapons were they associated with? The Allies needed to find out all this stuff and figure out how to confuse it and make it ineffective.

So the U.S. set up a top secret, 800-person lab to do just that, first, to gather signals intelligence to understand the "Radar Order of Battle" and then, to wage "electronic warfare" by building mechanical and electronic devices to severely hamper the Germans' ability to target and aim their weapons.

254

Ferrets and Crows – Signals Intelligence

The first job of the secret lab was to find and understand the German air defense system. To do this, we invented the U.S. Signals Intelligence industry in about 12 months (with help from their British counterparts at the Telecommunications Research Establishment.) The mission of the planes called Ferrets, manned by crews called Crows, was to find and understand the German electronic air defense system. We stripped out B-17 bombers in the Mediterranean theater and B-24 bombers over Occupied Germany, removed all the bomb racks, took out all the bombs and even took out all the guns. Then we filled it with racks of receivers and displays, wire and strip recorders and communications intercept equipment that could search the electromagnetic spectrum from 50 megahertz to 3 gigahertz.

These unarmed planes flew in and out of Germany alongside our bombers and basically built up the "radar order of battle." We now understood where the German radars were, their technical details, and what weapons they controlled.

Tin Foil Rain – Chaff

The Allies first decided to shut down the German radars that were directing the anti-aircraft guns and the fighter planes. And to do that *we dropped tin foil on the Germans.* No kidding. Radar engineers had observed if you cut a strip of aluminum foil to 1/2 the wavelength of a radar transmitter and throw it in front of the radars antenna, the radar signal would reflect perfectly. The radar operator would see noise instead of airplanes.

Well, you couldn't stand in front of the German radars and throw out tin foil, but you could if you had a fleet of airplanes. Each plane threw out packets of aluminum foil (called "chaff".) The raid on Hamburg in July 1943 was the first use of chaff in World War II. It completely shut down the German air defense system in and around Hamburg. The British firebombed the city with minimal air losses.

Chaff consumed three-fourths of all the aluminum foil in the U.S. in World War II because by the end of the war, every bomber stream was dumping chaff on every mission.

Jam It and Shut it Down - Electronic Warfare

Since this secret lab was focused on electronic warfare, they systematically designed electronic devices called "jammers" to shut down each part of the German air defense system. Think of a "jammer" as a radio transmitter broadcasting noise on the same frequency of the enemy radar set. The goal is to overwhelm the enemy radar with noise so they couldn't see the bombers. We built electronic jammers to target each part of the German air defense system: their early warning radars, the short range radars, the antiaircraft gun radars, the Ground Control Intercept Radars, the air to ground radio links and even the radars onboard the German night fighters. By the end of the war we had put multiple jammers on every one of our bombers. While their power output was ridiculously low, these jammers were flying in formation with 1,000 other planes fitted with jammers so the combined power was enough to confuse the radar operators.

Just to give you a sense of scale of how big this electronic warfare effort was, we built over 30,000 jammers, with entire factories running 24/7 in the U.S. making nothing but jammers to put on our bombers.

By the end of World War II, over Europe, a bomber stream no longer consisted of only planes with bombs. Now the bombers were accompanied by electronics intelligence planes looking for new radar signals, escort bombers full of jammers and others full of chaff, as well as P-51 fighter planes patrolling alongside our bomber stream. (Ultimately it would be the P-51 fighter escorts that would reduce U.S. daylight bomber losses to German fighters.)

Every WWII Movie and Book with a Bomber was Wrong
While there were lots of stories about how the British early warning radar system, called "Chain Home" saved England during the Battle of Britain by giving the Spitfire pilots time to scramble to intercept German bombers, there wasn't a coherent story about American and British bombers encountering the German radar-guided air defense system.

This lack of information meant that every World War II movie or book with airplanes on bombing missions in it was wrong. Every one of them. (To someone who had grown up with reruns of WWII war movies on TV, this was a shock.) Every movie I had seen – *12 O'clock High*, *Memphis Belle*, etc. – assumed that there were no electronics other than radios on these bombers. Wrong. Not only the moviemakers but also the actual pilots and crews did not know the size and scale of the German radar guided system trying to kill them. Nor did they know the full extent of resources put in place to provide the electronic shield being assembled to try to protect them.

But while this may be a great story, what the does this have to do with the history of Silicon Valley?

The answer lies with who ran this lab, the man who became the father of electronic warfare and signals intelligence in the Cold War for the next 20 years.

Who Ran the Most Secret Lab You Never Heard of?

The man was *Fred Terman of Stanford*. The Harvard Radio Research Lab was his creation. A Stanford professor was at Harvard in World War II because the head of the Office of Scientific Research and Development thought Terman was the best radio engineer in the country. (Why couldn't he have set up a lab at Stanford? Apparently, the Office of Scientific Research thought that Stanford's engineering department was second rate.)

Finally, I had an answer to the question I had asked 35 years earlier when I was in Thailand: "How did electronic warfare get started?" Now I knew that it began in the early days of World War II as a crash program to reduce the losses of bombers to the German air defense network. *Electronic warfare and signals intelligence in the U.S. started with Fred Terman and the Harvard Radio Research Lab.*

Spooky Music

Reading about Terman was like finding the missing link in my career. Here was the guy who invented the field where I had spent the first five years of my adult life working on. And 30 years later, I was teaching in a building named after him and never knew a thing about him. Play spooky music here.

I began to realize that everything the U.S. had done in electronic warfare in the Vietnam War was just a slightly more modern version of what we had done over occupied Europe in World War II. (And in hindsight, we seemed a bit more agile and innovative in WWII.)

Unbelievably, in less than two years, Terman's Radio Research lab invented an industry and had turned out a flurry of new electronic devices, the likes of which had never been seen. Yet decades later the military lacked the agility to write a spec in two years, let alone get 10's of thousands of new systems deployed on aircraft as Terman had done. How was this possible? *In 21ˢᵗ century terminology, we'd say that Terman built the Radio Research lab into a customer-centric organization doing agile development.*

Just the Beginning

The public history of Terman's involvement with the military ends when he returns back to Stanford at the end of the war. Nothing in his biography or any Stanford history mentions anything as exciting as his work in World War II. The public story of his last 20 years at Stanford, in the 1950's and '60's, has him settle into the role of the kindly dean and innovative provost.

Nothing could be further from the truth.

We Fought a War You Never Heard Of

Posted on August 3, 2009 by steveblank |

The Birth of Entrepreneurship in The Hot Cold War

Silicon Valley entrepreneurship was born in the middle of a secret war with the Soviet Union. It's a war you probably never heard of since most of it was classified, and both parties never wanted it public lest it got out of hand. Yet it was a war in which tens of thousands of Americans fought and hundreds died. Frederick Terman, Stanford's Dean of Engineering, enlisted Stanford University as a major arms supplier in this war. In doing so he accidentally launched entrepreneurship in Silicon Valley – with the help of the U.S. military, the CIA and the National Security Agency.

Stanford as a Center of Microwave and Electronics

In 1946 after running the military's secret 800 person Electronic Warfare Lab at Harvard, Fred Terman returned to Stanford as the dean of the Engineering School. Terman's goal was to build Stanford's electrical engineering department into a center of excellence focused on microwaves and electronics. Having already assembled one of most advanced electronic labs in World War II, Terman was one of the few academics who could do it.

Terman's first step was to recruit 11 former members of his staff from the Harvard Radio Research Lab — "Congratulations, you're now Stanford faculty." Not only were they all great researchers, but they also had just spent three years building electronic warfare systems that were used in World War II. They would become the core of Stanford's new Electronics Research Lab (ERL.) While officially in the electrical engineering department, the lab reported directly to Terman.

Next, Terman used his military contacts to secure funding for the Lab from the Office of Naval Research, the Air Force and the Army Signal Corps. (Although the country had returned to peace, some in the military wanted to preserve our ability to fight the next war.) By 1947 the U.S. military was funding half of Stanford's engineering school budget. Terman proudly pointed out that only Stanford, MIT and Harvard had a military sponsored electronics program.

Stanford Leads in Electronic Intelligence and Electronic Warfare

In the 1950's Stanford Engineering Research Lab (ERL) made major contributions to electronic intelligence and electronic warfare. Its basic research focused on three areas: microwave receiving and transmitting tubes, radar detection and deception techniques and the study of the earth's ionosphere.

258

Stanford became one of the leading research centers in advancing the state of microwave tubes including the klystron which provided high-power microwave in pulses, magnetrons which provided continuous wave microwave power, and backward wave oscillators and traveling wave tubes – both electronically tunable microwave tubes.

Stanford's research on the earth's ionosphere would lead to meteor-burst communication systems and Over the Horizon Radar used by the NSA and CIA to detect Soviet and Chinese missile tests and ultimately to the research that made Stealth technologies possible.

Its studies in radar detection and deception techniques would lead Stanford to the applied part of it mission. Stanford would build prototypes of electronic intelligence receivers (high probability of intercept/rapid scan receivers) for use by the military. These applied systems were prototypes of the jamming devices found on our bombers and receivers found in NSA ground stations and the fleet of ELINT aircraft flying around and in the Soviet Union and later on in the U-2, SR-71 and ELINT ferret subsatellites.

Later posts will talk about these technologies and the startups that spun out of Stanford to build them. But first, to understand what happened at Stanford and in Silicon Valley under Fred Terman, some context about the Cold War is helpful. (Skip the next section if you're a history major.)

The Cold War

After World War II ended, our wartime ally, the Soviet Union, kept its army in Eastern Europe and forcibly installed Communist governments in its occupied territories. Meanwhile, the U.S. demobilized its army, sent its troops home, scrapped most of its Air Force and mothballed almost all its Navy. As tensions rose, there was a growing fear that the Soviets could invade and occupy all of Western Europe.

In 1949, the Soviets exploded their first nuclear weapon and ended the U.S monopoly on atomic weaponry. That same year China fell to the communists under Mao Zedong, and the Nationalist government retreated to Taiwan. A year later the Korean War turned the cold war hot, as communist North Koreans attacked and overran most of South Korea (except for a small defensive perimeter in the south.) American and United Nations troops entered the war fighting North Koreans and then Communist Chinese ground troops, and Soviet fighter pilots for three years. 34,000 U.S. soldiers died in battle.

To the U.S., the Soviet Union seemed bent on world conquest, with Korea just a warm-up for an atomic war with massive casualties. (This was not an unreasonable supposition after a conventional world war that had left 50 million dead.) Faced with the reality of the Korean War, the U.S. began to rebuild its military. But now the Soviet Union was its target enemy, and nuclear weapons had become the principal instrument of offense. Instead of rebuilding its WWII forces, the U.S. military embraced new technologies (jets, electronics, missiles, nuclear subs) and built entirely new weapon systems (bombers with nuclear weapons, ICBMs, SLBM's) for a new era of international conflict.

Europe, completely outnumbered and outgunned by the Soviet Union, built the North Atlantic Treaty Organization (NATO) as a bulwark against ground Soviet attack. And the U.S. planned strikes with nuclear-armed bombers if war in Europe broke out.

Stanford's Electronic Research Lab (ERL) whic had focused on basic research on microwave tubes from 1946 was about to scale up for the Cold War.

Smarter Intelligence

One of the major differences between the war with Germany and the cold war confrontation with the Soviet Union had to do with access. The Soviet Union was a closed country. Unlike Germany in World War II, the U.S. could not fly across the Soviet Union to learn how their defenses were set up. We did not have radar maps of their cities. The Soviet's secrecy fed our cold war paranoia. The U.S. was determined to find out what was going on inside. And the way we were going to do it was with electronic/signals intelligence.

But the technology that supported intelligence gathering against our WW II enemies was not sufficient to penetrate the Soviet Union. The U.S. military had to develop new ways to collect intelligence. The engineering department and labs that Fred Terman established at Stanford University would play a key role in advancing electronic intercept and jamming technology to support the more sophisticated intelligence systems that the Cold War required.

The Air Force Needs to Know

By the Korean War, U.S. policy held that the Air Force, carrying nuclear weapons into the Soviet Union, would be the means to fight World War III.

Through World War II, the U.S. Air Force had been a part of the U.S. Army. It split off into a separate service in 1947. By the 1950's, the Strategic Air Command (SAC) had become the U.S. Air Force's long range bombing arm and the designated instrument of Armageddon.

On the other side of the Iron Curtain, the defense of the Soviet Motherland lay with the Soviet Air Defense Forces, called PVO Strany, a separate branch of the Soviet military formed in 1948 designed to detect U.S. bomber raids, target and aim radar-guided weapons and destroy the U.S. bombers.

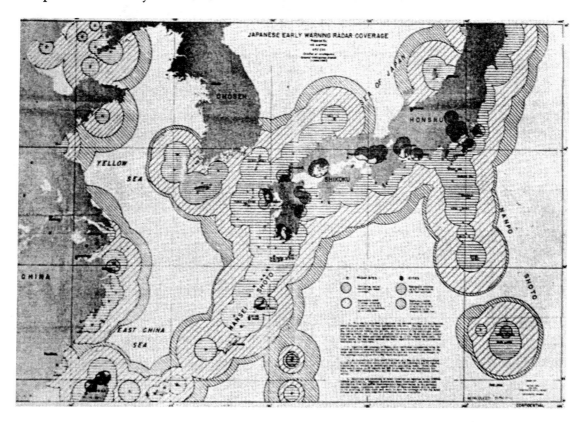

Example of Early Warning Radar Coverage – Japan in WWII

SAC needed intelligence to understand the components of the PVO Strany air defense system in order to shut them down and make them ineffective so our bombers with their nuclear payloads could reach their targets. (The information we collected would be passed on to contractors who would build jamming devices the bombers would carry.) It sought answers to tactical questions like: What was the Radar Order of Battle a penetrating bomber would face? (Were there holes in their radar coverage our bombers could sneak through? What was the best altitude to avoid the Soviet defenses?) What were the different types of Soviet fighter planes? How many? How effective? What about the anti-aircraft (AAA) gun defenses? In addition the Soviets were adding a new type of defensive radar-guided weapon called the Surface to Air Missile (SAM).

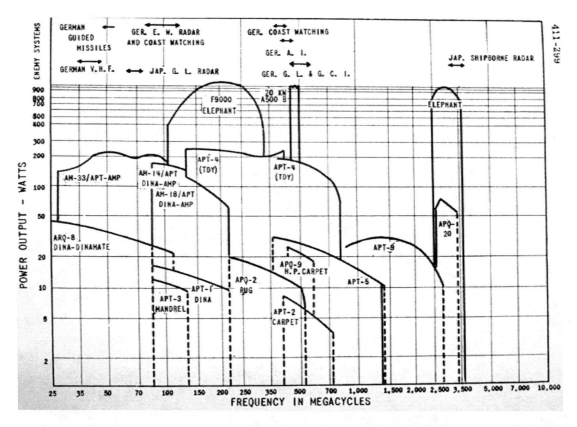

Example of Jammer versus Radar Coverage - Allied Jammers over Germany in WW11

The Strategic Air Command also needed to know what the navigational waypoints and the target would look like on their air-to-ground bombing radars. (These radars painted a map-like picture of the ground and prior to GPS. This is how bombers navigated their way to the target.)

And on top of all this the Strategic Air Command needed to understand the current state of the Soviet Air Defense Force readiness and deployment updated on a daily basis.

The CIA Needs to Know

While the Air Force was working on collecting intelligence to execute their tactical missions, the CIA, founded in 1947, was responsible for providing U.S. political leadership with a much bigger picture. They developed the National Intelligence Estimate – a series of reports which summarized their judgment about the size of the Russian threat. Also seeking to learn more about the Soviet Union's offensive weapon systems, the CIA wanted intelligence to help them understand: What type of strategic bombers did the Soviets have? How many did they have? How would they reach the U.S.? How would we know if they were coming? (Have they moved to their forward operating bases in the Arctic?) The same was true about the Soviet defensive systems – how many fighters would they build and of what type? How many Surface to Air Missiles – what was their range and accuracy?

By the mid 1950's the Soviets were testing ballistic missiles, both intermediate range which could reach Europe and intercontinental range which could reach the U.S. What was their range? What was their accuracy? How big of a nuclear warhead could they carry (throw weight and yield)? The military needed to answer these same questions about the nuclear-armed missiles the Soviets were using on their submarine force.

To give our leadership an estimate of the Soviet's nuclear production capacity, the CIA also had to estimate how many nuclear weapons the Soviet Union could make. Where were their production facilities? What was the yield of the weapons and their weight and size?

Throughout the 1950's the CIA's Office of Scientific Intelligence was heavily involved in the development of Electronics Intercept and Electronic Warfare Intelligence – and Stanford and the emerging startups around it would provide the systems and concepts to help.

The NSA and ELINT

In the 1950's the Strategic Air Command and the U.S. Navy were the airborne ELINT assets for the U.S. Beginning in the mid/late 1950's the National Security Agency (NSA) starting taking more and more responsibility for collection – first in communications intelligence, then in signals and telemetry intelligence. The NSA ultimately built up hundreds of ground stations, satellites and aircraft manned by tens of thousands servicemen (under the cover of the Air Force Security Service, Army Security Agency and the Naval Security Group.)

The "Hot" Cold War

Remember the Soviet Union was a closed country. To collect the intelligence to answer its questions about the Soviet threat, the U.S. military resurrected the signals Intelligence lessons and skills we invented in World War II. Starting in 1946, ELINT aircraft had probed and overflown the Soviet Union. SAC, the CIA, the Navy and our British allies flew modified planes called Ferrets around the periphery of the Soviet Union to understand their air defense system (the crews were called Crows). (What isn't well known is that the U.S. and Britain flew planes on deep penetration missions into and across the Soviet Union numerous times – well before a U-2 spy plane was shot down over the Soviet Union in 1960.)

The Air Force adopted a cover story that these were weather data gathering missions. These flights were no secret to the Soviets, (given the sheer number of surveillance flights around the Soviet Union it's surprising they didn't need their own air traffic control system,) and they started to protest diplomatically in 1948. When our flights continued, the Soviets took direct action. In 1950, two months before the Korean War started, the Soviets shot down an ELINT plane over the Baltic. All ten crewmembers were killed. This was the beginning of a Soviet policy to stop ignoring incursions. They would attempt to force the ELINT planes to land in the Soviet Union or they would destroy them. Every year through the 1950's and the early '60's the Soviets attacked and shot down at least one of our ELINT ferret aircraft. This was a deadly game.

Convinced that it was in our national interest to continue, we kept on probing their defenses. The low-level conflict continued until the height of the Cuban Missile Crisis when the local Soviet commander shot down a U-2 over Cuba. Both countries realized that a miscalculation could have been a catalyst for World War III, and the Soviets stopped attacks on U.S. spy planes. (The Communist Chinese continued to shoot down U-2's flown by Nationalist Chinese pilots until 1970, and the Soviet Union accidently attacked two Korean airline passenger planes in the Far East, one damaged in 1978 and one destroyed in 1983.)

During the Cold War, 32 U.S. ELINT planes were shot down by Soviet pilots, with 225 U.S. airmen killed. (The numbers vary depending on the sources you read.) Regardless of the number, this was a deadly shooting war.

Stanford and an emerging set of Silicon Valley startups would be deeply involved in designing the technologies, techniques and ELINT systems on these planes. Microwave Valley was about to take off.

264

A Wilderness of Mirrors

Posted on July 1, 2009 by steveblank |

Excuse the non-Customer Development, non-entrepreneurial post, semi-Secret History post. I can't get this one out of my head.

The VENONA Project

One of the most interesting (declassified) stories of cryptography is the deciphering of Soviet communications to their diplomatic missions in the U.S during World War II. What was amazing about these decrypts was the Soviets used one-time pads, which were theoretically unbreakable. The National Security Agency has a great website on the subject.

I had dinner last week with someone involved in the VENONA project (now retired.) We talked about one of the spies unearthed in the decoded messages. Ted Hall, a 19-year scientist at Los Alamos working on the Manhattan Project. For lots of complicated reasons, Hall was never arrested nor charged with a crime. Hall's interest in Communism came from literature his older brother Ed brought home from college.

When Ted Hall went to work on the Atomic Bomb during World War II, his older brother Ed joined the Air Force.

My Brothers Keeper

During the Cold War, when Ted Hall was under suspicion of being a Soviet spy, his brother Ed Hall, stayed in the Air Force and worked on every U.S. military missile program in the 1950's (Atlas, Thor, Titan Minuteman, etc.)

The Soviet Union's first practical ICBM the SS-7 (Soviet designation R-16) used storable fuels strikingly similar to the Titan II.

Ed Hall eventually became the father of the Minuteman missile project, our land-based ICBM carrying nuclear weapons to destroy the Soviet Union.

Surely the KGB, who ran Ted Hall as a spy, knew about his brother? Perhaps even first?

A Wilderness of Mirrors

My dinner companion, (who had a hand in his agencies counterintelligence group,) "acted" surprised about the connection between the two

Oh, what a wilderness of mirrors we live in.

The Rise of Entrepreneurship

Posted on August 6, 2009 by steveblank |

The Korean War catapulted Stanford University's Electronics Research Laboratory (ERL) into becoming a major player in electronic intelligence and electronic warfare systems. Encouraged by their Dean, Fred Terman, scientists and engineers left Stanford Electronics Research Laboratory to set up companies to build microwave tubes and systems for the military. Funded by military contracts, these 1950's startups would help build Silicon Valley's entrepreneurial culture and environment.

The Beginnings – "Vacuum Tube Valley" Ecosystem circa 1950

From its founding in 1946 Stanford's *Electronics Research Laboratory (ERL)* did basic research into vacuum tubes that could operate at microwave frequencies. The research was funded and paid for by the Office of Naval Research (ONR) and later by the Air Force and Army. Much of the basic research work was done by advanced students or by recent Ph.Ds doing postdoctoral internships, supervised by Stanford engineering faculty members or senior research associates (staff.)

In a 1950 proposal to the Navy, Fred Terman noted that the work that Stanford proposed "correlates almost ideally with related industrial activities in this area." There were already "tube manufacturers in the area (Eitel-McCullough, Litton Industries, Varian Industries, Henitz and Kaufman and Lewis and Kaufman) that represented an integrated set of tube facilities for basic research, advanced development, engineering of new tubes, model shop and pilot and quantity production. And that circuit work is carried on by several organizations in the neighborhood, with Hewlett Packard Company being especially notable in this regard." Terman was describing the valley's already existing ecosystem for building vacuum tubes in 1950.

But unlike the majority of existing tube manufacturers in the valley who were making products for radios, Stanford Electronics Research Lab tube group had a special customer with very special needs – the U.S. Air Force and its Strategic Air Command.

So what exactly was the Electronics Research Lab designing? What were these microwave tubes? Why were they so important to the military? And what were these electronic intelligence and warfare systems used for?

Stanford Joins the Cold War - Microwave Power Tubes

Stanford's work in microwave power tubes would solve two of the Strategic Air Command's most important cold war problems.

266

During a nuclear war in the 1950's, the Strategic Air Command was going to fly its bombers with nuclear weapons into the Soviet Union. To protect their country, the Soviets were building an air defense network to warn, track and destroy these attacking bombers. Our bombers used jammers to confuse the Soviet air defense radars. But the jammers that we built in WWII were no longer sufficient to protect the planes we wanted to send into the Soviet Union.

These 1940's jammers (built by the wartime lab headed up by Terman and his team now at Stanford) had been built around tubes originally designed for radio applications and put out 5 watts of power. This miniscule amount of jamming power was acceptable because each WWII bomber flew in formation with hundreds of other planes, together attacking just a single target each day. The *combined jamming power* of all the bombers on a mission was enough to saturate and confuse German radar. But in a potential cold war attack on the Soviet Union, our bombers were not going to fly in a massed formation to attack one target. Instead we would attack multiple targets in the Soviet Union at the same time. And while a few bombers would penetrate the periphery of the Soviet Union together, each plane — now able to carry more explosive power than all the bombs dropped in WWII — would *approach its target individually*. As a result of this change in strategy (and explosive capacity), *each bomber had to supply enough jamming power to defend itself.*

As a result, to protect its bombers flying over the Soviet Union the U.S. Air Force needed power tubes that had *hundreds of times more power* than WWII devices.

The U.S. Air Force also needed improvements in *frequency agility* to protect its cold war bombers. Frequency agility can be best described by what happened over Germany in WWII. As the allies jammed Germany radar, the Germans tried to avoid the effect of jamming by changing the frequency on which their radars transmitted. This was possible since the jammers in U.S. planes' could only transmit on a narrow band of frequencies (providing *spot jamming)* and could not be retuned in the air. To cover all the possible frequencies German radars might be operating on, allied technicians pretuned the jammers before each bomber raid so that each plane transmitted on a different frequency. The combined effect of hundreds of planes in the bomber stream was to cover a broader frequency range than one jammer could by itself. (This technique of covering a broad range of frequencies was known as *barrage jamming.)*

But nuclear warfare over the Soviet Union in the 1950's meant that a single bomber needed jammers that could cover multiple frequencies, and could be tuned *instantaneously.* Not only did the US need more powerful microwave power tubes, the power tubes had to be *frequency agile,* (able to be tuned in the air to different frequencies) to jam the Soviet radars. (For example, the Soviet P-20 Token was an early warning radar our bombers would encounter. It transmitted on 5 different frequencies over a band 300mhz wide. To jam it, all five frequencies had to be jammed at the same time. Our WWII jammers couldn't do the job.)

Terman's Systems Engineering Research Lab at Stanford would develop microwave power tubes that offered a solution to both challenges and would be a game changer for electronic warfare at the time.

High Power, Instant Tuning – Stanford's contribution
Stanford's Electronics Research Laboratory first contribution to high power microwave tubes for airborne electronic warfare in the 1950's was the Backward Wave Oscillator (BWO). Stanford engineers realized that this tube, which had been invented in France, could *electronically tune through microwave frequencies* while producing almost a 1,000 watts of power – (equivalent to the output of 200 jammers over Germany in WWII.) Perfecting this tube for use as an airborne jammer became one of the lab's primary objectives.

This was a critical development to support the new tactics of single bombers penetrating the Soviet Union. Equipping a bomber with several jammers built around Backward Wave Oscillator could give it enough power to use barrage jamming against multiple radars and get it through to its target. Stanford gave its Backward Wave Oscillator design drawings to tube manufacturers throughout the U.S. By the 1960's, the U.S. Air Force would ultimately equip its B-52 bombers with 6,000 jammers using these oscillators.

The Rise of "Microwave Valley" Stanford Tube Spinouts
A technician in Stanford's ERL tube shop, Ray Stewart, thought he could build these Backward Wave Oscillators commercially, and left to start Stewart Engineering in Scotts Valley near Santa Cruz. The company had more orders from the military than it could handle. (Stewart would sell his company to Watkins Johnson, one of the most financially successful of the Stanford microwave tube spinoffs. More about Watkins-Johnson in the next post.) Stewart joined a growing list of other microwave startups beginning to populate the valley.

One of the early microwave spinouts from Stanford was built around a microwave power tube called the Klystron, invented by Terman's students Russell and Sigurd Varian and William Hansen. In 1948 the Varian brothers along with Stanford professors Edward Ginzton and Marvin Chodorow founded Varian Corporation in Palo Alto to produce klystrons for military applications. (Fred Terman and David Packard of HP joined Varian's board.) While the Klystrons of the 1950's had too narrow bandwidth and were too large for airborne use, they could be scaled up to generate megawatts of power and were used to power the U.S. ground-based Ballistic Missile Early Warning System (BMEWS) radars (and the Stanford Linear Accelerator.)

Another of Terman's students, Charles Litton, also started several Silicon Valley companies. In the 1950's Litton Industries would become the leader in pulse and continuous wave magnetrons used in jammers and missiles. Magnetrons were the first high power microwave device invented in WWII. Used in radars systems and missiles, magnetrons could produce hundreds of watts of power.

More to Come

These first microwave tubes were just the beginning of a flood of innovative products for the military. The next Stanford tubes and systems would revolutionize the Electronic Intelligence aircraft that were circling (and flying over) the Soviet Union.

Entrepreneurship in "Microwave Valley"

Posted on August 10, 2009 by steveblank |

In the 1950's Stanford University's Electronics Research Laboratory (ERL) continued to develop innovative microwave tubes for the U.S. military. This next product, the Traveling Wave Tube, would have a major impact on electronic intelligence. Stanford's Dean of Engineering, Fred Terman, encouraged scientists and engineers to set up companies to build these microwave tubes for the military. Funded by military contracts, these 1950's microwave tube startups would help build Silicon Valley's entrepreneurial culture and environment.

Why Electronics Intelligence?

Starting in 1946 Electronic Intelligence aircraft (ELINT) had been probing and overflying the Soviet Union to understand their air defense system. During the 1950's, the U.S. Air Force Strategic Air Command, U.S. Navy and the CIA were the primary collectors of tactical and operational ELINT on the Soviet PVO Strany Air Defense system. (The NSA owned COMINT collection.) They flew an alphabet soup of Air Force and Navy planes (Navy PB4Y-2's, P2V's, P4M's and EA-3's, Air Force B-17s, EC-47's, RB-29s, RB-50's, and the ultimate ELINT collector of the 1950's – the RB-47H.) Common to all these planes (generically called Ferrets) is that they were loaded with ELINT receivers, manned by crews called Crows.

The Strategic Air Command needed this intelligence to understand the Soviet air defense system: early warning radars, Soviet fighter plane radar, Ground Control Intercept radar, Anti-Aircraft gun radar, and radars guiding Soviet Surface to Air Missiles. We needed this data to build radar jammers that could make the Soviet air defense radars ineffective so our bombers with their nuclear payloads could reach their targets. The information we collected would be passed on to defense contractors who would build the jammers to confuse the Soviet air defense radars.

ELINT Tasking

The ELINT program sought answers to operational questions like: What was the Radar Order of Battle a penetrating bomber would face? Were there holes in their radar coverage our bombers could sneak through? What was the best altitude to avoid the Soviet defenses? ELINT operators on each flight were tasked to gather basic data about the characteristics of the radar: Is this a new type of radar or an existing one? What is its frequency, power, pulse repetition interval, rotation rate, scan rate, polarization, carrier modulation characteristics? etc. Then they would use direction-finding equipment on their aircraft to locate its position.

270

ELINT Receivers

Early ELINT receivers were not much different then the radios you had at home – someone had to manually turn a dial to tune them to the correct frequency. By the 1950's these receivers could automatically "sweep" a frequency band, but this action was mechanical and slow. That was fine if the Soviet radar was operating continuously, but if it were just a brief radar transmission or burst communication (which Soviet submarines used), we would probably miss hearing it. (The Soviets kept their radars turned off to stop us from recording their signals. So at times multiple ELINT planes would fly on a mission – one to run at the Soviet border appearing to attack, the other to pick up the signals from the air defense network as it responded to the intrusion. Keep in mind that 23 of these planes were shot down in the Cold War.)

The ultimate dream of ELINT equipment designers was a "high-probability of intercept" receiver, one which could pick up a signal that appeared on any frequency and capture even a single pulse, however brief.

This was a two-pronged challenge: the U.S. needed near instantaneous speed - receivers *that could tune much faster* than any of the manual methods that existed, and it needed broadband range - receivers that could *tune a much broader range of frequencies* along the electromagnetic spectrum. Again, Stanford technology would solve these challenges.

Rapid Scan/High Probability of Intercept – Stanford's contribution

In the last post we described Stanford's high power, electronically tuned microwave tube (the Backward Wave Oscillator) which made high power, frequency agile airborne jammers possible.

Now Stanford's Electronics Research Laboratory delivered another tube which forever changed electronic intelligence receivers - the Traveling Wave Tube (TWT.) Invented in Britain and further developed at Bell Labs, this tube would deliver the "holy grail" for ELINT receivers - *instantaneous scan speed* and *extremely broad frequency range.* A Traveling Wave Tube (TWT) could electronically tune through microwave frequencies *at 1000 times faster* than any other device, and it could operate in a frequency range measured in gigahertz. As a microwave preamp, it had high gain, low noise and extremely wide bandwidth. It was perfect for a new generation of ELINT receivers to be built into the Ferret planes searching for signals around the Soviet Union. Later on, TWTs would be built that could not only be used in receivers, but also actually transmit broadband microwaves at high power.

Invention Versus Commercialization

While Stanford was doing its share of pure research, what's interesting about the Electronics Research Laboratory (ERL) was its emphasis on delivering useful products for its customers – the military – from inside a research university. The military had specific intelligence requirements which meant that a TWT needed to be rugged enough to withstand being installed on airplanes. This military / university collaboration for deliverable products is where the Electronics Research Laboratory (ERL) excelled – and ultimately this collaboration would end up leading to its destruction.

The Rise of "Microwave Valley" – More Stanford Tube Startups

The Traveling Wave Tube generated another series of startups from Stanford's Electronics Research Laboratory. R. A. Huggins, a research associate at the Stanford's Engineering Research Lab, left in 1948 to start *Huggins Laboratories* in Palo Alto and introduced the first commercially manufactured traveling wave tube to the market. With a boost from military R&D contracts, Huggins Labs continued to expand, diversifying into backward-wave oscillators, low-noise TWTs, and electrostatic focused tubes. (In the 1970's Huggins Labs sold to an east coast company, Microwave Associates which became M/A-COM.)

Stanley Kaisel, another research associate at the Stanford ERL tube laboratory, left to join Litton's startup. He left Litton in 1959 and started *Microwave Electronics Corporation* (MEC) to make low power, low noise TWTs. He sold the company to Teledyne in 1965.

Venture Capital, Microwaves and the OSS

Dean Watkins, the leader of TWT research at Stanford's Electronic Laboratory, left Stanford in 1957 and along with R.H. Johnson, the head of Hughes Aircraft microwave tube department, co-founded *Watkins-Johnson* to market advanced TWTs to the military. Unlike the other Stanford tube spinouts that were funded with military contracts, Watkins-Johnson would be one of the first venture capital funded companies in the valley. Its first round of funding came from Tommy Davis (an ex-WWII OSS agent) then at the Kern County Land Company who knew Fred Terman through his military contacts. Terman and Davis negotiated the Watkins-Johnson investment and would sit on the Watkins-Johnson board together.

Frustrated with Kern's lack of interest in investing in more technology companies, Tommy Davis would go on to found one of Silicon Valley's first VC firms with Arthur Rock, creating Davis and Rock in 1961. They were one the first venture firms to organize their firm as a partnership rather than an SBIC or public company. They also set the standard for the 20% carry for general partners. Tommy Davis would go on to found the Mayfield Fund in 1969.

These Stanford tube spinoffs joined the growing list of other microwave tube manufacturers in the valley including *Eitel-McCullough, Varian, Litton Industries and Stewart Industries.* Others would soon join them. By the early 1960s, a third of the nation's TWT business and a substantial share of the klystron and magnetron industry was located in the Santa Clara Valley– and almost all of these companies emerged from one engineering lab at Stanford.

But microwave tubes were just the beginning of Stanford's relationship with the military. Fred Terman was just getting warmed up. Much more was to come.

Stanford Crosses the Rubicon

Posted on August 17, 2009 by steveblank |

Swords Into Plowshares

After the end of World War II, returning veterans were happy to beat swords into plowshares (and microwave tubes) on the Stanford campus. From 1946 until 1950, Stanford's Electronic Research Lab conducted basic research in microwave tubes. Although this research would lead to the development of the Backward Wave Oscillator and Traveling Wave Tube for military applications, Stanford was building tubes and circuits not entire systems. The labs basic research was done by graduate students or PhDs doing postdoctoral internships, supervised by faculty members or hired staff, many from Fred Terman's WWII Electronic Warfare lab.

In 1949, with the detection of the first Soviet nuclear weapons test, the rise of the Iron Curtain across Europe and the fall of China to the Communists, Cold War paranoia drove the U.S. military to rearm and mobilize.

We'll Do Great in the Next War

Early in 1950, just months before the outbreak of the Korean War, the Office of Naval Research asked Fred Terman to build an *Applied* electronics program for electronic warfare. All branches of the military (the Air Force and Army would fund the program as well) wanted Stanford to build prototypes of electronic intelligence and electronic warfare systems that could be put into production by partners in industry. The Navy informed Terman that "money was not a problem but time was."

Pitching the idea to the President of Stanford, Terman enthusiastically said, "In the event of all-out war, Stanford would become one of the giant electronic research centers " (A bit optimistic about the outcome perhaps, given that both the U.S. and the Soviet Union had nuclear weapons at this point.)

Crossing the Rubicon – The *Applied* Electronics Lab

The *Applied Electronics Lab* used the ideas and discoveries (on microwave tubes and receiver circuits) from Terman's basic research program in the *Electronic Research Lab* which had been started in 1946.

Setting up a separate *Applied Electronics Lab* for military funded programs doubled the size of the electronics program at Stanford. The new Applied Electronics Laboratory was built with Navy money and a gift from Hewlett-Packard. With the memories of WWII only five years old, and the Cold War now a shooting war in Korea, there was very little discussion (or dissension) about turning a university into a center for the production of military intelligence and electronic warfare systems.

274

The work in the applied program focused in fields in which faculty members or senior research associates specialized. Many of the other staff in the applied program were full-time employees hired to work solely on these military programs.

ELINT, Jammers and OTH

The Applied Lab would build prototypes of complete *systems* such as Electronic Intelligence systems, Electronic Warfare Jammers, and Over the Horizon Radar. The Applied Electronics Lab also continued work on the Klystron, pushing the tube to produce megawatts in transmitted power. (Stanford-designed Klystrons producing 2½ Megawatts were manufactured by Varian and Litton powered the radar in the BMEWS (Ballistic Missile Early Warning System) built at the height of the cold war.)

The close tie between the Electronic Research Lab and the new Applied Lab was a unique aspect of the Stanford organization. Stanford had a Customer Development loop going on inside their own lab. The discoveries in tube and circuit research suggested new electronic intelligence and countermeasure techniques and systems; in turn the needs of the Applied Lab pushed tube and circuit development. With the Applied Electronics Lab, Stanford was becoming something akin to a federal or corporate lab run under university contract. The university found government contracts profitable as the government reimbursed their overhead charges (their indirect costs.) This meant they could fund other non-military academic programs from this overhead.

The *Stanford Applied Electronics Lab* built prototypes which were handed off to the military labs for their evaluation. Subsequently, military labs would contract with companies to build the devices in volume. In some cases, branches of the military contracted directly with Stanford which worked with local contractors in Silicon Valley to build these components or systems for the military. The prototype ELINT receivers built by the Applied Electronics Lab used the Stanford Traveling Wave Tubes. They quickly went into production at Sylvania Electronic Defense Labs down the street in Mountain View and Hallicrafters in Chicago. Later versions would be built by numerous industry contractors and installed on the fleet of ELINT planes orbiting the Soviet Union. These traveling wave tubes would also become the heart of the panoramic receiver used on the B-52 by the electronic warfare officer to get the bomber through the Soviet Air Defense system.

Jammers built by the Stanford Applied Electronics Lab used the Stanford Backward Wave Oscillators to produce high power microwaves. Unlike the simple noise jammers used in World War II, Soviet radars were becoming more sophisticated and newer designs were fairly immune to noise. Instead the jamming signal needed to be much smarter with a deep understanding of how the targeted radar worked. Taking the information gleaned from our ELINT aircraft, Stanford built prototypes of jammers modulated with two new deception jamming techniques – angle jamming and range-gate pull-off. Some form of these deception jammers would eventually find its way into most electronic warfare defense systems used in the Cold War; including the U-2, A-12 and SR-71. (Ironically, the B-52 bomber, which would become the airborne leg of our nuclear triad, would use dumb noise jammers for two more decades – the Air Force opting to put the smart jammers on the B-58 and B-70, high altitude supersonic bombers – one soon obsolete while the other never made it into production.)

The Applied Electronics Lab group's last major area of research was studying how radio signals propagated within the earth's ionosphere. Over the next fifteen years this *Radio Science Laboratory* would receive the most funding of all departments in the lab (from the CIA) to build a ground-based ELINT system. Stanford would build and deploy two Over The Horizon Radar (OTHR) systems to detect Soviet and Chinese ballistic missile tests using ground based radars.

Guards at the Door – Stanford Joins the Cold War
In 1953 the Office of Naval Research told Terman that all military-funded projects (basic or applied, classified or not) needed to be housed in their own separate physical building. As a result Stanford moved the Applied work from the Electronics Research Lab into its own building.

In 1955, the pretense of keeping unclassified and classified work separate imposed too much of an administrative overhead and Stanford merged the *Applied Electronics Lab* and the *Electronics Research Laboratory* into the *Systems Engineering Lab.* The *Applied Electronics* portion of the lab was now the size of a small company. It had 100 people, 18 of them full time faculty, 33 research associates and assistants and 33 other tube technicians, draftsman, machinists, etc. Over half this lab would hold clearances for military secrets. (Top Secret: Terman, Harris, McGhie, Secret; 44 others, Confidential: 8 others. Terman, Harris and Rambo also had Atomic Energy Commission "Q" clearances.) Some students earning their engineering graduate degrees wrote masters and PhD thesis that were classified. Unless you had the proper clearances, you couldn't read them. Terman and Stanford had just made a major bet on the cold war, and Stanford now ranked sixth among university defense contractors.

A security guard was stationed at the door of the *Applied Electronics Lab* to ensure that only those with proper security clearance could enter. The law of unintended consequences meant that this most casual addition in front of a university building would result in the occupation and destruction of the lab (and its twin at MIT) and the end of the program 14 years later.

Show and Tell – The Stanford ELINT and Electronic Warfare Contractors Meeting

During a typical year, the *Applied Electronics Lab* would host classified visits from military labs and defense contractors. By early 1950's, Stanford started holding a two day meeting for contractors and the military.

The 1955 attendee list gives you a feeling of the "who's who" of the military/industrial establishment: RCA, GE, Motorola, AIL, Bendix, Convair, Melpar, Crosley, Westinghouse, McDonnell Aircraft, Douglas Aircraft, Boeing, Lockheed, Hughes Aircraft, North American, Bell Aircraft, Glen Martin, Ryan Aeronautics, Farnsworth, Sperry, Litton, Polarad, Hallicrafters, Varian, Emerson, Dumont, Maxson, Collins Radio. Other universities doing classified ELINT and Electronic Warfare work also attended including University of Michigan, Georgia Institute of Technology and Cornell. Over a hundred government contractors reviewed Stanford's work on tubes and systems.

This was a *classified* conference at a university. The contractors not only heard the conference lectures, but also visited exhibits on the devices and systems the lab had built. The lab would repeat the conference the following week for government agencies doing military work.

Barely noticed at the 1955 conference, a year before the first transistor company opened in Silicon Valley, one of the sessions described how to use a new device called a "transistor" to build wide-band amplifiers. (Terman had sent faculty and graduate students to the University of Illinois in 1953 to learn transistor physics.)

The World Turned Upside Down

The *Applied Electronics Lab* solidified Stanford's lead as one of, if not *the* place in the U.S. military for advanced thinking in ELINT and Electronic Warfare. It would turn on its head the relationship of universities and corporations.

Traditionally, universities chased corporations for funding and patronage, but the military's dependence on Stanford's and Fred Terman's judgment turned that relationship upside down. Now the military listened to Terman's advice about which military contractors should get the order to mass-produce the Stanford systems, the contractors were now dependent on Stanford.

Terman the Rainmaker

During the 1950's Fred Terman was an advisor to every major branch of the U.S. military. He was on the Army Signal Corps R&D Advisory Council, the Air Force Electronic Countermeasures Scientific Advisory board, a Trustee of the Institute of Defense Analysis, the Naval Research Advisory Committee, the Defense Science Board, and a consultant to the President's Science Advisory Committee. His commercial activities had him on the board of directors of HP, Watkins-Johnson, Ampex, and Director and Vice Chairman of SRI. It's amazing this guy ever slept. Terman was the ultimate networking machine for Stanford and its military contracts.

Stanford Industrial Park – Microwave Valley Booms

By the early 1950's, many of the corporations which attended the yearly Stanford Electronic Warfare conferences would establish research labs centered around Stanford for just this reason – to learn from Stanford's basic and applied research and get a piece of the ELINT and Electronic Warfare contracting pie.

Stanford Industrial Park was the first technology office park set up to house local and out of state microwave and electronics startups. First occupied in 1953, it would include Varian, Watkins Johnson, Admiral, HP, General Electric, Kodak, Lockheed. Other east coast companies which established branches in Microwave valley in the 1950's included IBM, Sylvania, Philco, Zenith and ITT.

The Future is Clear – Microwave Valley Forever

By 1956 Fred Terman had every right to be pleased with what he had helped build in the last ten years in and around Stanford. The Stanford Electronics Lab was now the center of ELINT and Electronic Warfare.

Startups were sprouting all over Microwave Valley slowiy replacing the orchards and fruit trees while delivering microwave tubes and complete military systems. Granger Associates was a 1956 startup founded by Bill Ayer, a graduate student in the Applied Electronics Radioscience Lab, and John Granger, a former RRL researcher, building ELINT and Electronic Warfare systems. (The Granger jammer was carried on the U-2.) Four years later Ayer and another Granger engineer would leave Granger and found one of the preeminent electronic warfare and ELINT companies: *Applied Technologies*.

The future of the valley was clear – *microwaves*.

1956 – Change Everything

Yet in 1956 two events would change everything. At the time neither appeared earthshaking or momentous. First, a Bell Labs researcher who had grown up in Palo Alto, had his own interesting World War II career, and recently had served as a military advisor on cold war weapons systems, decided to follow Fred Terman's advice to locate his semiconductor company near Stanford.

The second was when a Southern Californian aircraft company decided to break into the missiles and space field by partnering with Stanford electronics expertise. It moved its electronics research group from Burbank to the new Stanford Industrial Park and built its manufacturing facility in Sunnyvale.

In 1956 Shockley Semiconductor Laboratory and Lockheed Missiles Systems Division would change everything.

The Rise of "Risk Capital" Part 1

Posted on October 26, 2009 by steveblank |

This is the first of two posts about the rise of "risk capital" and how it came to be associated with what became Silicon Valley.

Building Blocks of Entrepreneurship
By the mid 1950's, the groundwork for a culture and environment of entrepreneurship were taking shape on the east and west coasts of the United States. Stanford and MIT were building on the technology breakthroughs of World War II and graduating a generation of engineers into a consumer and cold war economy that seemed limitless. Communication between scientists, engineers and corporations were relatively open, and ideas flowed freely. There was an emerging culture of cooperation and entrepreneurial spirit illustrated in this chart:

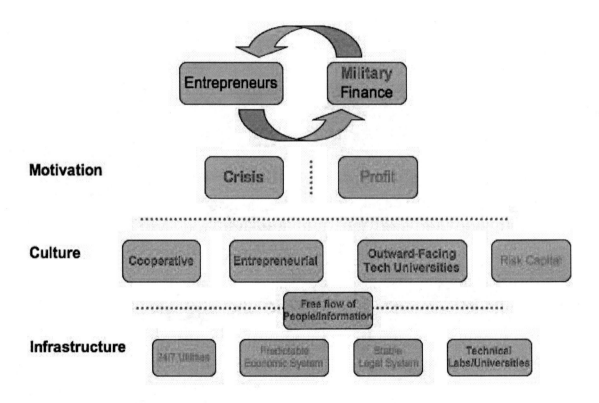

Terman and the Cold War – Silicon Valley's 1ˢᵗ Engine of Entreprenuership

At Stanford, Dean of Engineering Fred Terman wanted companies outside the university to take Stanford's prototype microwave tubes and electronic intelligence systems and produce them in volume for the military. While existing companies took some of the business, often it was a graduate student or professor who started a new company. The motivation in the mid 1950's for these new startups was a crisis – the U.S. was in the midst of the cold war and the United States military and intelligence agencies were rearming as fast as they could.

Yet one of the most remarkable things about the boom in microwave and silicon startups which occurred in the 1950's and 60's was that it was *done without venture capital.* There was none. Funding for the companies spinning out of Stanford's engineering department in the 1950's benefited from the tight integration and web of relationships between Fred Terman, Stanford, the U.S. military and intelligence agencies and defense contractors.

These technology startups had no risk capital – just customers/purchase orders from government/military/intelligence agencies.

This post is about the rise of "risk capital" and how it came to be associated with what became Silicon Valley.

Risk Capital via Family Money   1940's

During the 1930's, the heirs to U.S. family fortunes made in the late 19th century – Rockefeller, Whitney, Bessemer - started to dabble in personal investments in new, risky ventures. Post World War II this generation recognized that:

1. Technology spin-offs coming out of WWII military research and development could lead to new, profitable companies.
2. Entrepreneurs attempting to commercialize these new technologies could not get funding. At this time commercial and investment banks didn't fund new companies, just the expansion of existing firms, and existing companies would buy up entrepreneurs and their ideas, not fund them.
3. There was no organized company to seek out and evaluate new ventures, manage investments in them and nurture their growth.
4. Several wealthy families in the U.S. set up companies to do just that – find and formalize investments in new and emerging industries.

In 1946 Jock Whitney started J.H. Whitney Company by writing a personal check for $5M and hiring Benno Schmidt as the first partner. (Schmidt turned Whitney's description of "private adventure capital" into the term "venture capital.")

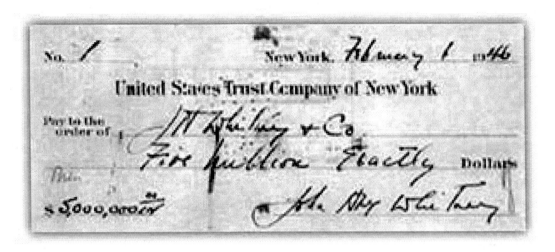

Jock Whitney writes himself a check to fund J.H. Whitney Co.

That same year Laurance Rockefeller founded Rockefeller Brothers, Inc., with a check for $1.5 million. (23 years later they would rename the firm Venrock.)

Bessemer Securities was set up to invest the Phipps family fortune. (Phipps was Andrew Carnegie's partner.)

These early family investment efforts are worth noting for:

- They were "*risk capital*," investing where others feared
- They invested in a wide variety of new industries – from orange juice to airplanes
- They almost exclusively focused on the East Coast
- They used *family* money as the source of their investment funds

East Coast Venture Capital Experiments

In 1946, George Doriot founded what is considered the first "venture capital firm" – American Research & Development (ARD). A Harvard Business School professor and early evangelist for entrepreneurs and entrepreneurship, Doriot was the Fred Terman of the East Coast. Doroit had the right idea with ARD (funding startups out of MIT and Harvard and raising money from outsiders who weren't part of a private family) but picked the wrong model for raising capital for his firm. ARD was a *publicly traded* venture capital firm raising $3.5 Million in 1946 as a closed-end mutual fund, which meant ARD was regulated by the Securities and Exchange Commission (SEC.) For reasons too numerous to mention here, this turned out to be a very bad idea. (It would take another three decades of experimentation before the majority of venture firms organized as limited partnerships.)

The region around Boston's Route 128 would boom in the 1950's-70's with technology startups, many of them funded by ARD. ARD's most famous investment was the $70,000 they invested in Digital Equipment Corporation (DEC) in 1957 for 77% of the company, worth hundreds of millions by DEC's 1968 IPO. It wasn't until the rise of the semiconductor industry and a unique startup culture in Silicon Valley that entrepreneurship became associated with the West Coast.

Doriot and American Research and Development are worth noting for:

- Some of the very early VC's got their venture capital education at Harvard as Doriot's students (Arthur Rock, Peter Crisp, Charles Waite.)
- ARD was almost exclusively focused on the East Coast.
- ARD proved that institutional investors, not just family money, had an appetite for investing *into* venture capital firms.

Corporate Finance

One of the ironies in Silicon Valley is that the two companies which gave birth to its entire semiconductor industry weren't funded by venture capital. Since neither of these startups were yet doing any business with the military—and venture capital as we know it today did not exist, they had to look elsewhere for funding. Instead, in 1956/57, Shockley Semiconductor Laboratory and Fairchild Semiconductor were both funded by corporate partners – Shockley by Beckman Instruments, Fairchild by Fairchild Camera and Instrument.

More on the rise of SBIC's, Limited Partnerships and the venture capital industry as we know it today in the next post.

The Rise of "Risk Capital" Part 2

Posted on October 29, 2009 by steveblank |

The First Valley IPO's
Silicon Valley first caught the eyes of east coast investors in the late 1950's when the Valleys first three IPO's took place: Varian in 1956, Hewlett Packard (HP) in 1957, and Ampex in 1958. These IPOs meant that technology companies didn't have to get acquired to raise money or get their founders and investors liquid. Interestingly enough, Fred Terman, Dean of Stanford Engineering, was tied to all three companies.

Varian made a high power microwave tube called the Klystron, invented by Terman's students Russell and Sigurd Varian and William Hansen. In 1948, the Varian brothers along with Stanford professors Edward Ginzton and Marvin Chodorow, founded *Varian Corporation* in Palo Alto to produce klystrons for military applications. Fred Terman and David Packard of HP joined Varian's board.

Terman was also on the board of HP. Terman arranged for a research assistantship to bring his former student, David Packard, back from a job at General Electric in New York to collaborate with William Hewlett, another of Terman's graduate students. Terman sat on the HP board from 1957-1973.

Ampex made the first tape recorders in the U.S (copied from captured German models,) and Terman was on its board as well. Ampex's first customer was Bing Crosby who wanted to record his radio programs for rebroadcast (and had exclusive distribution rights.) Ampex business took off when Terman introduced Ampex founder Alex Poniatoff to Joseph and Henry McMicking. The McMickings bought 50% of Ampex for $365,000 (some liken this to the first VC investment in the valley.) McMicking and Terman introduced Ampex to the National Security Agency, and Ampex sales boomed when their audio and video recorders became the standard for Electronic Intelligence and telemetry signal collection recorders.

Meanwhile on the West Coast – "The Group" 1950's
When Ampex was raising its money in 1952, an employee of Fireman's Fund in San Francisco, Reid Dennis, managed to put $20,000 in the deal. Five years later, Dennis and a small group of angel investors who called themselves "The Group" started investing in new electronics companies being formed in the valley south of San Francisco. These angels, who were all working in their day jobs at various financial institutions, would invite startup electronics companies up to San Francisco to pitch their deals and then invest an average of $75 -$300K per deal.

The Group is worth noting for:

- Investing their own private money,
- Reid Dennis would found Institutional Venture Partners in 1974
- First group specifically investing in the valley's *electronics industry*

SBIC Act of 1958

During the cold war, the launch of Sputnik-1 by the Soviet Union in 1957 both traumatized and galvanized the United States. Having the first earth satellite launched by a country considered as a third-world backwater with a bellicose foreign policy shocked the U.S. into the belief that it was behind the Soviet Union in innovation. In response, one of the many U.S. national initiatives (DARPA, NASA, Space Race, etc.) to spur innovation was a new government agency to fund new companies. The Small Business Investment Company (SBIC) Act in 1958 guaranteed that for every dollar a bank or financial institution invested in a new company, the U.S. government would invest three (up to $300,000.) So for every dollar that a fund invested, it would have four dollars to invest.

While SBICs were set up around the country, companies in Northern California including Bank of America, Firemans Fund and American Express (Reid Dennis of the Group ran theirs) began to set up SBIC funds to tap the emerging microwave and semiconductor startups setting up shop south of San Francisco. And for the first time, private companies like Continental Capital, Pitch Johnson & Bill Draper and Sutter Hill were formed to take advantage of the government largesse from the SBA. Like all government programs, the SBIC was fond of paperwork, but it began to formalize, professionalize and standardize the way investors evaluated risk.

SBIC's were worth noting for:

- The good news – government money for startups encouraged a "risk capital" culture at large financial institutions.
- The better news – government money encouraged private companies to form to invest in new startups.
- The bad news – the government was more interested in rules, regulations and accounting then startups (because some SBICs saw the government funds as a license to steal).
- By 1968 over 600 SBIC funds provided 75% of all venture funding in the U.S.
- In 1988, after the rise of the limited partnership, that number would fall to 7%.

Limited Partnerships

By the end of the 1950's, there was still no clear consensus about how to best organize an investment company for risky ventures. Was it like George Doriot's ARD venture fund – a publicly traded closed end mutual fund? Was it using government money as a private SBIC firm? Or was it some other form of organization? Many investors weren't interested in working for a large company for a salary and bonus, and most hated the paperwork and salary limitations that the SBIC imposed. Was there some other structure?

The limited partnership offered one way to structure an investment company. The fund would have limited life. It would charge its investors annual "management fees" to pay for the firm's salaries, building, etc. In a typical venture fund, the partners receive a 2% management fee.

But the biggest innovation was the "carried interest" (called the "carry".) This is where the partners would make their money. They would get a share of the profits of the fund (typically 20%.) For the first time, venture investors would have a very strong performance incentive.

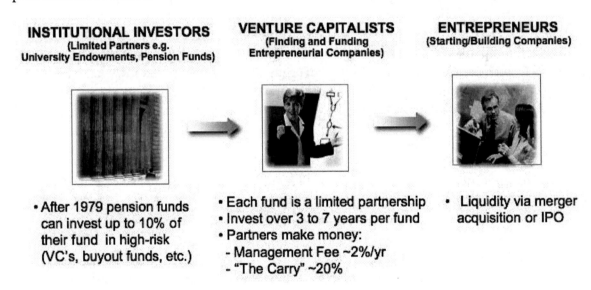

INSTITUTIONAL INVESTORS
(Limited Partners e.g.
University Endowments, Pension Funds)

VENTURE CAPITALISTS
(Finding and Funding
Entrepreneurial Companies)

ENTREPRENEURS
(Starting/Building Companies)

- After 1979 pension funds can invest up to 10% of their fund in high-risk (VC's, buyout funds, etc.)

- Each fund is a limited partnership
- Invest over 3 to 7 years per fund
- Partners make money:
  - Management Fee ~2%/yr
  - "The Carry" ~20%

- Liquidity via merger acquisition or IPO

In 1958 General William Draper, Rowan Gaither (founder of the RAND corporation) and Fred Anderson (a retired Air Force general) founded Draper, Gaither and Anderson, Silicon Valley's (and possible the world's) first limited partnership. The firm was funded by Laurance Rockefeller and Lazard Freres, but after a dispute lost to the sands of time, Rockefeller pulled his financing, and the firm dissolved after the first fund.

Davis and Rock, formed in 1961, also claim to be the first limited partnership. Arthur Rock, an investment banker at Hayden Stone in New York who helped broker the financing of Fairchild moved out to San Francisco in 1961 and partnered with Tommy Davis. Davis an ex-WWII OSS agent and then a VP at the Kern Land Company, got involved with investing in technology companies through Fred Terman. Davis's first investment in 1957 was *Watkins-Johnson,* the maker of microwave Traveling Wave Tubes for electronic intelligence systems, where he sat on its board with Fred Terman. Rock and Davis would raise a $5M fund from east coast institutions and while they invested only $3.4 million of it by the time they dissolved their partnership in 1968, they returned $90 million to their limited partners, a 54% compound growth rate.

Limited partnerships are worth noting for:

- By the 1970's, the limited partnership would become the preferred organizational form for venture investors.
- The "carried interest" (the "carry") assured that the venture partners would only make real money if their investments were successful thus aligning their interests with their limited investors and the entrepreneurs they were investing in.
- The limited life of each fund, 7-10 years of which 3-5 years would be spent actively investing, focused the firms on investments that could reasonably expect to have "exits" during the life of the fund.
- The limited life of each fund allowed venture firms to be flexible. They could change the split of the carry in follow-on funds, add partners with carry in subsequent funds, change investing strategy and focus in follow-on funds, etc.

Silicon Innovation Collides with Risk Capital

Lacking a "risk capital" infrastructure in the 1950's, military contracts and traditional bank loans were the only options microwave startups had for capital. The first semiconductor companies couldn't even get that – Shockley and Fairchild could only be funded through corporate partners. But by the 1960's, the tidal wave of semiconductor startups would find a valley with a growing number of SBIC backed venture firms and limited partnerships.

A wave of silicon innovation was about to meet a pile of risk capital.

Steve Blank

Put to a vote I might have been chosen "least likely to succeed" in my New York City high school class. My path has taken me from repairing fighter planes in Thailand during the Vietnam War, to spook stuff in undisclosed location(s), and I was lucky enough to arrive at the beginning of the boom times of Silicon Valley in 1978.

After 21 years in 8 high technology companies, I retired in 1999. I started my last company, E.piphany, in my living room in 1996. My other startups include two semiconductor companies, Zilog and MIPS Computers, a workstation company, Convergent Technologies, a consulting stint for a graphics hardware/software spinout, Pixar, a supercomputer firm, Ardent, a computer peripheral supplier, SuperMac, a military intelligence systems supplier, ESL and a video game company, Rocket Science Games.

Total score: two large craters (Rocket Science and Ardent), one dot.com bubble home run (E.piphany) and several base hits.

After I retired, I took some time to reflect on my experience and wrote a book (actually my class text) about building early stage companies called *Four Steps to the Epiphany*. I moved from being an entrepreneur to teaching entrepreneurship to both undergraduate and graduate students at U.C. Berkeley, Stanford University and the Columbia University/Berkeley Joint Executive MBA program. The "Customer Development" model that I developed in my book is one of the core themes in these classes. In 2009 I was awarded the Stanford University Undergraduate Teaching Award in the department of Management Science and Engineering. The same year, the *San Jose Mercury News* listed me as one of the 10 Influencers in Silicon Valley.

In 2007 Governor Arnold Schwarzenegger appointed me to serve on the California Coastal Commission, the public body which regulates land use and public access on the California coast.

I am on the board of Audubon California (and its past chair) and spent several years on the Audubon National Board. I'm also a board member of Peninsula Open Space Land Trust (POST). In 2009 I became a trustee of U.C. Santa Cruz and joined the board of the California League of Conservation Voters (CLCV).